diabetic LIVING™ slow cooker recipes

Meredith® Books
Des Moines, Iowa

1

Diabetic Slow Cooker Recipes
Editor: Carrie E. Holcomb
Contributing Editors: Ellen Boeke, Mary Williams
Contributing Writers: Wini Moranville, Jessica Saari
Contributing Designer: Brad Ruppert
Copy Chief: Terri Fredrickson
Publishing Operations Manager: Karen Schirm
Senior Editor, Asset and Information Manager:
   Phillip Morgan
Edit and Design Production Coordinator:
   Mary Lee Gavin
Editorial Assistant: Cheryl Eckert
Book Production Managers: Pam Kvitne,
   Marjorie J. Schenkelberg, Rick vonHoldt,
   Mark Weaver
Contributing Copy Editor: Judy Friedman
Contributing Proofreaders: Emmy Clausing,
   Donna Segal, Jody Speer
Indexer: Elizabeth Parson
Test Kitchen Director: Lynn Blanchard
Test Kitchen Product Supervisor: Juliana Hale
Test Kitchen Home Economists: Marilyn Cornelius;
   Juliana Hale, Laura Harms, R.D.; Jennifer Kalinowski,
   R.D.; Maryellyn Krantz; Jill Moberly; Dianna Nolin;
   Colleen Weeden; Lori Wilson; Charles Worthington

Meredith® Books
Executive Director, Editorial: Gregory H. Kayko
Executive Director, Design: Matt Strelecki
Senior Editor/Group Manager: Jan Miller, R.D.
Marketing Product Manager: Gina Rickert

Publisher and Editor in Chief: James D. Blume
Editorial Director: Linda Raglan Cunningham
Executive Director, New Business Development:
   Todd M. Davis
Executive Director, Sales: Ken Zagor
Director, Operations: George A. Susral
Director, Production: Douglas M. Johnston
Director, Marketing: Amy Nichols
Business Director: Jim Leonard

Vice President and General Manager: Douglas J. Guendel

Better Homes and Gardens® Magazine
Editor in Chief: Karol DeWulf Nickell
Deputy Editor, Food and Entertaining: Nancy Hopkins

Meredith Publishing Group
President: Jack Griffin
Executive Vice President: Bob Mate

Meredith Corporation
Chairman and Chief Executive Officer: William T. Kerr
President and Chief Operating Officer: Stephen M. Lacy

In Memoriam: E.T. Meredith III (1933-2003)

All of us at Meredith® Books are dedicated to providing you with the information and ideas you need to create delicious foods. We welcome your comments and suggestions. Write to us at: Meredith Books, Cookbook Editorial Department, 1716 Locust St., Des Moines, IA 50309-3023.

If you would like to purchase any of our cooking, crafts, gardening, home improvement, or home decorating and design books, check wherever quality books are sold. Or visit us at: meredithbooks.com

Our seal assures you that every recipe in *Diabetic Living™ Slow Cooker Recipes* has been tested in the Better Homes and Gardens® Test Kitchen. This means that each recipe is practical and reliable, and meets our high standards of taste appeal. We guarantee your satisfaction with this book for as long as you own it.

Pictured on the front cover: Fireside Beef Stew, page 96   Pictured on the back cover: Beef in Red Wine Gravy, page 55

contents

introduction

Finding nutritious, wholesome foods to accommodate a carb-conscious diabetic lifestyle can be difficult—especially with increasing trends toward convenient foods that are fast, fast, fast! Time is of the essence these days, and even people with special dietary requirements are looking for ways to speed up the process of cooking and eating. Look no further—this slow cooker book is just for you! Whether you're a diabetic, a low-carb dieter, or someone who is just looking for an easy way to make nutritious food, our collection of more than 200 recipes will keep you coming back for more.

To aid in the important diabetic decision of how many carbs to eat in a meal, the chapters in this book have been divided according to the carb-level — from fewer than 5 grams up to 30 grams — of each recipe, which makes recipe selection simple. Additionally, you can count on *Better Homes and Gardens*® to supply you with useful tips and hints for using your slow cooker, complete nutritional analyses, daily values, and exchanges for every recipe. We've also included a special bonus chapter with low-carb, low-fat side dishes, snacks, and desserts.

You'll be delighted by the wide selection of diabetic-friendly recipes available in this book, and with this many choices, nutritious and delicious dinners will be easier than you ever thought possible!

chapter one

0 to 5
grams of carbs

spicy beef roast

Horseradish is the star in this spicy beef roast. For those who prefer even a little more heat, increase the amount to 2 tablespoons.

Prep: 15 minutes Cook: 10 to 12 hours (low) or 5 to 6 hours (high), plus 10 minutes Makes: 10 servings

1	3½- to 4-pound boneless beef chuck pot roast
	Salt and black pepper
2	tablespoons cooking oil (optional)
½	cup water
1	tablespoon Worcestershire sauce
1	tablespoon tomato paste
2	cloves garlic, minced
	Several dashes bottled hot pepper sauce
1	tablespoon cornstarch
1	tablespoon cold water
1	tablespoon prepared horseradish
½	teaspoon salt

---

1 Trim fat from meat. If necessary, cut meat to fit into a 3½- to 4½-quart slow cooker. Sprinkle meat with salt and pepper. If desired, in a large skillet cook meat in hot oil over medium heat until brown on all sides. Drain off fat. Place meat in cooker. In a small bowl combine the ½ cup water, the Worcestershire sauce, tomato paste, garlic, and hot pepper sauce. Pour over meat in cooker.

2 Cover and cook on low-heat setting for 10 to 12 hours or on high-heat setting for 5 to 6 hours.

3 Transfer meat to a serving platter, reserving cooking liquid. Cover meat with foil to keep warm.

4 For gravy, strain cooking liquid and skim fat. Transfer liquid to a medium saucepan. In a small bowl combine cornstarch and the 1 tablespoon water; stir into liquid in saucepan. Cook and stir over medium heat until thickened and bubbly. Cook and stir for 2 minutes more. Stir in horseradish and the ½ teaspoon salt. Serve gravy with meat.

Nutrition Facts per serving: 203 cal., 6 g total fat (2 g sat. fat), 94 mg chol., 278 mg sodium, 2 g carbo., 0 g fiber, 34 g pro.
Daily Values: 1% vit. C, 1% calcium, 23% iron
Exchanges: 4 Lean Meat

pot roast with dill

To season meat, some cooks prefer the taste and texture of kosher salt, which is coarsely ground and additive-free.

Prep: 20 minutes Cook: 10 to 12 hours (low) or 5 to 6 hours (high), plus 10 minutes Makes: 6 servings

1	2½- to 3-pound boneless beef chuck pot roast
1	tablespoon cooking oil
½	cup water
1	tablespoon snipped fresh dill
½	teaspoon coarse salt or regular salt
½	teaspoon black pepper
½	cup plain yogurt
2	tablespoons all-purpose flour
	Hot cooked whole wheat pasta (optional)

1 Trim fat from meat. If necessary, cut meat to fit into a 3½- or 4-quart slow cooker. In a large skillet cook meat in hot oil over medium heat until brown on all sides. Drain off fat. Place meat in cooker. Add water. Sprinkle meat with 2 teaspoons fresh dill, the salt, and pepper.

2 Cover and cook on low-heat setting for 10 to 12 hours or on high-heat setting for 5 to 6 hours. Transfer meat to a serving plater, reserving cooking liquid. Cover meat with foil to keep warm.

3 For sauce, pour cooking liquid into a glass measuring cup. Skim off fat. Measure 1 cup cooking liquid; set aside (discard any remaining liquid). In a small saucepan combine yogurt and flour. Stir in the reserved 1 cup liquid and remaining dill. Cook and stir over medium heat until thickened and bubbly. Cook and stir for 1 minute more. Pour some of the sauce over meat; pass remaining sauce. If desired, serve with hot cooked pasta.

Nutrition Facts per serving: 275 cal., 10 g total fat (3 g sat. fat), 113 mg chol., 302 mg sodium, 3 g carbo., 0 g fiber, 42 g pro.
Daily Values: 1% vit. C, 5% calcium, 27% iron
Exchanges: 6 Very Lean Meat, 1½ Fat

bloody mary-style pot roast

The kick for this perfect Sunday-dinner dish comes from the lively combination of flavors—no vodka needed.

Prep: 20 minutes Cook: 10 to 12 hours (low) or 5 to 6 hours (high), plus 10 minutes Makes: 10 servings

1	3- to 3½-pound boneless beef chuck pot roast
2	tablespoons cooking oil (optional)
¾	cup hot-style tomato juice
¼	cup water
1	teaspoon Worcestershire sauce
2	cloves garlic, minced
2	tablespoons cold water
4	teaspoons cornstarch
1	tablespoon prepared horseradish
	Salt and black pepper

---

1 Trim fat from meat. If necessary, cut meat to fit into a 3½- or 4-quart slow cooker. If desired, in a large skillet cook meat in hot oil over medium heat until brown on all sides. Drain off fat. Place meat in slow cooker.

2 In a small bowl combine tomato juice, the ¼ cup water, the Worcestershire sauce, and garlic. Pour over meat in cooker.

3 Cover and cook on low-heat setting for 10 to 12 hours or on high-heat setting for 5 to 6 hours.

4 Transfer meat to a serving platter, reserving cooking liquid. Cover meat with foil to keep warm.

5 For gravy, pour cooking liquid into a glass measuring cup. Skim off fat. Measure 1½ cups cooking liquid; set aside (discard any remaining liquid). In a small saucepan combine the 2 tablespoons water and the cornstarch. Stir in the reserved 1½ cups liquid. Cook and stir over medium heat until thickened and bubbly. Cook and stir for 2 minutes more. Stir in horseradish. Season gravy to taste with salt and pepper. Serve meat with gravy.

Nutrition Facts per serving: 180 cal., 5 g total fat (2 g sat. fat), 81 mg chol., 255 mg sodium, 2 g carbo., 0 g fiber, 29 g pro.
Daily Values: 2% vit. A, 5% vit. C, 1% calcium, 19% iron
Exchanges: 4 Very Lean Meat, 1 Fat

dried tomato-sauced beef

This perfectly seasoned roast is ideal for a blustery Sunday dinner. Be sure to serve it with plenty of the cream cheese-infused sauce—it is divine!

Prep: 15 minutes Cook: 8 to 10 hours (low) or 4 to 5 hours (high), plus 15 minutes (high) Makes: 10 servings

1	3- to 4-pound boneless beef chuck pot roast
1	teaspoon coarse salt
1	teaspoon black pepper
4	cloves garlic, minced
1	tablespoon olive oil
¼	cup oil-packed dried tomatoes, drained and snipped
½	cup reduced-sodium beef broth
2	tablespoons cornstarch
2	tablespoons cold water
½	of an 8-ounce package reduced-fat cream cheese (Neufchâtel), cubed and softened

---

1 Trim fat from meat. If necessary, cut meat to fit into a 4- to 5-quart slow cooker. In a small bowl combine salt, pepper, and garlic. Sprinkle mixture evenly over meat; rub in with your fingers. In a large skillet cook meat in hot oil over medium heat until brown on all sides. Drain off fat. Place meat in cooker. Sprinkle with dried tomatoes. Add broth.

2 Cover and cook on low-heat setting for 8 to 10 hours or on high-heat setting for 4 to 5 hours. Transfer meat to a serving platter, reserving cooking liquid. Cover meat with foil to keep warm.

3 If using low-heat setting, turn to high-heat setting. In a small bowl combine cornstarch and water. Stir into liquid in cooker. Cover and cook 15 minutes more or until thickened and bubbly. Add cream cheese; whisk until smooth. Spoon sauce over meat.

Nutrition Facts per serving: 224 cal., 9 g total fat (4 g sat. fat), 89 mg chol., 359 mg sodium, 3 g carbo., 0 g fiber, 30 g pro.
Daily Values: 3% vit. A, 5% vit. C, 2% calcium, 20% iron
Exchanges: 4 Lean Meat

asian lettuce wraps

These Asian-inspired wraps bring a windfall of flavor to the table. Serve with a steaming bowl of hot cooked brown rice to round out the meal, if desired.

Prep: 20 minutes Cook: 8 to 10 hours (low) or 4 to 5 hours (high), plus 15 minutes (high) Makes: 12 servings

1	3-pound boneless beef chuck pot roast
1½	cups diced, peeled jicama (1 small) or chopped celery (3 stalks)
½	cup chopped green onions (4)
¼	cup rice vinegar
¼	cup reduced-sodium soy sauce
2	tablespoons hoisin sauce
1	tablespoon finely chopped fresh ginger
½	teaspoon salt
½	teaspoon chili oil
¼	teaspoon black pepper
2	tablespoons cornstarch
2	tablespoons cold water
24	Bibb or Boston lettuce leaves

1 Trim fat from meat. If necessary, cut meat to fit into in a 3½- or 4-quart slow cooker. Place meat in cooker. In a medium bowl combine jicama, green onions, vinegar, soy sauce, hoisin sauce, ginger, salt, chili oil, and pepper. Pour over meat in cooker.

2 Cover and cook on low-heat setting for 8 to 10 hours or on high-heat setting for 4 to 5 hours.

3 If using low-heat setting, turn to high-heat setting. In a small bowl combine cornstarch and water. Stir cornstarch mixture into liquid around the meat. Cover and cook about 15 minutes more or until thickened.

4 Remove meat from cooker. Using two forks, pull meat apart into shreds. Return meat to cooker. Spoon meat mixture onto lettuce leaves. Fold bottom edge of each lettuce leaf up and over filling. Fold in opposite sides; roll up from bottom.

Nutrition Facts per serving: 168 cal., 4 g total fat (1 g sat. fat), 67 mg chol., 401 mg sodium, 5 g carbo., 0 g fiber, 25 g pro.
Daily Values: 11% vit. A, 9% vit. C, 2% calcium, 18% iron
Exchanges: 1 Vegetable, 3 Very Lean Meat

brisket and cabbage

This traditional Irish combination is moist and tender. Mustard and horseradish add just the right flavor accents.

Prep: 20 minutes Cook: 10 to 12 hours (low) or 5 to 6 hours (high) Makes: 10 servings

1	medium head (1½ to 2 pounds) cabbage, cut into wedges
1	tablespoon quick-cooking tapioca
1	3- to 3½-pound fresh beef brisket
1½	teaspoons ground allspice
1½	teaspoons dried thyme, crushed
1	teaspoon cracked black pepper
½	teaspoon salt
¼	teaspoon dried sage, crushed
½	teaspoon paprika
¼	cup water
2	tablespoons Dijon-style mustard
1	to 2 tablespoons prepared horseradish

1 In a 4½- or 5-quart slow cooker place cabbage wedges. Sprinkle with tapioca. Trim fat from meat. Place meat on top of cabbage in cooker. Sprinkle with allspice, thyme, pepper, salt, sage, and paprika. In a small bowl combine water, mustard, and horseradish. Pour over mixture in cooker.

2 Cover and cook on low-heat setting for 10 to 12 hours or on high-heat setting for 5 to 6 hours.

Nutrition Facts per serving: 218 cal., 8 g total fat (3 g sat. fat), 82 mg chol., 311 mg sodium, 5 g carbo., 2 g fiber, 30 g pro.
Daily Values: 4% vit. A, 26% vit. C, 4% calcium, 18% iron
Exchanges: ½ Vegetable, 4 Very Lean Meat, 1½ Fat

round steak with herbs

Ladle wonderfully rich gravy over tender steak and noodles for a real homestyle main dish the family will love.

Prep: 10 minutes Cook: 10 to 12 hours (low) or 5 to 6 hours (high) Makes: 8 servings

2	to 2½ pounds beef round steak, cut ¾ inch thick
1	medium onion, sliced
1	10¾-ounce can reduced-fat and reduced-sodium condensed cream of celery soup
½	teaspoon dried oregano, crushed
¼	teaspoon dried thyme, crushed
¼	teaspoon black pepper
3	cups hot cooked noodles (optional)

1 Trim fat from meat. Cut meat into serving-size pieces. Place onion in a 3½- or 4-quart slow cooker. Add meat. In a small bowl combine soup, oregano, thyme, and pepper; pour over meat.

2 Cover and cook on low-heat setting for 10 to 12 hours or on high-heat setting for 5 to 6 hours. If desired, serve over hot cooked noodles.

Nutrition Facts per serving: 177 cal., 6 g total fat (2 g sat. fat), 67 mg chol., 199 mg sodium, 5 g carbo., 1 g fiber, 25 g pro.
Daily Values: 1% vit. A, 1% vit. C, 4% calcium, 16% iron
Exchanges: 3½ Very Lean Meat, 1 Fat

german-style pork roast

Serve the pork, flavored with caraway seeds and a splash of vinegar, with noodles or spaetzle (tiny dumplings) and creamy gravy for an unbeatable cold-weather meal.

Prep: 30 minutes Cook: 7 to 9 hours (low) or 3½ to 4½ hours (high), plus 10 minutes Makes: 8 servings

1	2½- to 3-pound boneless pork shoulder roast
1	tablespoon caraway seeds
1½	teaspoons dried marjoram, crushed
1	teaspoon salt
½	teaspoon black pepper
1	tablespoon olive oil
½	cup water
2	tablespoons white wine vinegar
1	8-ounce carton light dairy sour cream
4	teaspoons cornstarch

1 Trim fat from meat. If necessary, cut meat to fit into a 3½- or 4-quart slow cooker. In a small bowl combine caraway seeds, marjoram, salt, and pepper. Sprinkle caraway mixture evenly over meat; rub in with your fingers. In a large skillet cook meat in hot oil over medium heat until brown on all sides. Drain off fat. Place meat in slow cooker. Add water to skillet; bring to boiling, stirring to loosen browned bits from bottom of skillet. Add skillet juices and vinegar to cooker.

2 Cover and cook on low-heat setting for 7 to 9 hours or on high-heat setting for 3½ to 4½ hours.

3 Remove the meat from cooker, reserving the cooking liquid. Cover meat with foil to keep warm.

4 For gravy, pour cooking liquid into a glass measuring cup. Skim off fat. Measure 1¼ cups liquid (add water, if necessary, to make 1¼ cups). Pour liquid into a small saucepan; bring to boiling. In a medium bowl combine sour cream and cornstarch. Stir some of the hot liquid into sour cream mixture; return all to saucepan. Cook and stir over medium heat until mixture is thickened (do not boil). Cut meat into slices. Serve meat with gravy.

Nutrition Facts per serving: 257 cal., 12 g total fat (4 g sat. fat), 101 mg chol., 426 mg sodium, 4 g carbo., 0.421 g fiber, 30 g pro.
Daily Values: 4% vit. A, 2% vit. C, 7% calcium, 13% iron
Exchanges: 4 Very Lean Meat, 1 Fat

seeded pork roast

The savory blend of anise, fennel, caraway, dill, and celery seeds creates a crusty coating for this pork roast. Apple juice in the cooking liquid lends a subtle sweetness.

Prep: 25 minutes Cook: 9 to 11 hours (low) or 4½ to 5½ hours (high), plus 10 minutes Makes: 8 servings

1	2½- to 3-pound boneless pork shoulder roast
1	tablespoon reduced-sodium soy sauce
2	teaspoons anise seeds, crushed
2	teaspoons fennel seeds, crushed
2	teaspoons caraway seeds, crushed
2	teaspoons dillseeds, crushed
2	teaspoons celery seeds, crushed
½	cup reduced-sodium beef broth
⅔	cup apple juice
1	tablespoon cornstarch

1 Trim fat from meat. If necessary, cut meat to fit into a 3½- to 5-quart slow cooker. Brush soy sauce over meat. On a large piece of foil combine anise seeds, fennel seeds, caraway seeds, dillseeds, and celery seeds. Roll roast in seeds to coat evenly. Place meat in cooker. Pour broth and ⅓ cup of the apple juice around meat.

2 Cover and cook on low-heat setting for 9 to 11 hours or on high-heat setting for 4½ to 5½ hours.

3 Transfer meat to a serving platter, reserving cooking liquid. Cover meat with foil to keep warm.

4 For gravy, strain cooking liquid and skim fat. Transfer liquid to a small saucepan. In a small bowl combine remaining ⅓ cup apple juice and cornstarch; stir into liquid in saucepan. Cook and stir over medium heat until thickened and bubbly. Cook and stir for 2 minutes more. Serve gravy with meat.

Nutrition Facts per serving: 220 cal., 9 g total fat (3 g sat. fat), 92 mg chol., 269 mg sodium, 5 g carbo., 0 g fiber, 29 g pro.
Daily Values: 3% vit. C, 4% calcium, 14% iron
Exchanges: 4 Lean Meat

sauerkraut and pork shoulder roast

Look for sauerkraut with caraway seeds next to the plain sauerkraut in your supermarket's canned vegetable aisle. You'll be amazed at the flavor it adds to this hearty dish.

Prep: 15 minutes Cook: 8 to 10 hours (low) or 4 to 5 hours (high) Makes: 8 servings

1	2½-pound boneless pork shoulder or sirloin roast
	Salt and black pepper
2	tablespoons creamy Dijon-style mustard blend
1	14½-ounce can sauerkraut with caraway seeds, rinsed and drained
1	cup regular or nonalcoholic beer

1 Trim fat from meat. If necessary, cut meat to fit into a 3½- or 4-quart slow cooker. Lightly sprinkle meat with salt and pepper. Spread mustard blend over meat. Set aside.

2 Place sauerkraut in the slow cooker. Add meat. Pour beer over mixture in cooker.

3 Cover and cook on low-heat setting for 8 to 10 hours or on high-heat setting for 4 to 5 hours. Remove meat from cooker. If present, remove string or netting from meat. Cut meat into slices. Serve meat with sauerkraut.

Nutrition Facts per serving: 230 cal., 10 g total fat (3 g sat. fat), 92 mg chol.,
546 mg sodium, 4 g carbo., 1 g fiber, 29 g pro.
Daily Values: 15% vit. C, 3% calcium, 14% iron
Exchanges: 4 Lean Meat

herbed pork

You'll definitely want a bright, colorful side dish to complement this intriguingly spiced meaty main dish. Try the Green Beans in Shallot Butter, page 228.

Prep: 10 minutes   Cook: 8 to 10 hours (low) or 4 to 5 hours (high)   Makes: 10 servings

1	3½- to 4-pound boneless pork shoulder roast
2	teaspoons fennel seeds, crushed
1	teaspoon ground sage
1	teaspoon dried marjoram, crushed
1	teaspoon celery seeds, crushed
1	teaspoon dry mustard
¼	teaspoon salt
¼	teaspoon black pepper
¾	cup light beer or water

1 Trim fat from meat. If necessary, cut meat to fit into a 3½- to 4½-quart slow cooker. In a small bowl combine fennel seeds, sage, marjoram, celery seeds, mustard, salt, and pepper. Sprinkle fennel mixture evenly over meat; rub in with your fingers. Place meat in cooker. Pour beer over meat.

2 Cover and cook on low-heat setting for 8 to 10 hours or on high-heat setting for 4 to 5 hours. Transfer meat to a serving platter; discard cooking liquid.

Nutrition Facts per serving: 227 cal., 9 g total fat (3 g sat. fat), 103 mg chol.,
190 mg sodium, 1 g carbo., 0 g fiber, 32 g pro.
Daily Values: 2% vit. C, 2% calcium, 13% iron
Exchanges: 4 Lean Meat

shredded pork salad

Shredded meat is a welcome change from sliced roast. This slow cooker method makes it especially tender.

Prep: 15 minutes Cook: 8 to 10 hours (low) or 4 to 5 hours (high) Makes: 8 servings

1	**2-pound boneless pork shoulder roast**
1	**cup water**
2	**large onions, quartered**
3	**fresh jalapeño chile peppers, cut up***
8	**cloves garlic, minced**
2	**teaspoons ground coriander**
2	**teaspoons ground cumin**
2	**teaspoons dried oregano, crushed**
1/2	**teaspoon salt**
1/2	**teaspoon black pepper**
4	**cups shredded lettuce**
1/2	**cup finely shredded reduced-fat Monterey Jack cheese (2 ounces)**
	Bottled salsa (optional)
	Light dairy sour cream (optional)

1 Trim fat from meat. If necessary, cut meat to fit into a 3½- or 4-quart slow cooker. Place meat in the cooker. Add water, onions, jalapeño peppers, garlic, coriander, cumin, oregano, salt, and black pepper.

2 Cover and cook on low-heat setting for 8 to 10 hours or on high-heat setting for 4 to 5 hours.

3 Remove meat from cooker; discard cooking liquid. Using two forks, pull meat apart into shreds. To serve, spoon warm meat on lettuce. Top with cheese, and if desired, salsa and sour cream.

*Note: Because hot chile peppers, such as jalapeños, contain volatile oils that can burn your skin and eyes, avoid direct contact with chiles as much as possible. When working with chile peppers, wear plastic or rubber gloves. If your bare hands do touch the chile peppers, wash your hands well with soap and water.

Nutrition Facts per serving: 217 cal., 10 g total fat (4 g sat. fat), 82 mg chol.,
275 mg sodium, 5 g carbo., 2 g fiber, 25 g pro.
Daily Values: 34% vit. A, 19% vit. C, 11% calcium, 12% iron
Exchanges: 1 Vegetable, 3½ Lean Meat

sassy pork chops

The sass in these chops comes from the chipotle chile peppers! Note: Freeze leftover chipotle peppers, covered in some of the adobo sauce, in a tightly sealed freezer container.

Prep: 25 minutes Cook: 6 to 7 hours (low) or 3 to 3½ hours (high) Makes: 8 servings

2	medium red, green, and/or yellow sweet peppers, cut into strips
1	cup thinly sliced celery (2 stalks)
½	cup chopped onion (1 medium)
8	pork loin chops (with bone), cut ¾ inch thick
½	teaspoon garlic salt
¼	teaspoon black pepper
2	tablespoons cooking oil
¼	cup reduced-sodium chicken broth
¼	cup orange juice
1	tablespoon chopped chipotle chile peppers in adobo sauce
½	teaspoon dried oregano, crushed

1 In a 4- to 5-quart slow cooker place sweet peppers, celery, and onion; set aside. Season chops with garlic salt and black pepper. In a 12-inch skillet cook chops, half at a time, in hot oil over medium heat until brown on both sides. Drain off fat. Add chops to cooker. In a small bowl combine chicken broth, orange juice, chipotle peppers, and oregano. Pour over mixture in cooker.

2 Cover and cook on low-heat setting for 6 to 7 hours or on high-heat setting for 3 to 3½ hours. Using a slotted spoon transfer chops and vegetables to a serving platter; discard cooking liquid.

Nutrition Facts per serving: 215 cal., 7 g total fat (1 g sat. fat), 78 mg chol., 363 mg sodium, 4 g carbo., 1 g fiber, 33 g pro.
Daily Values: 21% vit. A, 103% vit. C, 2% calcium, 6% iron
Exchanges: 1 Vegetable, 4 Lean Meat

thai pork chops

With ginger, lime, red pepper, coconut milk, and cilantro, this recipe expertly melds hallmark Thai ingredients into one very authentic-tasting dish!

Prep: 15 minutes Cook: 5 hours (low) or 2½ hours (high), plus 15 minutes (high) Makes: 8 servings

8	pork rib chops (with bone), cut ¾ inch thick
	Nonstick cooking spray
1	tablespoon cooking oil
½	cup reduced-sodium beef broth
1	tablespoon grated fresh ginger
1	tablespoon reduced-sodium soy sauce
2	teaspoons finely shredded lime peel
½	to 1 teaspoon crushed red pepper
1	cup unsweetened light coconut milk
2	tablespoons cornstarch
2	tablespoons snipped fresh cilantro

1 Trim fat from chops. Coat a large skillet with cooking spray. Cook half of the chops in hot skillet over medium-high heat until brown on both sides. Place in a 4- to 5-quart slow cooker. Add oil to skillet. Brown remaining chops in hot oil. Drain off fat. Set aside.

2 In a small bowl combine beef broth, ginger, soy sauce, lime peel, and crushed red pepper. Pour half of the broth mixture over chops in cooker. Place remaining chops in cooker; pour remaining broth mixture over all.

3 Cover and cook on low-heat setting for 5 hours or on high-heat setting for 2½ hours.

4 Transfer pork chops to a serving platter, reserving the cooking liquid. Cover the chops with foil to keep warm.

5 If using low-heat setting, turn to high-heat setting. For sauce, strain cooking liquid and skim off fat. Return liquid to slow cooker. In a small bowl combine coconut milk, cornstarch, and cilantro. Stir into liquid in cooker. Cover and cook for 15 minutes more. Serve sauce over chops.

Nutrition Facts per serving: 186 cal., 9 g total fat (3 g sat. fat), 53 mg chol., 152 mg sodium, 3 g carbo., 0 g fiber, 22 g pro.
Daily Values: 2% vit. A, 2% vit. C, 2% calcium, 6% iron
Exchanges: 3 Lean Meat, ½ Fat

ham and spinach soup

Fresh spinach provides a healthy dose of iron and vitamins A and C in this brothy soup.

Prep: 10 minutes Cook: 8 to 10 hours (low) or 4 to 5 hours (high) Makes: 6 servings

2	cups diced low-fat reduced-sodium cooked ham (about 10 ounces)
1	cup shredded carrots (2 medium)
1	cup sliced celery (2 stalks)
1½	teaspoons dried oregano, crushed
¼	teaspoon black pepper
2	14-ounce cans reduced-sodium chicken broth
1¾	cups water
1	6-ounce package baby spinach leaves (about 8 cups)

1 In a 3½- to 5-quart slow cooker combine ham, carrots, celery, oregano, and pepper. Add chicken broth and water.

2 Cover and cook on low-heat setting for 8 to 10 hours or on high-heat setting for 4 to 5 hours. Stir spinach into soup.

Nutrition Facts per serving: 74 cal., 2 g total fat (1 g sat. fat), 20 mg chol., 885 mg sodium, 5 g carbo., 2 g fiber, 11 g pro.
Daily Values: 104% vit. A, 38% vit. C, 5% calcium, 8% iron
Exchanges: 1½ Vegetable, 1 Very Lean Meat

chicken with lemon-caper sauce

Love Chicken Piccata at your favorite restaurant? Then this slow cooker version—bursting with flavors of lemon and capers—is just for you.

Prep: 20 minutes Cook: 5 to 6 hours (low) or 2½ to 3 hours (high), plus 10 minutes Makes: 8 servings

3½	to 4 pounds meaty chicken pieces (breast halves, thighs, and drumsticks), skinned
¼	teaspoon salt
¼	teaspoon black pepper
3	tablespoons capers, drained
1	tablespoon finely shredded lemon peel
½	cup reduced-sodium chicken broth
1	8-ounce package reduced-fat cream cheese (Neufchâtel), cubed
1	tablespoon cornstarch
1	tablespoon cold water

1 Sprinkle chicken with salt and pepper. Place chicken in a 4- to 5-quart slow cooker. Sprinkle with capers and lemon peel. Add chicken broth.

2 Cover and cook on low-heat setting for 5 to 6 hours or on high-heat setting for 2½ to 3 hours.

3 Transfer chicken to a serving platter, reserving the cooking liquid. Cover the chicken with foil to keep warm.

4 For sauce, pour cooking liquid into a glass measuring cup. Measure 1 cup liquid. In a medium saucepan whisk together the 1 cup liquid and the cream cheese until combined. In a small bowl combine cornstarch and water. Whisk cornstarch mixture into cream cheese mixture. Cook and stir over medium heat until thickened and bubbly. Cook and stir for 2 minutes more. Serve sauce over chicken.

Nutrition Facts per serving: 191 cal., 9 g total fat (5 g sat. fat), 88 mg chol., 389 mg sodium, 2 g carbo., 0 g fiber, 23 g pro.
Daily Values: 7% vit. A, 6% vit. C, 4% calcium, 6% iron
Exchanges: 3½ Lean Meat

chicken and portobellos with mustard cream

Mushrooms, garlic, chicken, rosemary, and wine—these are simple secrets to a fabulous dish. Top it off with the easiest sauce in the world: a luscious combo of sour cream and mustard.

Prep: 15 minutes Cook: 5 to 6 hours (low) or 2½ to 3 hours (high) Makes: 6 servings

3	portobello mushroom caps, sliced
2	cloves garlic, minced
3½	to 4 pounds meaty chicken pieces (breast halves, thighs, and drumsticks), skinned
2	teaspoons dried rosemary, crushed
½	teaspoon salt
¼	teaspoon black pepper
¼	cup reduced-sodium chicken broth
¼	cup dry white wine
½	cup light dairy sour cream
1	tablespoon coarse-grain Dijon-style mustard

1 In a 4- to 5-quart slow cooker place mushrooms and garlic. Sprinkle chicken with rosemary, salt, and pepper. Add chicken to cooker. Pour chicken broth and wine over mixture in cooker.

2 Cover and cook on low-heat setting for 5 to 6 hours or on high-heat setting for 2½ to 3 hours.

3 Transfer chicken and mushrooms to a serving platter; discard cooking liquid.

4 For mustard cream, in a small bowl combine sour cream and mustard. Serve mustard cream with chicken and mushrooms.

Nutrition Facts per serving: 207 cal., 7 g total fat (2 g sat. fat), 96 mg chol., 392 mg sodium, 4 g carbo., 1 g fiber, 31 g pro.
Daily Values: 4% vit. A, 5% vit. C, 7% calcium, 9% iron
Exchanges: ½ Vegetable, 4 Lean Meat

chicken and pepperoni

Craving pizza but don't want takeout again? This dish brings pizza's zesty flavors—pepperoni, olives, an herby tomato sauce, and mozzarella—to a family-friendly supper.

Prep: 25 minutes Cook: 6 to 7 hours (low) or 3 to 3½ hours (high) Stand: 5 minutes Makes: 6 servings

3½	to 4 pounds meaty chicken pieces (breast halves, thighs, and drumsticks), skinned
⅛	teaspoon salt
⅛	teaspoon black pepper
2	ounces sliced turkey pepperoni
¼	cup sliced pitted ripe olives
½	cup reduced-sodium chicken broth
1	tablespoon tomato paste
1	teaspoon dried Italian seasoning, crushed
½	cup shredded part-skim mozzarella cheese (2 ounces)

1 Place chicken in a 3½- to 5-quart slow cooker. Sprinkle chicken with salt and pepper. Cut pepperoni slices in half. Add pepperoni and olives to cooker. In a small bowl whisk together chicken broth, tomato paste, and Italian seasoning. Add to mixture in cooker.

2 Cover and cook on low-heat setting for 6 to 7 hours or on high-heat setting for 3 to 3½ hours.

3 Using a slotted spoon, transfer chicken, pepperoni, and olives to a serving platter. Discard cooking liquid. Sprinkle chicken with cheese. Cover loosely with foil and let stand for 5 minutes to melt cheese.

Nutrition Facts per serving: 209 cal., 7 g total fat (2 g sat. fat), 105 mg chol., 484 mg sodium, 1 g carbo., 0 g fiber, 33 g pro.
Daily Values: 4% vit. A, 6% vit. C, 9% calcium, 9% iron
Exchanges: 4 Lean Meat

teriyaki chicken

Fresh slices of bok choy—added at the very end of cooking—offer a nice contrast of color and crunch to the rich brown sauce.

Prep: 20 minutes Cook: 5 to 6 hours (low) or 2½ to 3 hours (high) Stand: 5 minutes Makes: 6 to 8 servings

3	to 3½ pounds meaty chicken pieces (breast halves, thighs, and drumsticks), skinned
¼	cup reduced-sodium soy sauce
¼	cup dry sherry
¼	cup water
1	tablespoon toasted sesame oil
1	tablespoon grated fresh ginger
1	tablespoon rice vinegar
2	cloves garlic, minced
6	cups sliced bok choy or shredded Chinese cabbage
	Toasted sesame seeds (optional)

1 In a 3½- or 4-quart slow cooker place chicken. In a small bowl combine soy sauce, sherry, water, sesame oil, ginger, vinegar, and garlic. Pour over chicken.

2 Cover and cook on low-heat setting for 5 to 6 hours or on high-heat setting for 2½ to 3 hours.

3 Transfer the chicken to a serving platter, reserving cooking liquid. Cover chicken with foil to keep warm.

4 Stir bok choy into liquid in cooker. Cover and let stand for 5 minutes. Transfer bok choy to serving dish with chicken. If desired, sprinkle with sesame seeds. Spoon a little of the cooking liquid over chicken and bok choy. Discard remaining liquid.

Nutrition Facts per serving: 191 cal., 6 g total fat (1 g sat. fat), 76 mg chol., 514 mg sodium, 4 g carbo., 1 g fiber, 25 g pro.
Daily Values: 64% vit. A, 58% vit. C, 10% calcium, 10% iron
Exchanges: 1 Vegetable, 3 Lean Meat

feta-topped chicken

Feta cheese and snipped fresh parsley make a pretty garnish on this Mediterranean-inspired chicken dish.

Prep: 15 minutes Cook: 5 to 6 hours (low) or 2½ to 3 hours (high) Makes: 6 servings

1	teaspoon finely shredded lemon peel
1	teaspoon dried basil, crushed
1	teaspoon dried rosemary, crushed
½	teaspoon salt
¼	teaspoon black pepper
2	cloves garlic, minced
3½	to 4 pounds meaty chicken pieces (breast halves, thighs, and drumsticks), skinned
½	cup reduced-sodium chicken broth
½	cup crumbled feta cheese (2 ounces)
2	tablespoons snipped fresh Italian (flat-leaf) parsley

1 In a small bowl combine lemon peel, basil, rosemary, salt, pepper, and garlic. Sprinkle lemon peel mixture over chicken pieces; rub in with your fingers. Place chicken pieces in a 4- to 5-quart slow cooker. Add chicken broth.

2 Cover and cook on low-heat setting for 5 to 6 hours or on high-heat setting for 2½ to 3 hours.

3 Transfer chicken to a serving platter. Discard cooking liquid. Sprinkle chicken with feta cheese and parsley.

Nutrition Facts per serving: 179 cal., 6 g total fat (2 g sat. fat), 97 mg chol., 425 mg sodium, 1 g carbo., 0 g fiber, 29 g pro.
Daily Values: 4% vit. A, 8% vit. C, 7% calcium, 7% iron
Exchanges: 3½ Lean Meat

moroccan-spiced chicken

Hot cooked couscous or rice would be the perfect accompaniment to this flavorful chicken dish inspired by Moroccan cuisine.

Prep: 10 minutes Cook: 6 to 8 hours (low) or 3 to 4 hours (high) Makes: 6 servings

1½	teaspoons ground cumin
1	teaspoon salt
½	teaspoon ground cinnamon
½	teaspoon ground coriander
¼	teaspoon ground turmeric
¼	teaspoon black pepper
3½	to 4 pounds meaty chicken pieces (breast halves, thighs, and drumsticks), skinned
½	cup reduced-sodium chicken broth

---

1 In a small bowl combine cumin, salt, cinnamon, coriander, turmeric, and pepper. Sprinkle over chicken pieces; rub in with your fingers. Pour chicken broth into a 3½- or 4-quart slow cooker. Add chicken.

2 Cover and cook on low-heat setting for 6 to 8 hours or on high-heat setting for 3 to 4 hours.

Nutrition Facts per serving: 155 cal., 4 g total fat (1 g sat. fat), 89 mg chol., 534 mg sodium, 1 g carbo., 0 g fiber, 27 g pro.
Daily Values: 1% vit. A, 5% vit. C, 2% calcium, 7% iron
Exchanges: 3½ Lean Meat

caesar-style chicken

Serve this brand-new take on a traditional Caesar salad with a side of hot cooked brown rice to soak up the juices.

Prep: 30 minutes Cook: 5 to 6 hours (low) or 2½ to 3 hours (high), plus 10 minutes Makes: 8 servings

3½	to 4 pounds meaty chicken pieces (breast halves, thighs, and drumsticks), skinned
1	teaspoon paprika
½	teaspoon salt
¼	teaspoon black pepper
	Nonstick cooking spray
1	tablespoon cooking oil
½	cup reduced-sodium chicken broth
⅓	cup dry white wine
4	anchovy fillets, finely chopped
¼	cup sliced green onions (2)
2	cloves garlic, minced
1	teaspoon finely shredded lemon peel
2	tablespoons cornstarch
2	tablespoons cold water
4	slices turkey bacon, crisp-cooked, drained, and crumbled
	Shredded Parmesan cheese (optional)

1 Sprinkle chicken with paprika, salt, and pepper. Lightly coat a large skillet with cooking spray; heat skillet over medium heat. Cook chicken, half at a time, in hot skillet until brown on all sides, adding cooking oil, if necessary. Drain off fat.

2 Place chicken in a 4- to 6-quart slow cooker. In a small bowl combine chicken broth, wine, anchovies, green onions, garlic, and lemon peel. Pour over chicken.

3 Cover and cook on low-heat setting for 5 to 6 hours or on high-heat setting for 2½ to 3 hours.

4 Transfer the chicken to a serving platter, reserving cooking liquid. Cover chicken with foil to keep warm.

5 For sauce, transfer cooking liquid to a small saucepan. In a small bowl combine cornstarch and water. Stir into liquid in saucepan. Cook and stir over medium-high heat until thickened and bubbly. Cook and stir for 2 minutes more. Spoon sauce over chicken. Sprinkle chicken with bacon and, if desired, Parmesan cheese.

Nutrition Facts per serving: 150 cal., 4 g total fat (1 g sat. fat), 73 mg chol., 424 mg sodium, 3 g carbo., 0 g fiber, 22 g pro.
Daily Values: 4% vit. A, 6% vit. C, 2% calcium, 6% iron
Exchanges: 3 Lean Meat

blue cheese-sauced chicken

Calling all blue cheese lovers! This dish will become addictive. For added crunch top with toasted walnuts.

Prep: 20 minutes **Cook:** 5 hours (low) or 2½ hours (high), plus 10 minutes **Makes:** 8 servings

8	medium chicken breast halves, skinned
½	teaspoon salt
¼	teaspoon black pepper
¾	cup reduced-sodium chicken broth
⅓	cup finely crumbled blue cheese (1 ounce)
⅔	cup fat-free half-and-half
2	teaspoons cornstarch
2	tablespoons finely chopped walnuts, toasted (optional)
	Finely crumbled blue cheese (optional)

1 Place chicken in a 5- to 6-quart slow cooker. Sprinkle with salt and pepper. Pour broth over chicken; sprinkle with ⅓ cup blue cheese.

2 Cover and cook on low-heat setting for 5 hours or on high-heat setting for 2½ hours.

3 Transfer the chicken to a serving platter; discard cooking liquid. Cover chicken with foil to keep warm.

4 For sauce, in a small saucepan combine half-and-half and cornstarch. Cook and stir over medium heat until thickened and bubbly. Cook and stir for 2 minutes more. Spoon sauce over chicken. If desired, sprinkle with nuts and additional blue cheese.

Nutrition Facts per serving: 225 cal., 4 g total fat (1 g sat. fat), 102 mg chol.,
262 mg sodium, 3 g carbo., 0 g fiber, 41 g pro.
Daily Values: 1% vit. A, 5% calcium, 6% iron
Exchanges: 6 Very Lean Meat, ½ Fat

jalapeño and bacon chicken breasts

If using the optional bacon garnish, be sure to sprinkle it on just before serving so it stays nice and crispy.

Prep: 15 minutes Cook: 5 to 6 hours (low) or 2½ to 3 hours (high), plus 15 minutes (high) Makes: 6 servings

6	chicken breast halves, skinned
1	tablespoon chili powder
	Salt
½	cup reduced-sodium chicken broth
2	tablespoons lemon juice
⅓	cup bottled pickled jalapeño pepper slices, drained
1	tablespoon cornstarch
1	tablespoon cold water
1	8-ounce package reduced-fat cream cheese (Neufchâtel), softened and cut into cubes
2	slices bacon or turkey bacon, crisp-cooked, drained, and crumbled (optional)

1 Sprinkle chicken with chili powder and a little salt. Arrange chicken, bone-side down, in a 4½- to 6-quart slow cooker. Pour chicken broth and lemon juice around chicken in cooker. Top with jalapeño pepper slices.

2 Cover and cook on low-heat setting for 5 to 6 hours or on high-heat setting for 2½ to 3 hours.

3 Transfer chicken and jalapeño peppers to a serving platter, reserving cooking liquid. Cover chicken with foil to keep warm.

4 If using low-heat setting, turn to high-heat setting. For sauce, in a small bowl combine cornstarch and water; stir into liquid in cooker. Add cream cheese, whisking until combined. Cover and cook about 15 minutes more or until thickened. If desired, sprinkle chicken with bacon. Serve sauce with chicken.

Nutrition Facts per serving: 329 cal., 11 g total fat (6 g sat. fat), 143 mg chol., 489 mg sodium, 5 g carbo., 1 g fiber, 49 g pro.
Daily Values: 19% vit. A, 10% vit. C, 8% calcium, 9% iron
Exchanges: 7 Very Lean Meat, 2 Fat

chicken with thyme and garlic sauce

Thyme, garlic, a little orange juice, and a splash of balsamic vinegar flavor these moist, fork-tender chicken breasts.

Prep: 15 minutes Cook: 5 to 6 hours (low) or 2½ to 3 hours (high), plus 10 minutes Makes: 6 to 8 servings

3	to 4 pounds chicken breast halves, skinned
6	cloves garlic, minced
1½	teaspoons dried thyme, crushed
¼	cup orange juice
1	tablespoon balsamic vinegar

1 Place chicken in a 3½- or 4-quart slow cooker. Sprinkle chicken with garlic and thyme. Add orange juice and vinegar.

2 Cover and cook on low-heat setting for 5 to 6 hours or on high-heat setting for 2½ to 3 hours.

3 Transfer the chicken to a serving platter, reserving cooking liquid. Cover chicken with foil to keep warm.

4 For sauce, skim fat from cooking liquid. Strain liquid into a small saucepan. Bring to boiling; reduce heat. Boil gently, uncovered, about 10 minutes or until reduced to 1 cup. Spoon a little sauce over chicken; pass remaining sauce.

Nutrition Facts per serving: 178 cal., 2 g total fat (0 g sat. fat), 85 mg chol., 78 mg sodium, 3 g carbo., 0 g fiber, 34 g pro.
Daily Values: 13% vit. C, 3% calcium, 7% iron
Exchanges: 5 Very Lean Meat

chicken in herbed cream sauce

Prepare for an elegant meal in just two easy steps. First, poach the chicken in a delicate herbed broth. Then transform the enriched broth into a luscious Parmesan cheese sauce.

Prep: 20 minutes **Cook:** 5 to 6 hours (low) or 2½ to 3 hours (high), plus 10 minutes **Makes:** 8 servings

8	medium chicken breast halves, skinned
2	teaspoons dried basil, crushed
¼	teaspoon salt
¼	teaspoon black pepper
½	cup reduced-sodium chicken broth
½	cup fat-free half-and-half
4	teaspoons cornstarch
½	8-ounce package reduced-fat cream cheese (Neufchâtel), cubed
½	cup shredded Parmesan cheese (2 ounces)

1 Place chicken in a 5- to 6-quart slow cooker. Sprinkle chicken with basil, salt, and pepper. Add chicken broth.

2 Cover and cook on low-heat setting for 5 to 6 hours or on high-heat setting for 2½ to 3 hours. Transfer chicken to a serving platter, reserving cooking liquid. Cover chicken with foil to keep warm.

3 For sauce, in a small saucepan combine half-and-half and cornstarch. Stir in cooking liquid. Cook and stir over medium heat until thickened and bubbly. Stir in cream cheese and Parmesan cheese. Cook and stir just until the cheese melts. Spoon the sauce over the chicken.

Nutrition Facts per serving: 235 cal., 7 g total fat (4 g sat. fat), 96 mg chol., 341 mg sodium, 4 g carbo., 0 g fiber, 37 g pro.
Daily Values: 5% vit. A, 10% calcium, 6% iron
Exchanges: 5½ Very Lean Meat, 1 Fat

mediterranean chicken thighs

Recipes featuring chicken, eggplant, and olives are common in both Greek and Italian cuisines so choose either Greek or Italian seasoning to flavor this fresh-tasting dish.

Prep: 20 minutes Cook: 5 to 6 hours (low) or 2½ to 3 hours (high) Makes: 6 servings

½	of a medium eggplant, peeled and cubed (8 ounces)
1	medium onion, cut into wedges
¼	cup pitted ripe olives, halved
2	cloves garlic, minced
3	pounds chicken thighs, skinned
2	teaspoons finely shredded lemon peel
1	teaspoon Greek seasoning or Italian seasoning, crushed
⅛	teaspoon salt
¼	teaspoon black pepper
⅓	cup reduced-sodium chicken broth
⅔	cup coarsely chopped roma tomatoes (2 medium)
½	cup shredded Parmesan cheese (optional)

1 In a 4- or 5-quart slow cooker combine eggplant, onion, olives, and garlic. Top with chicken. Sprinkle chicken with lemon peel, Greek seasoning, salt, and pepper. Pour broth over all.

2 Cover and cook on low-heat setting for 5 to 6 hours or on high-heat setting for 2½ to 3 hours.

3 Using a slotted spoon, transfer chicken and eggplant mixture to a serving platter. Discard cooking liquid. Sprinkle chicken with tomatoes and cheese.

Nutrition Facts per serving: 179 cal., 6 g total fat (1 g sat. fat), 107 mg chol.,
234 mg sodium, 5 g carbo., 2 g fiber, 26 g pro.
Daily Values: 7% vit. A, 10% vit. C, 3% calcium, 9% iron
Exchanges: 1 Vegetable, 3 Lean Meat

smoky paprika chicken thighs

Smoked paprika can be difficult to find (try the internet or large supermarkets). Regular paprika found at any grocery store makes a fine substitute.

Prep: 20 minutes Cook: 6 to 7 hours (low) or 3 to 3½ hours (high), plus 15 minutes (high) Makes: 8 servings

1	tablespoon smoked paprika or paprika
1	teaspoon salt
¼	teaspoon garlic powder
¼	teaspoon black pepper
3	pounds chicken thighs, skinned
½	cup reduced-sodium chicken broth
1	tablespoon tomato paste
1	8-ounce carton light dairy sour cream
2	tablespoons cornstarch

1 In a small bowl combine paprika, salt, garlic powder, and pepper. Sprinkle over chicken; rub in with your fingers. Place chicken in a 4½- to 5½-quart slow cooker. In another bowl whisk together chicken broth and tomato paste. Pour over chicken in cooker.

2 Cover and cook on low-heat setting for 6 to 7 hours or on high-heat setting for 3 to 3½ hours.

3 Transfer the chicken to a serving platter, reserving cooking liquid. Cover the chicken with foil to keep warm.

4 If using low-heat setting, turn to high-heat setting. In a small bowl combine sour cream and cornstarch. Whisk into liquid in cooker until smooth. Cover and cook about 15 minutes more or until thickened. Spoon sauce over chicken.

Nutrition Facts per serving: 164 cal., 6 g total fat (2 g sat. fat), 89 mg chol., 414 mg sodium, 5 g carbo., 0 g fiber, 21 g pro.
Daily Values: 12% vit. A, 1% vit. C, 7% calcium, 6% iron
Exchanges: 3 Lean Meat

turkey chablis

Spoon some of the gravy over the turkey. Pass the rest and serve with mashed potatoes for a comforting meal.

Prep: 15 minutes Cook: 9 to 10 hours (low) or 4½ to 5 hours (high),
plus 10 minutes Makes: 6 to 8 servings

¾	cup Chablis or other dry white wine
½	cup chopped onion (1 medium)
1	clove garlic, minced
1	bay leaf
1	3½- to 4-pound frozen boneless turkey, thawed
1	teaspoon dried rosemary, crushed
¼	teaspoon black pepper
⅓	cup fat-free half-and-half
2	tablespoons cornstarch

---

1 In a 3½- to 6-quart slow cooker combine white wine, onion, garlic, and bay leaf. If turkey is wrapped in netting, remove netting and discard. If gravy packet is present, remove and refrigerate for another use. Combine rosemary and pepper. Sprinkle rosemary mixture over turkey; rub in with your fingers. Place turkey in cooker.

2 Cover and cook on low-heat setting for 9 to 10 hours or on high-heat setting for 4½ to 5 hours.

3 Transfer the turkey to a serving platter, reserving cooking liquid. Cover the turkey with foil to keep warm.

4 For gravy, strain cooking liquid into a glass measuring cup. Skim off fat. Measure 1⅓ cups liquid. Pour into a small saucepan. In a small bowl combine half-and-half and and cornstarch. Stir into liquid in saucepan. Cook and stir over medium heat until thickened and bubbly. Cook and stir for 2 minutes more. Slice turkey. Spoon some gravy over turkey. Pass remaining gravy with turkey.

Nutrition Facts per serving: 208 cal., 4 g total fat (1 g sat. fat), 108 mg chol.,
125 mg sodium, 3 g carbo., 0 g fiber, 35 g pro.
Daily Values: 3% calcium, 12% iron
Exchanges: 5 Very Lean Meat, ½ Fat

sesame turkey

Sometimes called Asian or Oriental sesame oil, toasted sesame oil is made from toasted sesame seeds. Its rich, concentrated flavor nicely complements the soy and ginger flavors here.

Prep: 15 minutes **Cook:** 5 to 6 hours (low) or 2½ to 3 hours (high), plus 10 minutes **Makes:** 8 servings

3	pounds turkey breast tenderloins
¼	teaspoon black pepper
⅛	teaspoon cayenne pepper
¼	cup reduced-sodium chicken broth
¼	cup soy sauce or reduced-sodium soy sauce
4	teaspoons grated fresh ginger
1	tablespoon lemon juice
1	tablespoon toasted sesame oil
2	cloves garlic, minced
2	tablespoons cornstarch
2	tablespoons cold water
2	tablespoons sliced green onion (1)
1	tablespoon sesame seeds, toasted

---

1 In a 3½- or 4-quart slow cooker place turkey. Sprinkle with black pepper and cayenne pepper. In a small bowl combine chicken broth, soy sauce, ginger, lemon juice, sesame oil, and garlic. Pour over turkey in cooker.

2 Cover and cook on low-heat setting for 5 to 6 hours or on high-heat setting for 2½ to 3 hours.

3 Transfer the turkey to a serving platter, reserving cooking liquid. Cover the turkey with foil to keep warm.

4 For sauce, strain cooking liquid into a small saucepan. In a small bowl combine cornstarch and water. Stir into liquid in saucepan. Cook and stir over medium heat until thickened and bubbly. Cook and stir for 2 minutes more. If desired, slice turkey. Spoon sauce over turkey. Sprinkle with green onion and sesame seeds.

Nutrition Facts per serving: 222 cal., 3 g total fat (1 g sat. fat), 112 mg chol.,
373 mg sodium, 3 g carbo., 0 g fiber, 42 g pro.
Daily Values: 1% vit. A, 3% vit. C, 3% calcium, 12% iron
Exchanges: 6 Very Lean Meat

turkey and sausage stew

This creamy stew is extra satisfying, thanks to a double dose of turkey—both breast tenderloins and turkey kielbasa. The vinegar adds a pleasantly tangy note.

Prep: 10 minutes Cook: 5 hours (low) or 2½ hours (high) Makes: 6 servings

1	pound turkey breast tenderloins
8	ounces cooked turkey kielbasa
2	14-ounce cans reduced-sodium chicken broth
¼	cup bottled reduced-calorie Italian salad dressing
2	tablespoons vinegar
3	cups shredded cabbage
½	cup light dairy sour cream (optional)
1	cup shredded Swiss cheese (4 ounces) (optional)

---

1 Cut turkey into 1½-inch pieces. Cut kielbasa into 1-inch pieces. In a 3½- or 4-quart slow cooker combine turkey, kielbasa, chicken broth, salad dressing, and vinegar.

2 Cover and cook on low-heat setting for 5 hours or on high-heat setting for 2½ hours. Stir in cabbage. If desired, top each serving with sour cream and Swiss cheese.

Nutrition Facts per serving: 230 cal., 12 g total fat (5 g sat. fat), 67 mg chol.,
796 mg sodium, 5 g carbo., 1 g fiber, 25 g pro.
Daily Values: 1% vit. A, 20% vit. C, 3% calcium, 8% iron
Exchanges: ½ Vegetable, 2½ Very Lean Meat, 1 Medium-Fat Meat, 1 Fat

peppercorn-topped turkey

To crush the peppercorns, use a pepper mill adjusted to the coarse-grind setting. The mixed peppercorns include black, white, pink, green and white varieties.

Prep: 15 minutes Cook: 5 to 6 hours (low) or 2½ to 3 hours (high) Makes: 8 servings

2	tablespoons mixed peppercorns, coarsely crushed
1	teaspoon coarse salt
1	teaspoon dried thyme, crushed
3	pounds turkey thighs
¼	cup reduced-sodium chicken broth
¼	cup dry white wine

1 In a small bowl combine crushed peppercorns, salt, and thyme. Sprinkle over turkey; rub in with your fingers. Place turkey in a 3½- or 4-quart slow cooker. Add chicken broth and wine.

2 Cover and cook on low-heat setting for 5 to 6 hours or on high-heat setting for 2½ to 3 hours.

3 Transfer turkey to a serving platter. Spoon some of the cooking liquid over the turkey. Discard remaining cooking liquid.

Nutrition Facts per serving: 132 cal., 3 g total fat (1 g sat. fat), 73 mg chol., 344 mg sodium, 1 g carbo., 0 g fiber, 22 g pro.
Daily Values: 1% vit. A, 1% vit. C, 3% calcium, 14% iron
Exchanges: 3 Very Lean Meat, ½ Fat

curry-sauced turkey thighs

Why save turkey for the holidays? Everyone loves it, and turkey parts are now widely available. Take advantage, and see how wonderfully these thighs cook up in the slow cooker.

Prep: 15 minutes Cook: 5 to 6 hours (low) or 2½ to 3 hours (high), plus 15 minutes (high) Makes: 6 servings

1	tablespoon curry powder
1	teaspoon salt
¼	teaspoon crushed red pepper
¼	teaspoon black pepper
3	to 3½ pounds turkey thighs, skinned
½	cup fat-free half-and-half
2	tablespoons cornstarch
2	tablespoons cold water

1 In a small bowl combine curry powder, salt, crushed red pepper, and black pepper. Sprinkle curry mixture over turkey; rub in with your fingers. Place turkey in a 3½- to 4½-quart slow cooker. Add half-and-half.

2 Cover and cook on low-heat setting for 5 to 6 hours or on high-heat setting for 2½ to 3 hours.

3 Transfer turkey to a serving platter, reserving cooking liquid. Cover turkey with foil to keep warm.

4 If using low-heat setting, turn to high-heat setting. For sauce, in a small bowl combine cornstarch and water. Stir cornstarch mixture into liquid in cooker. Cover and cook about 15 minutes more or until thickened. Spoon sauce over turkey.

Nutrition Facts per serving: 209 cal., 7 g total fat (2 g sat. fat), 100 mg chol.,
520 mg sodium, 5 g carbo., 0 g fiber, 30 g pro.
Daily Values: 4% calcium, 16% iron
Exchanges: 4 Lean Meat

spicy asian radish soup

This light side dish or starter soup has amazing flavor dimensions. Serve it the next time you cook (or carry out) Asian dishes.

Prep: 25 minutes Cook: 6 to 8 hours (low) or 3 to 4 hours (high)
Stand: 10 minutes Makes: 10 side-dish servings

3	14-ounce cans reduced-sodium chicken broth
2	cups sliced fresh mushrooms
1	cup sliced radishes
5	ounces daikon or jicama, peeled and cut into julienne strips (1 cup)
2	tablespoons reduced-sodium soy sauce
1	tablespoon grated fresh ginger
1/4	teaspoon crushed red pepper
3	cups shredded Chinese cabbage

1 In a 3½- or 4-quart slow cooker combine chicken broth, mushrooms, radishes, daikon, soy sauce, ginger, and crushed red pepper.

2 Cover and cook on low-heat setting for 6 to 8 hours or on high-heat setting for 3 to 4 hours. Stir in cabbage. Cover and let stand for 10 minutes before serving.

Nutrition Facts per serving: 21 cal., 0 g total fat (0 g sat. fat), 0 mg chol., 315 mg sodium, 3 g carbo., 1 g fiber, 2 g pro.
Daily Values: 2% vit. A, 19% vit. C, 3% calcium, 2% iron
Exchanges: Free

0 to 5 grams of carbs

cheesy cauliflower

Vary the kind of cheese you use in this creamy side dish. You could also substitute basil or oregano for the thyme.

Prep: 15 minutes Cook: 3 to 4 hours (low) or 1½ to 2 hours (high) Makes: 8 side-dish servings

1	large head cauliflower (about 2½ pounds), broken into 8 pieces
¼	teaspoon salt
¼	teaspoon black pepper
⅔	cup vegetable broth
½	of an 8-ounce package reduced-fat cream cheese (Neufchâtel), cubed
½	teaspoon dried thyme, crushed
½	cup shredded reduced-fat cheddar cheese (2 ounces)

---

1 Place cauliflower in a 4- to 5-quart slow cooker. Sprinkle with salt and pepper. Add vegetable broth.

2 Cover and cook on low-heat setting for 3 to 4 hours or on high-heat setting for 1½ to 2 hours. Using a slotted spoon, transfer cauliflower to a serving dish.

3 For sauce, add cream cheese and thyme to liquid in cooker; whisk until smooth. Spoon sauce over cauliflower. Sprinkle with cheddar cheese.

Nutrition Facts per serving: 68 cal., 5 g total fat (3 g sat. fat), 16 mg chol., 286 mg sodium, 2 g carbo., 1 g fiber, 4 g pro.
Daily Values: 6% vit. A, 43% vit. C, 12% calcium, 2% iron
Exchanges: 1 Vegetable, 1 Fat

chapter two

6 to 10
grams of carbs

beef with leeks and capers

Subtle, mellow leeks and bright, citrusy capers are favorite ingredient of gourmet cooks. They complement each other in this dish, and bring an upscale angle to this simple recipe.

Prep: 15 minutes Cook: 8 to 10 hours (low) or 4 to 5 hours (high), plus 15 minutes (high) Makes: 8 servings

1	3- to 4-pound boneless beef chuck pot roast
2	medium leeks, trimmed, halved, and sliced
3	tablespoons drained capers
2	teaspoons dried marjoram or oregano, crushed
$1/4$	teaspoon salt
$1/4$	teaspoon black pepper
$1/2$	cup reduced-sodium beef broth
$1/2$	cup fat-free half-and-half
2	tablespoons cornstarch

1 Trim fat from meat. If necessary, cut meat to fit into a 4- to 5-quart slow cooker. Place leeks in cooker. Place meat on leeks. Sprinkle with capers, marjoram, salt, and pepper. Add beef broth.

2 Cover and cook on low-heat setting for 8 to 10 hours or on high-heat setting for 4 to 5 hours.

3 Transfer meat to a serving platter, reserving cooking liquid. Cover meat with foil to keep warm.

4 If using low-heat setting, turn to high-heat setting. For sauce, in a small bowl combine half-and-half and cornstarch. Stir into the liquid in cooker. Cover and cook about 15 minutes more or until thickened. Spoon some of the sauce over meat. Pass the remaining sauce.

Nutrition Facts per serving: 243 cal., 6 g total fat (2 g sat. fat), 101 mg chol.,
330 mg sodium, 7 g carbo., 1 g fiber, 37 g pro.
Daily Values: 8% vit. A, 5% vit. C, 4% calcium, 29% iron
Exchanges: $1/2$ Other Carbo., $4^1/2$ Lean Meat

mediterranean-style pot roast

This savory roast gets its appeal from herbes de Provence. The mix typically includes basil, fennel, lavender, marjoram, rosemary, sage, savory, and thyme.

6 to 10 grams of carbs

Prep: 20 minutes **Cook:** 8 to 10 hours (low) or 4 to 5 hours (high) **Makes:** 6 servings

1	2- to 3-pound boneless beef chuck pot roast
1	tablespoon cooking oil
1	medium onion, sliced
1	14½-ounce can diced tomatoes with basil, oregano, and garlic; undrained
¼	cup sliced pitted ripe olives
1	tablespoon Worcestershire sauce
2	teaspoons dried herbes de Provence, crushed
1	teaspoon coarsely ground black pepper
½	cup crumbled feta cheese (2 ounces)

1 Trim fat from meat. If necessary, cut meat to fit into a 3½- or 4-quart slow cooker. In a large skillet cook meat in hot oil over medium heat until brown on all sides. Drain off fat. Place onion in cooker. Add meat. In a medium bowl combine undrained tomatoes, olives, Worcestershire sauce, herbes de Provence, and pepper. Pour over the mixture in cooker.

2 Cover and cook on low-heat setting for 8 to 10 hours or on high-heat setting for 4 to 5 hours.

3 Remove meat from cooker. Cut meat into serving-size pieces. Place meat on a serving platter. Using a slotted spoon, transfer vegetables and olives to serving platter, reserving cooking liquid. Spoon enough of the liquid over meat and vegetables to moisten. Sprinkle with feta cheese.

Nutrition Facts per serving: 274 cal., 10 g total fat (4 g sat. fat), 98 mg chol., 641 mg sodium, 9 g carbo., 1 g fiber, 35 g pro.
Daily Values: 10% vit. A, 10% vit. C, 11% calcium, 30% iron
Exchanges: 1 Vegetable, 4½ Very Lean Meat, 2 Fat

herbed-port pot roast

Port wine is the secret to this roast's outstanding flavor. No need to buy expensive port, which is aged for several years. The less expensive ruby port works just fine here.

6 to 10 grams of carbs

Prep: 15 minutes Cook: 8 to 10 hours (low) or 4 to 5 hours (high) Makes: 8 to 10 servings

1	2½- to 3-pound boneless beef chuck pot roast
½	cup chopped onion (1 medium)
½	cup port wine or apple juice
1	8-ounce can tomato sauce
3	tablespoons quick-cooking tapioca
1	tablespoon Worcestershire sauce
1	teaspoon dried thyme, crushed
1	teaspoon dried oregano, crushed
2	cloves garlic, minced
3	cups hot cooked whole wheat pasta (optional)

1 Trim fat from meat. If necessary, cut meat to fit into a 3½- or 4-quart slow cooker. Place meat in cooker. In a small bowl combine onion, port wine, tomato sauce, tapioca, Worcestershire sauce, thyme, oregano, and garlic. Pour over meat.

2 Cover and cook on low-heat setting for 8 to 10 hours or on high-heat setting for 4 to 5 hours. Transfer meat to a serving platter. Skim fat from gravy. Pass gravy with meat. If desired, serve with hot cooked pasta.

Nutrition Facts per serving: 230 cal., 5 g total fat (2 g sat. fat), 84 mg chol., 247 mg sodium, 9 g carbo., 1 g fiber, 31 g pro.
Daily Values: 1% vit. A, 1% vit. C, 2% calcium, 24% iron
Exchanges: ½ Other Carbo., 4½ Very Lean Meat. 1 Fat

cajun pot roast with sweet peppers

If you are monitoring your sodium intake, be sure to read the label on the Cajun seasoning. Some brands contain salt while others are salt-free.

Prep: 20 minutes Cook: 8 to 10 hours (low) or 4 to 5 hours (high) Makes: 6 servings

1	2- to 2½-pound boneless beef chuck pot roast
1	tablespoon Cajun seasoning
1	cup chopped green sweet pepper (1 large)
1	cup chopped yellow sweet pepper (1 large)
½	cup chopped onion (1 medium)
½	teaspoon bottled hot pepper sauce
⅛	teaspoon black pepper
1	14½-ounce can diced tomatoes, undrained

1 Trim fat from meat. Sprinkle Cajun seasoning evenly over meat; rub in with your fingers. If necessary, cut meat to fit into a 3½- to 4½-quart slow cooker. Place meat in cooker. Add sweet peppers, onion, hot pepper sauce, and black pepper. Pour undrained tomatoes over mixture in cooker.

2 Cover and cook on low-heat setting for 8 to 10 hours or on high-heat setting for 4 to 5 hours.

3 Remove meat from cooker. Drain vegetables, discarding cooking liquid. Serve meat with vegetables.

Nutrition Facts per serving: 229 cal., 6 g total fat (2 g sat. fat), 89 mg chol., 310 mg sodium, 9 g carbo., 1 g fiber, 33 g pro.
Daily Values: 3% vit. A, 149% vit. C, 6% calcium, 26% iron
Exchanges: 1 Vegetable, 4½ Very Lean Meat, 1 Fat

6 to 10 grams of carbs

asian-style pot roast

Black bean garlic sauce, a staple in Chinese cuisine, gives a rich, exotic flavor to pot roast. Look for the sauce in the Asian foods section of the supermarket or in Asian grocery stores.

Prep: 30 minutes Cook: 10 to 12 hours (low) or 5 to 6 hours (high), plus 15 minutes (high) Makes: 6 servings

1	2-pound boneless beef chuck pot roast
1	tablespoon cooking oil
1½	cups water
¼	cup black bean garlic sauce
1	teaspoon instant beef bouillon granules
8	ounces green beans, trimmed
1	medium red sweet pepper, cut into thin strips
½	of a medium onion, cut into thin strips
3	tablespoons cornstarch
3	tablespoons cold water
	Hot cooked brown rice (optional)

1 Trim fat from meat. If necessary, cut meat to fit into a 4- to 5½-quart slow cooker. In a large skillet cook meat in hot oil over medium heat until brown on all sides. Drain off fat. Set meat aside.

2 In cooker combine the 1½ cups water, the garlic sauce, and bouillon granules. Add green beans, sweet pepper, and onion. Add meat.

3 Cover and cook on low-heat setting for 10 to 12 hours or on high-heat setting for 5 to 6 hours.

4 Remove meat and vegetables from cooker, reserving cooking liquid. Cover meat and vegetables with foil to keep warm.

5 If using low-heat setting, turn to high-heat setting. For sauce, in a small bowl combine cornstarch and the 3 tablespoons water; stir into cooking liquid in cooker. Cover and cook about 15 minutes more or until sauce is slightly thickened. Using two forks, separate beef into serving pieces. Serve meat and vegetables with sauce. If desired, serve with hot cooked rice.

Nutrition Facts per serving: 261 cal., 9 g total fat (2 g sat. fat), 89 mg chol., 470 mg sodium, 10 g carbo., 2 g fiber, 34 g pro.
Daily Values: 16% vit. A, 62% vit. C, 3% calcium, 26% iron
Exchanges: 1 Vegetable, ½ Other Carbo., 4 Very Lean Meat, 1 Fat

german-style beef roast

In German cuisine, roast seems to have countless versions, all with layers of earthy tang and spice. Red wine, chopped dill pickles, and hearty mustard set this one apart.

Prep: 25 minutes Cook: 8 to 10 hours (low) or 4 to 5 hours (high), plus 10 minutes Makes: 8 servings

1	2½- to 3-pound boneless beef chuck pot roast
1	tablespoon cooking oil
2	cups sliced carrots (4 medium)
2	cups chopped onions (2 large)
1	cup sliced celery (2 stalks)
¾	cup chopped kosher-style dill pickles
½	cup dry red wine or reduced-sodium beef broth
⅓	cup German-style mustard
½	teaspoon coarsely ground black pepper
¼	teaspoon ground cloves
2	bay leaves
2	tablespoons all-purpose flour
2	tablespoons dry red wine or reduced-sodium beef broth
	Hot cooked whole wheat noodles (optional)
	Crumbled crisp-cooked bacon (optional)

1 Trim fat from meat. If necessary, cut meat to fit into a 3½- or 4-quart slow cooker. In a large skillet cook meat in hot oil over medium heat until brown on all sides. Drain off fat. Place carrots, onions, celery, and pickles in slow cooker. Place meat on top of mixture in cooker. In a small bowl combine the ½ cup wine, the mustard, pepper, cloves, and bay leaves. Pour over meat.

2 Cover and cook on low-heat setting for 8 to 10 hours or on high-heat setting for 4 to 5 hours.

3 Transfer meat to a serving platter. Cover meat with foil to keep warm. For gravy, transfer vegetables and cooking liquid to a 2-quart saucepan. Skim off fat. Remove and discard bay leaves. In a small bowl combine flour and the 2 tablespoons wine. Stir flour mixture into liquid in saucepan. Cook and stir over medium heat until thickened and bubbly. Cook and stir for 1 minute more. Serve meat and vegetables with gravy. If desired, serve with hot cooked noodles and sprinkle with bacon.

Nutrition Facts per serving: 256 cal., 7 g total fat (2 g sat. fat), 84 mg chol., 476 mg sodium, 10 g carbo., 2 g fiber, 31 g pro.
Daily Values: 68% vit. A, 7% vit. C, 4% calcium, 23% iron
Exchanges: 1½ Vegetable, 4 Lean Meat

spiced beef brisket

For a real time-saver, freeze half of this plentiful main course. It'll be ready in minutes for dinner on a busy day.

Prep: 15 minutes Cook: 10 to 11 hours (low) or 5 to 5 ½ hours (high), plus 10 minutes Makes: 10 to 12 servings

1	3½- to 4-pound fresh beef brisket
2	cups water
¼	cup ketchup
1	envelope (½ of a 2.2-ounce package) onion soup mix
2	tablespoons Worcestershire sauce
½	teaspoon ground cinnamon
1	clove garlic, minced
¼	teaspoon black pepper
¼	cup cold water
3	tablespoons all-purpose flour

1 Trim fat from meat. If necessary, cut meat to fit into a 3½- or 4-quart slow cooker. Place meat in cooker.

2 In a medium bowl combine the 2 cups water, the ketchup, soup mix, Worcestershire sauce, cinnamon, garlic, and pepper. Pour over brisket.

3 Cover and cook on low-heat setting for 10 to 11 hours or on high-heat setting for 5 to 5½ hours.

4 Transfer meat to a serving platter, reserving cooking liquid. Cover meat with foil to keep warm.

5 For gravy, pour cooking liquid into a glass measuring cup. Skim off fat. Measure 1½ cups cooking liquid; set aside (discard any remaining liquid). In a small saucepan stir the ¼ cup cold water into the flour. Stir in the reserved 1½ cups liquid. Cook and stir over medium heat until thickened and bubbly. Cook and stir for 1 minute more. Thinly slice beef across the grain. Serve with the hot gravy.

Nutrition Facts per serving: 250 cal., 9 g total fat (3 g sat. fat), 76 mg chol., 474 mg sodium, 6 g carbo., 0 g fiber, 33 g pro.
Daily Values: 1% vit. A, 2% vit. C, 2% calcium, 19% iron
Exchanges: ½ Other Carbo., 4½ Lean Meat

beef with winter vegetables

Instead of potatoes, this recipe calls on beets and turnips to add interest to this classic one-dish meal. You'll love the way beer, mustard, and horseradish flavor and enrich the sauce.

Prep: 30 minutes Cook: 10 to 12 hours (low) or 5 to 6 hours (high) Makes: 10 servings

1	pound beets, peeled and cut into 1-inch pieces
8	ounces turnips, peeled and cut into 1-inch pieces
1	large onion, cut into thick wedges
1	tablespoon quick-cooking tapioca
1	3- to 3½-pound fresh beef brisket
1½	teaspoons ground allspice
1½	teaspoons dried thyme, crushed
1	teaspoon cracked black pepper
½	teaspoon paprika
½	teaspoon dried sage, crushed
½	teaspoon salt
4	cups coarsely chopped cabbage
⅓	cup light beer
½	cup fat-free half-and-half
3	tablespoons stone-ground mustard
1	to 2 tablespoons prepared horseradish

---

1 In a 5- to 6-quart slow cooker place beets, turnips, and onion. Sprinkle tapioca over mixture in cooker. Trim fat from meat. Add meat to cooker. Sprinkle with allspice, thyme, pepper, paprika, sage, and salt. Add cabbage. Pour beer over mixture in cooker.

2 Cover and cook on low-heat setting for 10 to 12 hours or on high-heat setting for 5 to 6 hours.

3 Transfer meat to a serving platter. Cover meat with foil to keep warm.

4 In a small bowl combine half-and-half, mustard, and horseradish. Stir half-and-half mixture into vegetable mixture in slow cooker. Serve vegetable mixture with meat.

Nutrition Facts per serving: 248 cal., 8 g total fat (3 g sat. fat), 82 mg chol., 342 mg sodium, 10 g carbo., 2 g fiber, 30 g pro.
Daily Values: 3% vit. A, 21% vit. C, 5% calcium, 19% iron
Exchanges: 1 Vegetable, 4 Very Lean Meat, 2 Fat

gingered brisket

With sherry, garlic, ginger, crushed red pepper, and hoisin sauce, this flavorful brisket is definitely Asian-inspired!

Prep: 20 minutes Cook: 10 to 12 hours (low) or 5 to 6 hours (high) Makes: 8 to 10 servings

1	2$\frac{1}{2}$- to 3-pound fresh beef brisket
2	4$\frac{1}{2}$-ounce jars whole mushrooms, drained
2	tablespoons quick-cooking tapioca
$\frac{1}{4}$	cup bottled hoisin sauce
$\frac{1}{4}$	cup water
2	tablespoons reduced-sodium soy sauce
2	tablespoons dry sherry
1	tablespoon grated fresh ginger
$\frac{1}{2}$	teaspoon garlic powder
$\frac{1}{4}$	to $\frac{1}{2}$ teaspoon crushed red pepper
$\frac{1}{2}$	cup bias-sliced green onions (4)
	Hot cooked brown rice (optional)

1 Trim fat from meat. If necessary, cut meat to fit into a 3$\frac{1}{2}$- or 4-quart slow cooker. Place meat in cooker. Add mushrooms and tapioca.

2 For sauce, in a small bowl combine hoisin sauce, water, soy sauce, dry sherry, ginger, garlic powder, and crushed red pepper. Pour over mixture in cooker.

3 Cover and cook on low-heat setting for 10 to 12 hours or on high-heat setting for 5 to 6 hours.

4 Transfer meat and mushrooms to a serving platter. If necessary, skim fat from sauce. Spoon some of the sauce over meat and mushrooms and sprinkle with green onions. If desired, serve with hot cooked rice. Pass remaining sauce.

Nutrition Facts per serving: 242 cal., 9 g total fat (3 g sat. fat), 86 mg chol., 495 mg sodium, 8 g carbo., 1 g fiber, 31 g pro.
Daily Values: 3% vit. A, 2% vit. C, 3% calcium, 17% iron
Exchanges: $\frac{1}{2}$ Other Carbo., 4 Very Lean Meat, 1$\frac{1}{2}$ Fat

beef brisket with barbecue sauce

When you feel like barbecuing without cooking on the grill, here's the answer: Prepare a classic barbecue sauce from some of the cooking liquid and pass with the juicy, tender meat.

Prep: 25 minutes Cook: 10 to 12 hours (low) or 5 to 6 hours (high), plus 10 minutes Makes: 8 servings

1	2½-pound fresh beef brisket
¾	cup water
¼	cup Worcestershire sauce
1	tablespoon vinegar
1	teaspoon instant beef bouillon granules
½	teaspoon dry mustard
½	teaspoon chili powder
¼	teaspoon cayenne pepper
2	cloves garlic, minced
½	cup ketchup
2	tablespoons heat-stable granular sugar substitute
2	tablespoons butter

6 to 10 grams of carbs

1 Trim fat from meat. If necessary, cut meat to fit into a 3½- or 4-quart slow cooker. Set aside. In a medium bowl combine water, Worcestershire sauce, vinegar, bouillon granules, mustard, chili powder, cayenne pepper, and garlic. Reserve ½ cup mixture for sauce; set aside in refrigerator. Place meat in cooker. Add remaining Worcestershire sauce mixture.

2 Cover and cook on low-heat setting for 10 to 12 hours or on high-heat setting for 5 to 6 hours.

3 For sauce, in a small saucepan combine the ½ cup reserved Worcestershire sauce mixture, the ketchup, sugar substitute, and butter. Heat through over medium heat. Pass sauce with meat.

Nutrition Facts per serving: 194 cal., 9 g total fat (4 g sat. fat), 56 mg chol., 482 mg sodium, 7 g carbo., 0 g fiber, 21 g pro.
Daily Values: 8% vit. A, 5% vit. C, 2% calcium, 15% iron
Exchanges: ½ Other Carbo., 3 Lean Meat

short ribs with leeks

Lemon peel freshens the flavors of this succulent, savory dish. Try it when you have a house full of guests and want to spend time with them away from the kitchen.

6 to 10 grams of carbs

Prep: 30 minutes **Cook:** 7 to 8 hours (low) or 3½ to 4 hours (high), plus 10 minutes **Makes:** 8 servings

8	ounces fresh mushrooms, halved
4	medium carrots, cut into 1-inch pieces
4	medium leeks, cut into 1-inch slices
2	pounds boneless beef short ribs
2	teaspoons finely shredded lemon peel
½	teaspoon black pepper
½	teaspoon dried rosemary, crushed
½	teaspoon dried thyme, crushed
¼	teaspoon salt
¾	cup reduced-sodium beef broth
⅓	cup light dairy sour cream
2	teaspoons cornstarch

1 In a 3½- or 4-quart slow cooker place mushrooms, carrots, and leeks. Place meat on top of vegetables. Sprinkle with lemon peel, pepper, rosemary, thyme, and salt. Add beef broth.

2 Cover and cook on low-heat setting for 7 to 8 hours or on high-heat setting for 3½ to 4 hours.

3 Transfer meat and vegetables to a serving platter, reserving cooking liquid. Cover meat with foil to keep warm.

4 For sauce, pour cooking liquid into a glass measuring cup; skim off fat. Measure 1 cup cooking liquid. Pour liquid into a small saucepan. In a small bowl combine sour cream and cornstarch. Whisk sour cream mixture into liquid in saucepan. Cook and stir over medium heat until slightly thickened (do not boil). Spoon sauce over meat and vegetables.

Nutrition Facts per serving: 223 cal., 11 g total fat (4 g sat. fat), 68 mg chol.,
219 mg sodium, 7 g carbo., 2 g fiber, 24 g pro.
Daily Values: 72% vit. A, 6% vit. C, 5% calcium, 17% iron
Exchanges: 1½ Vegetable, 3 Lean Meat, ½ Fat

beef and garden vegetable soup

This rich and satisfying chili-flavored soup has chunks of beef and a basketful of vegetables. Stewing the bones adds beefy flavor and body to the broth.

Prep: 30 minutes Cook: 8 to 10 hours (low) or 4 to 5 hours (high) Makes: 6 to 8 servings (10 cups)

2	to 2½ pounds meaty beef shank crosscuts
1½	cups sliced celery (3 stalks)
½	cup bias-sliced carrot (1 medium)
2	cups coarsely chopped cabbage
1	cup coarsely chopped onion (1 large)
3	cups water
2	cups low-sodium tomato juice
1	tablespoon instant beef bouillon granules
1	tablespoon Worcestershire sauce
1	teaspoon chili powder
2	bay leaves

---

1 Trim fat from meat. Cut meat into 1-inch cubes, reserving bones. In a 3½- to 6-quart slow cooker layer celery, carrot, cabbage, onion, beef, and beef bones. Add water, tomato juice, bouillon granules, Worcestershire sauce, chili powder, and bay leaves.

2 Cover and cook on low-heat setting for 8 to 10 hours or on high-heat setting for 4 to 5 hours. Remove and discard bones and bay leaves. Skim off fat.

Nutrition Facts per serving: 157 cal., 3 g total fat (1 g sat. fat), 35 mg chol., 559 mg sodium, 10 g carbo., 2 g fiber, 21 g pro.
Daily Values: 33% vit. A, 49% vit. C, 6% calcium, 16% iron
Exchanges: 1 Vegetable, 2½ Very Lean Meat, ½ Fat

classic beef stroganoff

Beef Stroganoff usually calls for tenderloin or sirloin steak, but this recipe calls for less-expensive stew meat, and lets the slow-cooker work its slow-simmering magic for rich results.

Prep: 30 minutes Cook: 8 to 10 hours (low) or 4 to 5 hours (high), plus 30 minutes (high) Makes: 6 servings

$1\frac{1}{2}$	pounds beef stew meat
1	tablespoon cooking oil
2	cups sliced fresh mushrooms
$\frac{1}{2}$	cup sliced green onions (4) or chopped onion (1 medium)
2	cloves garlic, minced
$\frac{1}{2}$	teaspoon dried oregano, crushed
$\frac{1}{2}$	teaspoon salt
$\frac{1}{4}$	teaspoon dried thyme, crushed
$\frac{1}{4}$	teaspoon black pepper
1	bay leaf
$1\frac{1}{2}$	cups reduced-sodium beef broth
$\frac{1}{3}$	cup dry sherry
1	8-ounce carton light dairy sour cream
$\frac{1}{4}$	cup cold water
2	tablespoons cornstarch
	Snipped fresh parsley (optional)

1 Trim fat from meat. Cut meat into 1-inch pieces. In a large nonstick skillet cook meat, half at a time, in hot oil over medium heat until brown. Drain off fat. Set aside.

2 In a $3\frac{1}{2}$- or 4-quart slow cooker place mushrooms, green onions, garlic, oregano, salt, thyme, pepper, and bay leaf. Add meat. Pour beef broth and sherry over all.

3 Cover and cook on low-heat setting for 8 to 10 hours or on high-heat setting for 4 to 5 hours. Remove bay leaf.

4 If using low-heat setting, turn to high-heat setting. In a medium bowl combine sour cream, water, and cornstarch. Stir about 1 cup of the hot cooking liquid into sour cream mixture. Stir sour cream mixture into mixture in cooker. Cover and cook about 30 minutes more or until thickened. If desired, sprinkle each serving with parsley.

Nutrition Facts per serving: 248 cal., 9 g total fat (4 g sat. fat), 79 mg chol., 408 mg sodium, 8 g carbo., 1 g fiber, 28 g pro.
Daily Values: 7% vit. A, 3% vit. C, 9% calcium, 18% iron
Exchanges: 1 Vegetable, 4 Lean Meat

beef in red wine gravy

This stew is the perfect way to use a small amount of leftover red wine. If you buy a bottle of wine, choose one of the same quality you would drink. Pictured on the back cover.

6 to 10 grams of carbs

Prep: 15 minutes Cook: 10 to 12 hours (low) or 5 to 6 hours (high), plus 15 minutes (high) Makes: 6 servings

1½	pounds beef stew meat
1	cup coarsely chopped onion (1 large)
2	beef bouillon cubes
	Salt and black pepper (optional)
1½	cups dry red wine
3	tablespoons cornstarch
3	tablespoons cold water
	Hot cooked whole wheat pasta (optional)

1 Trim fat from meat. Cut meat into 1-inch pieces. In a 3½- or 4-quart slow cooker place meat and onion. Add bouillon cubes. If desired, sprinkle with salt and pepper. Add wine.

2 Cover and cook on low-heat setting for 10 to 12 hours or on high-heat setting for 5 to 6 hours.

3 If using low-heat setting, turn to high-heat setting. In a small bowl combine cornstarch and water. Stir into mixture in slow-cooker. Cover and cook about 15 minutes more or until thickened. If desired, serve with hot cooked pasta.

Nutrition Facts per serving: 215 cal., 4 g total fat (1 g sat. fat), 64 mg chol., 405 mg sodium, 7 g carbo., 1 g fiber, 26 g pro.
Daily Values: 2% vit. C, 2% calcium, 16% iron
Exchanges: ½ Other Carbo., 4 Very Lean Meat. 1 Fat

dijon-pepper steak

Pepper steak is a classic French dish that starts with pressing cracked black pepper into the meat and finishes with an easy sauce. This slow-cooker version follows that basic plan.

Prep: 20 minutes Cook: 8 to 10 hours (low) or 4 to 5 hours (high) Makes: 6 servings

2	pounds boneless beef sirloin steak, cut 1 inch thick
1½	teaspoons cracked black pepper
1	tablespoon cooking oil
2	cups packaged peeled baby carrots
1	medium onion, sliced
1	10¾-ounce can condensed cream of celery soup
¼	cup Dijon-style mustard
	Hot cooked whole wheat noodles (optional)

1 Trim fat from meat. Cut meat into 6 serving-size pieces. Sprinkle pepper evenly over meat; press in with your fingers. In a large skillet brown meat, half at a time, in hot oil over medium heat. Drain off fat. Set aside.

2 In a 3½- or 4-quart slow cooker place carrots and onion. Add meat. In a medium bowl combine celery soup and Dijon mustard. Pour over mixture in cooker.

3 Cover and cook on low-heat setting for 8 to 10 hours or on high-heat setting for 4 to 5 hours. If desired, serve over hot cooked noodles.

Nutrition Facts per serving: 256 cal., 8 g total fat (2 g sat. fat), 93 mg chol., 533 mg sodium, 10 g carbo., 1 g fiber, 33 g pro.
Daily Values: 82% vit. A, 4% vit. C, 3% calcium, 24% iron
Exchanges: 1 Vegetable, ½ Other Carbo., 4 Lean Meat

southwestern steak and green bean soup

Purchased salsa is the shortcut to the bold flavors in this soup. Choose your favorite brand for your own "house specialty" version.

Prep: 25 minutes **Cook:** 8 to 10 hours (low) or 4 to 5 hours (high) **Makes:** 6 servings (8 cups)

1½	pounds boneless beef sirloin steak, cut 1 inch thick
2	cups frozen cut green beans
1	small onion, sliced and separated into rings
1	16-ounce jar thick and chunky salsa
1	14-ounce can reduced-sodium beef broth
1	teaspoon dried basil, crushed
2	cloves garlic, minced
	Shredded reduced-fat Monterey Jack or Mexican blend cheese (optional)

1 Trim fat from meat. Cut meat into 1-inch pieces. In a 3½- or 4-quart slow cooker place green beans and onion. Add meat. In a medium bowl combine salsa, beef broth, basil, and garlic. Pour over mixture in cooker.

2 Cover and cook on low-heat setting for 8 to 10 hours or on high-heat setting for 4 to 5 hours. If desired, sprinkle each serving with cheese.

Nutrition Facts per serving: 187 cal., 4 g total fat (1 g sat. fat), 53 mg chol., 773 mg sodium, 9 g carbo., 1 g fiber, 26 g pro.
Daily Values: 9% vit. A, 9% vit. C, 4% calcium, 16% iron
Exchanges: 1½ Vegetable, 3 Lean Meat

6 to 10 grams of carbs

round steak with mustard pepper strips

Use both red and yellow sweet peppers to make this delicious dish stand out on the dinner table. A green salad with a vinaigrette would round out the meal.

Prep: 20 minutes Cook: 6 to 8 to hours (low) or 3 to 4 hours (high), plus 15 minutes (high) Makes: 8 servings

2	to 2½ pounds boneless beef round steak, cut ¾ inch thick
1	large onion, cut into wedges
2	cloves garlic, minced
½	teaspoon dried thyme, crushed
⅛	teaspoon black pepper
¼	cup beef broth or water
2	medium red and/or yellow sweet peppers, cut into ½-inch strips
½	cup fat-free half-and-half
3	tablespoons Dijon-style mustard
2	tablespoons cornstarch

1 Trim fat from meat. If necessary, cut meat to fit into a 3½- or 4-quart slow cooker. Place meat, onion, and garlic in cooker. Sprinkle with thyme and black pepper. Pour beef broth over mixture in cooker.

2 Cover and cook on low-heat setting for 6 to 8 hours or on high-heat setting for 3 to 4 hours.

3 Transfer meat and onion to a serving platter, reserving cooking liquid. Cover meat to keep warm.

4 If using low-heat setting, turn to high-heat setting. Stir sweet pepper strips into cooking liquid. In a small bowl combine half-and-half, mustard, and cornstarch. Stir into mixture in cooker. Cover and cook about 15 minutes more or until thickened. Spoon pepper strips and some of the sauce over meat and onion; pass remaining sauce.

Nutrition Facts per serving: 185 cal., 4 g total fat (1 g sat. fat), 66 mg chol., 244 mg sodium, 7 g carbo., 1 g fiber, 26 g pro.
Daily Values: 18% vit. A, 82% vit. C, 2% calcium, 15% iron
Exchanges: ½ Vegetable, 3½ Very Lean Meat, 1 Fat

salsa swiss steak

We turned up the flavor a bit by adding salsa to this ever-popular saucy steak. It's still as family pleasing (and easy) as ever.

Prep: 15 minutes Cook: 9 to 10 hours (low) or 4½ to 5 hours (high) Makes: 8 servings

2	to 2½ pounds boneless beef round steak, cut ¾ inch thick
1	large green sweet pepper, cut into bite-size strips
1	medium onion, sliced
1	10¾-ounce can reduced-fat and reduced-sodium condensed cream of mushroom soup
1	cup bottled salsa
2	tablespoons all-purpose flour
1	teaspoon dry mustard
	Hot cooked brown rice (optional)

1 Trim fat from meat. Cut meat into 6 serving-size pieces. In a 3½- or 4-quart slow cooker place meat, sweet pepper, and onion.

2 In a medium bowl combine mushroom soup, salsa, flour, and dry mustard. Pour over mixture in cooker.

3 Cover and cook on low-heat setting for 9 to 10 hours or on high-heat setting for 4½ to 5 hours. If desired, serve with hot cooked rice.

Nutrition Facts per serving: 191 cal., 6 g total fat (1 g sat. fat), 67 mg chol., 292 mg sodium, 7 g carbo., 1 g fiber, 26 g pro.
Daily Values: 3% vit. A, 26% vit. C, 1% calcium, 17% iron
Exchanges: ½ Vegetable, 3½ Very Lean Meat, 1 Fat

so-easy pepper steak

Vary the style of the stewed tomatoes each time you make this simple standby—Cajun, Mexican, or Italian—for a whole new dish.

Prep: 15 minutes Cook: 10 to 12 hours (low) or 5 to 6 hours (high) Makes: 8 servings

2	pounds boneless beef round steak, cut $^3/_4$ to 1 inch thick
	Salt and black pepper
1	14$^1/_2$-ounce can Cajun-, Mexican-, or Italian-style stewed tomatoes; undrained
$^1/_3$	cup tomato paste with Italian seasoning
$^1/_2$	teaspoon bottled hot pepper sauce
1	16-ounce package frozen pepper stir-fry vegetables (yellow, green, and red peppers with onion)
	Hot cooked whole wheat pasta (optional)

1 Trim fat from meat. Cut meat into serving-size pieces. Sprinkle lightly with salt and black pepper. Place meat in a 3½- or 4-quart slow cooker. In a medium bowl combine undrained tomatoes, tomato paste, and hot pepper sauce. Pour over meat in cooker. Top with frozen vegetables.

2 Cover and cook on low-heat setting for 10 to 12 hours or on high-heat setting for 5 to 6 hours. If desired, serve with hot cooked pasta.

Nutrition Facts per serving: 196 cal., 5 g total fat (2 g sat. fat), 54 mg chol., 411 mg sodium, 9 g carbo., 1 g fiber, 27 g pro.
Daily Values: 7% vit. A, 47% vit. C, 1% calcium, 15% iron
Exchanges: 1 Vegetable, 3½ Very Lean meat, 1 Fat

swiss steak café

Coffee may sound like a strange ingredient in a meat dish, but it helps enrich the flavor of the nicely bodied brown sauce.

Prep: 20 minutes Cook: 8 to 10 hours (low) or 4 to 5 hours (high), plus 15 minutes (high) Makes: 6 servings

2	pounds boneless beef round steak, cut ¾ inch thick
1	tablespoon cooking oil
3	medium onions, cut into wedges
1	cup brewed coffee
2	tablespoons reduced-sodium soy sauce
2	cloves garlic, minced
2	bay leaves
½	teaspoon dried oregano, crushed
4	teaspoons cornstarch
4	teaspoons cold water

6 to 10 grams of carbs

1 Trim fat from meat. Cut meat into serving-size pieces. In a large skillet cook meat, half at a time, in hot oil over medium heat until brown (add more oil, if necessary). Drain off fat. Place onions in a 3½- or 4-quart slow cooker. Add meat. In a small bowl combine coffee, soy sauce, garlic, bay leaves, and oregano. Pour over meat in cooker.

2 Cover and cook on low-heat setting for 8 to 10 hours or on high-heat setting for 4 to 5 hours.

3 Transfer meat and onions to a serving platter, reserving cooking liquid. Cover meat and onions with foil to keep warm.

4 If using low-heat setting, turn to high-heat setting. In a small bowl combine cornstarch and water. Stir into liquid in cooker. Cover and cook about 15 minutes more or until thickened. Remove and discard bay leaves. Spoon some of the sauce over meat and onions. Pass remaining sauce.

Nutrition Facts per serving: 224 cal., 6 g total fat (1 g sat. fat), 85 mg chol., 387 mg sodium, 6 g carbo., 1 g fiber, 36 g pro.
Daily Values: 1% vit. A, 4% vit. C, 2% calcium, 19% iron
Exchanges: 1 Vegetable, 4½ Very Lean Meat, 1 Fat

italian-style steak

You can use red wine for a hearty dish and white wine or beef broth for a mild dish. All choices are delicious.

Prep: 20 minutes Cook: 9 to 10 hours (low) or 4½ to 5 hours (high),
plus 15 minutes (high) Makes: 6 servings (about 7 cups)

1½	pounds boneless beef bottom round steak
2	medium carrots, cut into ½-inch pieces
2	stalks celery, cut into ½-inch pieces
1	cup quartered fresh mushrooms
½	cup sliced green onions (4)
1	14½-ounce can Italian-style stewed tomatoes, undrained
1	cup reduced-sodium beef broth
½	cup dry red wine, white wine, or reduced-sodium beef broth
1	teaspoon dried Italian seasoning, crushed
½	teaspoon salt
¼	teaspoon black pepper
1	bay leaf
3	tablespoons cornstarch
3	tablespoons cold water

1 Trim fat from meat. Cut meat into 1-inch pieces. Place meat in a 3½- or 4-quart slow cooker. Add carrots, celery, mushrooms, and green onions. In a medium bowl combine undrained tomatoes, beef broth, wine, Italian seasoning, salt, pepper, and bay leaf. Pour over meat and vegetables.

2 Cover and cook on low-heat setting for 9 to 10 hours or on high-heat setting for 4½ to 5 hours.

3 If using low-heat setting, turn to high-heat setting. In a small bowl combine cornstarch and water. Stir into mixture in cooker. Cover and cook about 15 minutes more or until thickened. Remove and discard bay leaf.

Nutrition Facts per serving: 216 cal., 6 g total fat (2 g sat. fat), 66 mg chol., 589 mg sodium, 9 g carbo., 2 g fiber, 27 g pro.
Daily Values: 47% vit. A, 6% vit. C, 5% calcium, 21% iron
Exchanges: 1 Vegetable, 3½ Very Lean Meat. 1½ Fat

mustard-sauced round steak

Dill mustard adds tremendous flavor to this round steak. Another time, use a different type of mustard, such as a horseradish variety, for a whole new take on the dish.

Prep: 25 minutes Cook: 6 to 8 hours (low) or 3 to 4 hours (high), plus 15 minutes (high) Makes: 4 servings

2	pounds boneless beef round steak, cut ³⁄₄ inch thick
¹⁄₄	teaspoon salt
¹⁄₂	teaspoon black pepper
2	medium fennel bulbs, trimmed and cut into wedges
¹⁄₂	cup reduced-sodium beef broth
3	tablespoons dill mustard
¹⁄₂	cup fat-free half-and-half
1	tablespoon cornstarch

1 Trim fat from meat. Sprinkle both sides of meat with salt and pepper. Cut meat into 4 serving-size pieces. Place fennel in a 3½- or 4-quart slow cooker. Place meat on top of fennel. In a small bowl combine beef broth and mustard. Pour over meat.

2 Cover and cook on low-heat setting for 6 to 8 hours or on high-heat setting for 3 to 4 hours.

3 Transfer meat and fennel to a serving platter, reserving cooking liquid. Cover meat with foil to keep warm.

4 If using low-heat setting, turn to high-heat setting. For sauce, in a small bowl combine half-and-half and cornstarch. Stir into cooking liquid. Cover and cook about 15 minutes more or until thickened. Serve meat and fennel with sauce.

Nutrition Facts per serving: 237 cal., 7 g total fat (2 g sat. fat), 87 mg chol., 438 mg sodium, 7 g carbo., 1 g fiber, 36 g pro.
Daily Values: 6% vit. C, 4% calcium, 21% iron
Exchanges: 1 Vegetable, 4 Lean Meat

balsamic beef salad

Although balsamic vinegar has been made in Italy for ages, this country took a while to adopt the ingredient. What a find! It contributes a rich fat-free flavor to this salad.

Prep: 30 minutes Cook: 6 to 7 hours (low) or 3 to 3½ hours (high) Makes: 8 to 10 servings

2½	pounds boneless beef round steak
1	medium onion, cut into thin wedges
⅓	cup reduced-sodium beef broth
⅓	cup balsamic vinegar
¼	teaspoon salt
⅛	teaspoon black pepper
2	cloves garlic, minced
12	cups torn mixed salad greens
8	slices turkey bacon, crisp-cooked, drained, and crumbled
4	hard-cooked eggs, peeled and chopped
1	cup shredded reduced-fat Monterey Jack cheese (4 ounces)
⅔	cup chopped roma tomatoes (2 medium)

1 Trim fat from meat. Cut meat across the grain into ½-inch strips. In a 3½- or 4-quart slow cooker place meat and onion. Stir in beef broth, vinegar, salt, pepper, and garlic.

2 Cover and cook on low-heat setting for 6 to 7 hours or on high-heat setting for 3 to 3½ hours.

3 Arrange greens on salad plates. Using tongs, remove meat and onions from cooker and place on greens. Top with bacon, eggs, cheese, and tomatoes. Strain cooking liquid. Drizzle each salad with a little of the strained liquid. Discard any remaining liquid.

Nutrition Facts per serving: 243 cal., 8 g total fat (3 g sat. fat), 150 mg chol.,
394 mg sodium, 6 g carbo., 1 g fiber, 34 g pro.
Daily Values: 9% vit. A, 9% vit. C, 11% calcium, 16% iron
Exchanges: 1 Vegetable, 4 Lean Meat

6 to 10 grams of carbs

italian steak rolls

These delicious steak rolls inherit their Italian flair from Parmesan cheese and spaghetti sauce. Serve with hot cooked whole wheat pasta, if desired.

6 to 10 grams of carbs

Prep: 30 minutes Cook: 8 to 10 hours (low) or 4 to 5 hours (high) Makes: 6 servings

1/2	cup shredded carrot (1 medium)
1/3	cup chopped zucchini
1/3	cup chopped red or green sweet pepper
1/4	cup sliced green onions (2)
2	tablespoons grated Parmesan cheese
1	tablespoon snipped fresh parsley
1	clove garlic, minced
1/4	teaspoon black pepper
6	tenderized beef round steaks (about 2 pounds total)*
2	cups low-carb spaghetti sauce
	Hot cooked whole wheat pasta (optional)

1 For filling, in a small bowl combine carrot, zucchini, sweet pepper, green onions, Parmesan cheese, parsley, garlic, and black pepper. Spoon ¼ cup of the filling onto each piece of meat. Roll up meat around the filling and tie each roll with 100-percent cotton string or secure with wooden toothpicks. Place the meat rolls in a 3½- or 4-quart slow cooker. Pour spaghetti sauce over the meat rolls.

2 Cover and cook on low-heat setting for 8 to 10 hours or on high-heat setting for 4 to 5 hours. Discard string or toothpicks. If desired, serve meat rolls and sauce with hot cooked pasta.

*Note: If you can't find tenderized round steak, ask a butcher to tenderize 2 pounds boneless beef round steak and cut it into 6 pieces. Or cut 2 pounds boneless beef round steak into 6 serving-size pieces. Place the meat between 2 pieces of plastic wrap and, using a meat mallet, pound the steak to ¼- to ½-inch thickness.

Nutrition Facts per serving: 270 cal., 11 g total fat (3 g sat. fat), 73 mg chol.,
504 mg sodium, 6 g carbo., 2 g fiber, 36 g pro.
Daily Values: 38% vit. A, 38% vit. C, 5% calcium, 21% iron
Exchanges: 1 Vegetable, 5 Very Lean Meat, 1½ Fat

chipotle country-style ribs

Great-tasting ribs with just five ingredients? Chipotle chiles make it happen. These flavor-charged babies are actually jalepeño peppers that have been dried and smoked.

Prep: 15 minutes **Cook:** 10 to 12 hours (low) or 5 to 6 hours (high), plus 15 minutes (high) **Makes:** 8 servings

2½	to 3 pounds boneless pork country-style ribs
1	12-ounce bottle barbecue sauce
2	canned chipotle chiles in adobo sauce, finely chopped
2	tablespoons cornstarch
2	tablespoons cold water

1 Place ribs in a 4- to 5-quart slow cooker. In a medium bowl combine barbecue sauce and chipotle chiles. Pour over ribs in cooker.

2 Cover and cook on low-heat setting for 10 to 12 hours or on high-heat setting for 5 to 6 hours.

3 Transfer ribs to a serving platter, reserving cooking liquid. Cover the ribs with foil to keep warm.

4 If using low-heat setting, turn to high-heat setting. In a small bowl combine cornstarch and water. Stir into liquid in cooker. Cover and cook about 15 minutes more or until thickened. Serve ribs with sauce.

Nutrition Facts per serving: 260 cal., 12 g total fat (4 g sat. fat), 90 mg chol., 459 mg sodium, 8 g carbo., 1 g fiber, 28 g pro.
Daily Values: 1% vit. A, 6% vit. C, 4% calcium, 10% iron
Exchanges: ½ Other Carbo., 4 Lean Meat

five-spice pork ribs

Add a windfall of colorful vegetables to this dish—without peeling and chopping—using frozen stir-fry vegetables. Five-spice powder enhances the dish with flavor.

Prep: 10 minutes Cook: 8 to 10 hours (low) or 4 to 5 hours (high) Makes: 6 to 8 servings

1	16-ounce package frozen pepper stir-fry vegetables (yellow, green, and red sweet peppers and onions)
3	pounds pork country-style ribs
1/4	teaspoon salt
1/4	teaspoon black pepper
1/4	cup reduced-sodium beef broth
3	tablespoons reduced-sodium soy sauce
1	teaspoon five-spice powder or Homemade Five-Spice Powder (see recipe, page 111)
1/4	teaspoon ground ginger
1	clove garlic, minced

1 Place frozen vegetables in a 4½- to 6-quart slow cooker. Top with ribs. Sprinkle with salt and pepper. In a small bowl combine beef broth, soy sauce, five-spice powder, ginger, and garlic. Pour over ribs in cooker.

2 Cover and cook on low-heat setting for 8 to 10 hours or on high-heat setting for 4 to 5 hours. Using a slotted spoon, transfer ribs and vegetables to a serving platter; discard cooking liquid.

Nutrition Facts per serving: 226 cal., 10 g total fat (3 g sat. fat), 81 mg chol., 498 mg sodium, 6 g carbo., 1 g fiber, 26 g pro.
Daily Values: 10% vit. A, 47% vit. C, 4% calcium, 11% iron
Exchanges: 1 Vegetable, 3½ Lean Meat

6 to 10 grams of carbs

pork chops with a kick

Hot-style vegetable juice is the convenient ingredient here. It transforms itself into a rich tomato sauce with just the right hint of peppery notes.

Prep: 25 minutes **Cook:** 5 to 6 hours (low) or 2 ½ to 3 hours (high), plus 10 minutes **Makes:** 8 servings

1	cup bias-sliced celery (2 stalks)
1	cup chopped onion (1 large)
8	boneless pork loin chops, cut ¾ inch thick
2	cups red and/or green sweet pepper strips (2 large)
½	teaspoon cracked black pepper
2	cups hot-style vegetable juice
2	tablespoons cornstarch
2	tablespoons cold water

1 In a 3½- or 4-quart slow cooker place celery and onion. Trim fat from chops. Add chops to cooker in layers, sprinkling sweet pepper strips and black pepper between chops. Pour vegetable juice over mixture in cooker.

2 Cover and cook on low-heat setting for 5 to 6 hours or on high-heat setting for 2½ to 3 hours.

3 Transfer chops and vegetables to a serving platter, reserving cooking liquid. Cover chops and vegetables with foil to keep warm.

4 For sauce, strain cooking liquid into a glass measuring cup; skim off fat. Measure 2 cups cooking liquid. Pour liquid into a medium saucepan. In a small bowl combine cornstarch and water. Stir into liquid in saucepan. Cook and stir over medium heat until thickened and bubbly. Cook and stir for 2 minutes more. Serve chops and vegetables with sauce.

Nutrition Facts per serving: 189 cal., 6 g total fat (2 g sat. fat), 54 mg chol., 254 mg sodium, 9 g carbo., 2 g fiber, 23 g pro.
Daily Values: 51% vit. A, 119% vit. C, 2% calcium, 7% iron
Exchanges: 1 Vegetable, 3 Very Lean Meat, 1 Fat

mediterranean pork stew

Mushrooms, sweet peppers, and artichoke hearts make up a melange of Mediterranean flavors to dress up otherwise plain pork.

Prep: 25 minutes Cook: 6 to 8 hours (low) or 3 to 4 hours (high), plus 15 minutes (high) Makes: 8 servings (11 cups)

2	pounds boneless pork shoulder
	Nonstick cooking spray
1	tablespoon olive oil or cooking oil
3	14-ounce cans reduced-sodium chicken broth
3	cups quartered mushrooms (8 ounces)
1	12-ounce jar roasted red sweet peppers, drained and chopped
2	tablespoons balsamic vinegar
¼	teaspoon black pepper
2	tablespoons cornstarch
2	tablespoons cold water
1	6-ounce jar marinated artichoke hearts, undrained
½	cup crumbled feta cheese (2 ounces)

1 Trim fat from meat. Cut meat into 1-inch pieces. Lightly coat a large skillet with cooking spray. Cook half of the meat in hot skillet over medium heat until brown. Remove meat from skillet. Add oil to skillet. Cook remaining meat in hot oil until brown. Drain off fat. In a 4- to 5½-quart slow cooker combine the meat, chicken broth, mushrooms, sweet peppers, vinegar, and black pepper.

2 Cover and cook on low-heat setting for 6 to 8 hours or on high-heat setting for 3 to 4 hours.

3 If using low-heat setting, turn to high-heat setting. In a small bowl combine cornstarch and water. Stir cornstarch mixture and undrained artichoke hearts into mixture in cooker. Cover and cook about 15 minutes more or until thickened. Top each serving with feta cheese.

Nutrition Facts per serving: 228 cal., 10 g total fat (3 g sat. fat), 73 mg chol., 516 mg sodium, 8 g carbo., 1 g fiber, 25 g pro.
Daily Values: 137% vit. C, 1% calcium, 12% iron
Exchanges: 1½ Vegetable, 3 Lean Meat, ½ Fat

pork and mushroom marengo

Marengo refers to the battle Napoléon Bonaparte won against Austria in 1800. To celebrate the victory, Napoléon's chef invented a dish similar to this one.

Prep: 30 minutes Cook: 8 to 10 hours (low) or 4 to 5 hours (high), plus 15 minutes (high) Makes: 6 servings

1½	pounds boneless pork shoulder
3	cups sliced fresh mushrooms (8 ounces)
½	cup chopped onion (1 medium)
1	14½-ounce can diced tomatoes, undrained
1	cup water
1	teaspoon dried marjoram, crushed
1	teaspoon dried thyme, crushed
1	teaspoon instant chicken bouillon granules
¼	teaspoon salt
	Dash black pepper
3	tablespoons cornstarch
3	tablespoons cold water
	Hot cooked brown rice (optional)

1 Trim fat from meat; cut meat into 1-inch pieces. In a 3½- or 4-quart slow cooker place mushrooms and onion. Add meat. In a medium bowl combine undrained tomatoes, the 1 cup water, the marjoram, thyme, bouillon granules, salt, and pepper. Pour over mixture in cooker.

2 Cover and cook on low-heat setting for 8 to 10 hours or on high-heat setting for 4 to 5 hours.

3 If using low-heat setting, turn to high-heat setting. In a small bowl combine cornstarch and the 3 tablespoons water. Stir into mixture in cooker. Cover and cook about 15 minutes more or until thickened. If desired, serve with hot cooked brown rice.

Nutrition Facts per serving: 208 cal., 7 g total fat (2 g sat. fat), 73 mg chol., 452 mg sodium, 10 g carbo., 1 g fiber, 24 g pro.
Daily Values: 1% vit. A, 17% vit. C, 4% calcium, 13% iron
Exchanges: 2 Vegetable, 3 Lean Meat

lamb and mushroom stew

If you're one of those lucky cooks who has a flourishing rosemary bush in the windowsill, go ahead and substitute fresh rosemary for dried, but bump it up to about a tablespoon.

Prep: 20 minutes Cook: 8½ to 9½ hours (low) or 4 to 4½ hours (high), plus 15 minutes (high) Makes: 6 servings

3	pounds lean boneless lamb
2	cups quartered fresh mushrooms
2	medium leeks, trimmed and cut into 1-inch pieces
½	teaspoon salt
½	cup reduced-sodium beef broth
1	teaspoon dried rosemary, crushed
½	teaspoon black pepper
2	tablespoons cornstarch
2	tablespoons cold water

6 to 10 grams of carbs

1 Trim fat from meat. Cut meat into 1½- to 2-inch pieces. In a 3½- or 4-quart slow cooker place the meat, mushrooms, and leeks. Sprinkle with salt. In a small bowl combine beef broth, rosemary, and pepper. Pour over mixture in cooker.

2 Cover and cook on low-heat setting for 8½ to 9½ hours or on high-heat setting for 4 to 4 ½ hours.

3 If using low-heat setting, turn to high-heat setting. In a small bowl combine cornstarch and water. Stir into mixture in cooker. Cover and cook about 15 minutes more or until thickened.

Nutrition Facts per serving: 239 cal., 7 g total fat (2 g sat. fat), 102 mg chol.,
370 mg sodium, 8 g carbo., 1 g fiber, 35 g pro.
Daily Values: 10% vit. A, 6% vit. C, 3% calcium, 20% iron
Exchanges: 1½ Vegetable, 4 Lean Meat

lamb shanks with rosemary and olives

Purchase lamb foreshanks, which are smaller than hindshanks, for this Mediterranean dish.

Prep: 15 minutes Cook: 11 to 12 hours (low) or 5 ½ to 6 hours (high) Makes: 4 to 6 servings

1	pound boiling onions, peeled
½	cup pitted kalamata olives
4	meaty lamb shanks (about 4 pounds) or meaty veal shank crosscuts (about 3 pounds)
4	cloves garlic, minced
2	teaspoons dried rosemary, crushed
¼	teaspoon salt
¼	teaspoon black pepper
1	cup reduced-sodium chicken broth
	Snipped fresh flat-leaf parsley

1 In a 5- to 6-quart slow cooker place onions and olives. Place meat in cooker. Sprinkle with garlic, rosemary, salt, and pepper. Pour chicken broth over all.

2 Cover and cook on low-heat setting for 11 to 12 hours or on high-heat setting for 5½ to 6 hours.

3 Using a slotted spoon, transfer the meat, onions, and olives to a serving platter. Skim fat from the cooking liquid. If desired, strain liquid and pass with the meat. Sprinkle with parsley.

Nutrition Facts per serving: 194 cal., 5 g total fat (1 g sat. fat), 85 mg chol., 417 mg sodium, 9 g carbo., 2 g fiber, 27 g pro.
Daily Values: 8% vit. C, 3% calcium, 14% iron
Exchanges: 1½ Vegetable, 3 Lean Meat

lemon-lime chili chicken

Both lemon and lime juice combined with chicken broth seep into the chicken pieces to make this dish ultra tender.

Prep: 15 minutes Cook: 5 to 6 hours (low) or 2 ½ to 3 hours (high) Makes: 6 to 8 servings

2	tablespoons chili powder
1	teaspoon salt
½	teaspoon black pepper
3	to 3½ pounds meaty chicken pieces (breast halves, thighs, and drumsticks), skinned
1	medium zucchini or yellow summer squash, halved lengthwise and cut into 1-inch pieces
1	medium onion, cut into wedges
¼	cup reduced-sodium chicken broth
¼	cup lime juice
¼	cup lemon juice
2	cloves garlic, minced

1 In a small bowl combine chili powder, salt, and pepper. Sprinkle spice mixture over chicken; rub in with your fingers. Place chicken in a 4- to 5-quart slow cooker. Add zucchini and onion. In a small bowl combine chicken broth, lime juice, lemon juice, and garlic. Pour over mixture in cooker.

2 Cover and cook on low-heat setting for 5 to 6 hours or on high-heat setting for 2½ to 3 hours.

3 Transfer chicken and vegetables to a serving platter. Discard cooking liquid.

Nutrition Facts per serving: 156 cal., 4 g total fat (1 g sat. fat), 76 mg chol., 525 mg sodium, 6 g carbo., 1 g fiber, 24 g pro.
Daily Values: 20% vit. A, 31% vit. C, 3% calcium, 9% iron
Exchanges: 1 Vegetable, 3 Lean Meat

herbed balsamic chicken

Balsamic vinegar, rosemary, and thyme are classic ingredients for an old-fashioned, Italian-style oven-roasted chicken. The flavorings also work nicely on slow-cooked chicken.

6 to 10 grams of carbs

Prep: 25 minutes Cook: 6 to 7 hours (low) or 3 to 3 ½ hours (high), plus 15 minutes (high) Makes: 6 to 8 servings

1	medium onion, cut into very thin wedges
1	9-ounce package frozen Italian green beans
2	tablespoons finely chopped shallot (1 medium)
3½	to 4 pounds meaty chicken pieces (breast halves, thighs, and drumsticks), skinned
1	teaspoon dried rosemary, crushed
1	teaspoon dried thyme, crushed
½	teaspoon salt
¼	teaspoon black pepper
¼	cup reduced-sodium chicken broth
2	tablespoons balsamic vinegar
1	tablespoon cornstarch
1	tablespoon cold water

1 In a 4- to 5-quart slow cooker combine onion, frozen green beans, and shallot. Add chicken. Sprinkle with rosemary, thyme, salt, and pepper. Add chicken broth and vinegar to mixture in cooker.

2 Cover and cook on low-heat setting for 6 to 7 hours or on high-heat setting for 3 to 3½ hours.

3 Transfer chicken and vegetables to a serving platter, reserving cooking liquid. Cover chicken and vegetables with foil to keep warm.

4 If using low-heat setting, turn to high-heat setting. In a small bowl combine cornstarch and water. Stir into liquid in cooker. Cover and cook about 15 minutes more or until thickened. Spoon sauce over chicken and vegetables.

Nutrition Facts per serving: 187 cal., 4 g total fat (1 g sat. fat), 89 mg chol., 319 mg sodium, 8 g carbo., 2 g fiber, 28 g pro.
Daily Values: 7% vit. A, 16% vit. C, 4% calcium, 10% iron
Exchanges: 1½ Vegetable, 3 Lean Meat

chicken with sweet peppers and mushrooms

If you have any leftover shallots, use them as you would garlic cloves in your favorite vinaigrette recipe for a mellower version.

Prep: 25 minutes **Cook:** 4 to 5 hours (low) or 2 to 2½ hours (high), plus 15 minutes (high) **Makes:** 6 servings

8	ounces fresh mushrooms, quartered
2	shallots, sliced
2½	pounds chicken thighs, skinned
¼	cup reduced-sodium chicken broth
¼	cup dry white wine
1	teaspoon dried basil, crushed
½	teaspoon salt
¼	teaspoon black pepper
2	tablespoons cornstarch
2	tablespoons cold water
1	medium yellow sweet pepper, cut into 1-inch strips
1	medium red sweet pepper, cut into 1-inch strips
⅔	cup chopped roma tomatoes (2 medium)
	Shredded Parmesan cheese (optional)

1 In a 3½- or 4-quart slow cooker place mushrooms and shallots. Add chicken. In a small bowl combine broth, wine, basil, salt, and black pepper. Pour over chicken in cooker.

2 Cover and cook on low-heat setting for 4 to 5 hours or on high-heat setting for 2 to 2½ hours. Transfer chicken and vegetables to a serving platter, reserving cooking liquid. Cover chicken and vegetables with foil to keep warm.

3 If using low-heat setting, turn to high-heat setting. In a small bowl combine cornstarch and water. Stir into liquid in cooker. Stir in sweet pepper strips. Cover and cook about 15 minutes more or until thickened. Spoon sauce over chicken and vegetables. Top with tomatoes and, if desired, Parmesan cheese.

Nutrition Facts per serving: 175 cal., 6 g total fat (2 g sat. fat), 70 mg chol., 360 mg sodium, 9 g carbo., 1 g fiber, 21 g pro.
Daily Values: 22% vit. A, 168% vit. C, 8% calcium, 9% iron
Exchanges: 2 Vegetable, 2½ Lean Meat

chow mein-style chicken thighs

Chicken, water chestnuts, snow peas, and almonds mingle in a delicate ginger-soy sauce for a Chinese-American favorite. Revisit this classic soon—it's easy to forget how satisfying it is.

Prep: 25 minutes Cook: 5 to 6 hours (low) or 2½ to 3 hours (high), plus 15 minutes (high) Makes: 8 servings

2¼	pounds skinless, boneless chicken thighs
1	tablespoon cooking oil
1	8-ounce can sliced water chestnuts, drained
1	4-ounce can sliced mushrooms, drained
1	cup bias-sliced celery (2 stalks)
½	cup bias-sliced carrot (1 medium)
½	cup chopped onion (1 medium)
2	cloves garlic, minced
	Black pepper
1	cup reduced-sodium chicken broth
2	tablespoons reduced-sodium soy sauce
2	teaspoons grated fresh ginger
2	tablespoons cornstarch
2	tablespoons cold water
1	cup fresh snow peas, halved crosswise
⅓	cup chopped almonds, toasted
	Hot cooked brown rice (optional)

1 In a large skillet cook chicken, half at a time, in hot oil over medium-high heat until brown on both sides. Drain off fat. In a 4- to 5-quart slow cooker combine water chestnuts, mushrooms, celery, carrot, onion, and garlic. Top with chicken. Sprinkle lightly with pepper. In a small bowl combine chicken broth, soy sauce, and ginger. Pour over mixture in slow cooker.

2 Cover and cook on low-heat setting for 5 to 6 hours or on high-heat setting for 2½ to 3 hours. Transfer chicken to a serving platter, reserving vegetable mixture in cooker. Cover chicken with foil to keep warm.

3 If using low-heat setting, turn to high-heat setting. In a small bowl combine cornstarch and water. Stir into vegetable mixture in cooker. Stir in snow peas. Cover and cook about 15 minutes more or until thickened. Spoon vegetable mixture over chicken. Sprinkle with almonds. If desired, serve with hot cooked rice.

Nutrition Facts per serving: 242 cal., 10 g total fat (2 g sat. fat), 102 mg chol.,
382 mg sodium, 9 g carbo., 2 g fiber, 28 g pro.
Daily Values: 23% vit. A, 18% vit. C, 5% calcium, 10% iron
Exchanges: 2 Vegetable, 3 Lean Meat, ½ Fat

chicken and vegetables with herbs

To peel pearl onions, submerge them, unpeeled, in boiling water for about 3 minutes. Cut off the root ends. Gently press the onions and the skin will slip off.

6 to 10 grams of carbs

Prep: 25 minutes Cook: 5 to 6 hours (low) or 2½ to 3 hours (high), plus 10 minutes Makes: 4 servings

8	ounces fresh mushrooms, halved
16	pearl onions (about 3 ounces), peeled
½	cup reduced-sodium chicken broth
¼	cup dry red wine
2	tablespoons tomato paste
½	teaspoon garlic salt
½	teaspoon dried rosemary, crushed
½	teaspoon dried thyme, crushed
¼	teaspoon black pepper
1	bay leaf
8	chicken thighs, skinned
¼	cup reduced-sodium chicken broth
1	tablespoon cornstarch
	Snipped fresh parsley (optional)

1 In a 5½- or 6-quart slow cooker place mushrooms and onions. Stir in the ½ cup chicken broth, the wine, tomato paste, garlic salt, rosemary, thyme, pepper, and bay leaf. Add chicken.

2 Cover and cook on low-heat setting for 5 to 6 hours or on high-heat setting for 2½ to 3 hours.

3 Using a slotted spoon, transfer chicken and vegetables to a serving platter. Remove and discard bay leaf. Cover chicken and vegetables with foil to keep warm.

4 For sauce, pour cooking liquid into a glass measuring cup. Skim off fat. Measure 2 cups cooking liquid (add additional chicken broth, if necessary, to make 2 cups). Pour liquid into a medium saucepan. In a small bowl combine the ¼ cup chicken broth and the cornstarch. Stir into liquid in saucepan. Cook and stir over medium-high heat until thickened and bubbly. Cook and stir for 2 minutes more. Spoon some of the sauce over chicken. If desired, sprinkle with parsley. Pass remaining sauce.

Nutrition Facts per serving: 220 cal., 6 g total fat (1 g sat. fat), 114 mg chol.,
332 mg sodium, 8 g carbo., 1 g fiber, 30 g pro.
Daily Values: 2% vit. A, 4% vit. C, 3% calcium, 12% iron
Exchanges: 1½ Vegetable, 3½ Lean Meat

zesty ginger-tomato chicken

Chicken drumsticks or thighs are great for the slow cooker. They stay moist and tender during the long cooking times.

6 to 10 grams of carbs

Prep: 20 minutes Cook: 6 to 7 hours (low) or 3 to 3½ hours (high) Makes: 6 servings

2½	to 3 pounds chicken drumsticks and/or thighs, skinned
2	14½-ounce cans tomatoes
2	tablespoons quick-cooking tapioca
1	tablespoon grated fresh ginger
1	tablespoon snipped fresh cilantro or parsley
4	cloves garlic, minced
½	teaspoon crushed red pepper
½	teaspoon salt
	Hot cooked brown rice (optional)

1 Place chicken in a 3½- or 4-quart slow cooker. Drain 1 can of the tomatoes; chop tomatoes from both cans. In a medium bowl combine chopped tomatoes and the juice from 1 can of tomatoes, the tapioca, ginger, cilantro, garlic, crushed red pepper, and salt. Pour over chicken in cooker.

2 Cover and cook on low-heat setting for 6 to 7 hours or on high-heat setting for 3 to 3½ hours. Skim off fat. Serve in shallow bowls. If desired, serve with hot cooked rice.

Nutrition Facts per serving: 168 cal., 4 g total fat (1 g sat. fat), 81 mg chol., 472 mg sodium, 10 g carbo., 1 g fiber, 23 g pro.
Daily Values: 5% vit. A, 21% vit. C, 5% calcium, 13% iron
Exchanges: 1 Vegetable, 3 Very Lean Meat, 1 Fat

curried chicken soup

You'll love the way this soup hits so many flavor buttons—a little heat from the spices, a little sweetness from the coconut milk, and some nuttiness from the peanuts.

6 to 10 grams of carbs

Prep: 25 minutes Cook: 5 hours (low) or 2 ½ hours (high), plus 15 minutes (high) Makes: 8 servings (10 cups)

1½	to 2 pounds skinless, boneless chicken thighs
2	14-ounce cans reduced-sodium chicken broth
3	cups cauliflower florets (1 small head)
1½	cups sliced celery (3 stalks)
¾	cup chopped red or yellow sweet pepper (1 medium)
⅓	cup chopped onion (1 small)
2	cloves garlic, minced
1	tablespoon curry powder
½	teaspoon salt
½	teaspoon ground cumin
¼	teaspoon crushed red pepper
1	13½-ounce can unsweetened light coconut milk
2	medium zucchini or yellow summer squash, halved lengthwise and sliced (2½ cups)
	Chopped peanuts (optional)

1 Cut chicken into 1-inch pieces. In a 3½- or 4-quart slow cooker combine chicken, chicken broth, cauliflower, celery, sweet pepper, onion, garlic, curry powder, salt, cumin, and crushed red pepper.

2 Cover and cook on low-heat setting for 5 hours or on high-heat setting for 2½ hours.

3 If using low-heat setting, turn to high-heat setting. Stir in coconut milk and zucchini. Cover and cook for 15 to 30 minutes more or until zucchini is tender. If desired, sprinkle each serving with peanuts.

Nutrition Facts per serving: 226 cal., 13 g total fat (9 g sat. fat), 69 mg chol., 654 mg sodium, 8 g carbo., 2 g fiber, 20 g pro.
Daily Values: 13% vit. A, 78% vit. C, 4% calcium, 11% iron
Exchanges: 1 Vegetable, 2½ Lean Meat, 1 Fat

rosemary chicken

Twelve cloves of garlic may sound like a lot, but the garlic mellows as it slowly envelops the chicken in a delightful flavor.

Prep: 20 minutes **Cook:** 6 to 7 hours (low) or 3 to 3½ hours (high), plus 15 minutes (high) **Makes:** 6 servings

12	cloves garlic, minced
½	cup chopped onion (1 medium)
1	tablespoon olive oil
1	8- or 9-ounce package frozen artichoke hearts
1	red sweet pepper, cut into strips
½	cup reduced-sodium chicken broth
2	teaspoons dried rosemary, crushed
1	teaspoon finely shredded lemon peel
½	teaspoon black pepper
1½	pounds skinless, boneless chicken breast halves or thighs
1	tablespoon cornstarch
1	tablespoon cold water

1 In a small skillet cook garlic and onion in hot oil over medium heat about 5 minutes or until tender, stirring occasionally. In a 3½- or 4-quart slow cooker combine the garlic mixture, frozen artichoke hearts, and sweet pepper. In a small bowl combine chicken broth, rosemary, lemon peel, and black pepper. Pour over vegetables in cooker. Add chicken; spoon some of the broth mixture over chicken.

2 Cover and cook on low-heat setting for 6 to 7 hours or on high-heat setting for 3 to 3½ hours.

3 Transfer chicken and artichokes to a serving platter, reserving cooking liquid. Cover chicken and artichokes with foil to keep warm.

4 If using low-heat setting, turn to high-heat setting. In a small bowl combine cornstarch and water. Stir into liquid in cooker. Cover and cook about 15 minutes more or until slightly thickened. Spoon sauce over chicken and artichokes.

Nutrition Facts per serving: 195 cal., 4 g total fat (1 g sat. fat), 66 mg chol., 136 mg sodium, 10 g carbo., 3 g fiber, 28 g pro.
Daily Values: 14% vit. A, 63% vit. C, 5% calcium, 7% iron
Exchanges: 2 Vegetable, 3½ Very Lean Meat, ½ Fat

chicken breasts with brandy sauce

You'll have plenty of this rich, creamy sauce. If you can afford the carbs, serve with low carb pasta or brown rice.

Prep: 15 minutes Cook: 5 to 6 hours (low) or 2½ to 3 hours (high), plus 10 minutes Makes: 6 servings

2	cups quartered fresh mushrooms
6	medium chicken breast halves, skinned
¼	teaspoon black pepper
3	ounces thinly sliced prosciutto, cut into thin strips
¼	cup reduced-sodium chicken broth
¼	cup brandy
½	teaspoon dried thyme, crushed
2	tablespoons cornstarch
2	tablespoons cold water
½	of an 8-ounce package reduced-fat cream cheese (Neufchâtel), cubed
½	cup fat-free half-and-half

1 Place mushrooms in a 4½- to 6-quart cooker. Sprinkle chicken with pepper. Add chicken to cooker. Top with prosciutto. In a small bowl combine chicken broth, brandy, and thyme. Add to mixture in cooker.

2 Cover and cook on low-heat setting for 5 to 6 hours or on high-heat setting for 2½ to 3 hours.

3 Transfer chicken and mushrooms to a serving platter, reserving cooking liquid. Cover chicken and mushrooms with foil to keep warm.

4 For sauce, pour cooking liquid into a medium saucepan. In a small bowl combine cornstarch and water. Add to liquid in saucepan. Cook and stir over medium-high heat until thickened and bubbly. Cook and stir for 2 minutes more. Add cream cheese and half-and-half, whisking until smooth. Serve sauce with chicken.

Nutrition Facts per serving: 323 cal., 9 g total fat (4 g sat. fat), 121 mg chol., 594 mg sodium, 6 g carbo., 0 g fiber, 46 g pro.
Daily Values: 6% vit. A, 3% vit. C, 5% calcium, 9% iron
Exchanges: ½ Other Carbo., 6 Very Lean Meat, 2 Fat

cheesy garlic chicken

Two doses of cheese—luscious cream cheese and oozy melted mozzarella—bring extra richness to this dish. Four cloves of garlic make the flavors really soar.

Prep: 20 minutes Cook: 3½ to 4½ hours (low) or 1½ to 2 hours (high),
plus 30 minutes Stand: 10 minutes Makes: 6 servings

2	pounds skinless, boneless chicken breast halves
1½	cups cauliflower florets
4	cloves garlic, minced
¾	cup reduced-sodium chicken broth
2	tablespoons quick-cooking tapioca
¼	teaspoon salt
1½	cups frozen cut green beans
½	of an 8-ounce package reduced-fat cream cheese (Neufchâtel), cubed
½	cup shredded part-skim mozzarella cheese (2 ounces)
⅔	cup chopped roma tomatoes (2 medium)

1 Cut chicken into 1½-inch pieces. In a 3½- or 4-quart slow cooker combine chicken, cauliflower, garlic, chicken broth, tapioca, and salt.

2 Cover and cook on low-heat setting for 3½ to 4½ hours or on high-heat setting for 1½ to 2 hours.

3 If using low-heat setting, turn to high-heat setting. Add beans to mixture in cooker. Cover and cook for 30 minutes more. Turn off cooker.

4 Stir cream cheese into mixture in cooker. Cover and let stand for 10 minutes. Remove cover and gently stir until cream cheese is melted and sauce is smooth. Sprinkle each serving with mozzarella cheese and tomatoes.

Nutrition Facts per serving: 283 cal., 8 g total fat (4 g sat. fat), 108 mg chol.,
393 mg sodium, 10 g carbo., 2 g fiber, 41 g pro.
Daily Values: 14% vit. A, 20% vit. C, 13% calcium, 9% iron
Exchanges: ½ Vegetable, ½ Other Carbo., 5½ Very Lean Meat, 1 Fat

chicken with artichokes and olives

Serve this curry-flavored dish with a steaming bowl of cooked brown rice to capture all of the delicious sauce!

Prep: 15 minutes Cook: 7 to 8 hours (low) or 3½ to 4 hours, plus 15 minutes (high) Makes: 8 servings

2	**cups sliced fresh mushrooms**
1	**14½-ounce can diced tomatoes, undrained**
1	**cup reduced-sodium chicken broth**
½	**cup chopped onion (1 medium)**
¼	**cup dry white wine or reduced-sodium chicken broth**
1	**2¼-ounce can sliced, pitted ripe olives or ¼ cup capers, drained**
2	**to 3 teaspoons curry powder**
1	**teaspoon dried thyme, crushed**
¼	**teaspoon salt**
¼	**teaspoon black pepper**
1	**8- or 9-ounce package frozen artichoke hearts**
2½	**pounds skinless, boneless chicken breast halves and/or thighs**
3	**tablespoons cornstarch**
3	**tablespoons cold water**

1 In a 4- to 5-quart slow cooker combine mushrooms, undrained tomatoes, chicken broth, onion, wine, olives, curry powder, thyme, salt, and pepper. Add artichoke hearts. Place chicken on top; spoon some of the tomato mixture over the chicken.

2 Cover and cook on low-heat setting for 7 to 8 hours or on high-heat setting for 3½ to 4 hours.

3 Using a slotted spoon, transfer chicken and artichokes to a serving bowl. Cover chicken and artichokes with foil to keep warm.

4 If using low-heat setting, turn to high-heat setting. In a small bowl combine cornstarch and water. Stir into mixture in cooker. Cover and cook about 15 minutes more or until thickened. Spoon tomato mixture over chicken and artichokes.

Nutrition Facts per serving: 229 cal., 4 g total fat (1 g sat. fat), 82 mg chol., 396 mg sodium, 10 g carbo., 3 g fiber, 35 g pro.
Daily Values: 3% vit. A, 15% vit. C, 7% calcium, 11% iron
Exchanges: 2 Vegetable, 4½ Very Lean Meat, ½ Fat

asian-style chicken soup

Pea pods, cabbage, and a well-beaten egg added toward the end of cooking transform this version of classic chicken soup into distinctively Asian cuisine.

6 to 10 grams of carbs

Prep: 25 minutes Cook: 5 to 6 hours (low) or 2½ to 3 hours (high), plus 10 minutes (high) Makes: 4 servings

1	pound skinless, boneless chicken breast halves
2	14-ounce cans reduced-sodium chicken broth
1	cup water
1	medium red sweet pepper, cut into ¾-inch pieces
⅓	cup thinly sliced green onions (3)
1	tablespoon reduced-sodium soy sauce
1	teaspoon grated fresh ginger
⅛	teaspoon crushed red pepper
1	cup fresh pea pods, halved crosswise, or ½ of a 6-ounce package frozen pea pods, thawed and halved crosswise
2	cups shredded Napa cabbage
1	egg

1 Cut the chicken into bite-size pieces. Place chicken in a 3½- or 4-quart slow cooker. Stir in chicken broth, water, sweet pepper, green onions, soy sauce, ginger, and crushed red pepper.

2 Cover and cook on low-heat setting for 5 to 6 hours or on high-heat setting for 2½ to 3 hours.

3 If using low-heat setting, turn to high-heat setting. Stir in pea pods and cabbage. In a small bowl beat egg well; slowly add egg to soup, stirring gently. Cover and cook for 10 minutes more.

Nutrition Facts per serving: 194 cal., 3 g total fat (1 g sat. fat), 119 mg chol.,
704 mg sodium, 7 g carbo., 2 g fiber, 31 g pro.
Daily Values: 31% vit. A, 111% vit. C, 7% calcium, 9% iron
Exchanges: 1½ Vegetable, 4 Very Lean Meat, ½ Fat

creamy tarragon turkey

To add to the flavor and appeal of this meal, serve with a side of nutritionally rich baked sweet potatoes.

Prep: 15 minutes **Cook:** 5 to 6 hours (low) or 2½ to 3 hours (high), plus 15 minutes (high) **Makes:** 6 servings

2	medium fennel bulbs, cored and cut into thin wedges (2 cups)
1	large onion, cut into thin wedges (1 cup)
3	turkey breast tenderloins (about 2¼ pounds)
½	cup reduced-sodium chicken broth
1	tablespoon Dijon-style mustard
½	teaspoon dried tarragon, crushed
¼	teaspoon salt
¼	teaspoon black pepper
¼	cup fat-free half-and-half
4	teaspoons cornstarch
2	ounces goat cheese (chèvre), crumbled (½ cup)
¼	cup snipped fresh parsley

1 In a 3 ½- or 4-quart slow cooker place fennel and onion. Add turkey. In a small bowl combine broth, mustard, tarragon, salt, and pepper. Pour over turkey in cooker.

2 Cover and cook on low-heat setting for 5 to 6 hours or on high-heat setting for 2½ to 3 hours.

3 Transfer turkey to a serving platter, reserving cooking liquid. Cover turkey with foil to keep warm.

4 If using low-heat setting, turn to high-heat setting. In a small bowl combine half-and-half and cornstarch. Stir into mixture in cooker. Cover and cook about 15 minutes more or until thickened. To serve, cut turkey into serving-size pieces. Spoon vegetable mixture over turkey. Sprinkle with goat cheese and parsley.

Nutrition Facts per serving: 258 cal., 5 g total fat (2 g sat. fat), 106 mg chol.,
347 mg sodium, 8 g carbo., 1 g fiber, 43 g pro.
Daily Values: 4% vit. A, 14% vit. C, 7% calcium, 13% iron
Exchanges: 1½ Vegetable, 5½ Very Lean Meat, ½ Fat

creamed turkey and smoked salmon

A downhome favorite goes uptown! Here, smoked salmon and dillweed add a gourmet angle to creamed turkey and mushrooms.

Prep: 15 minutes Cook: 3½ hours (low) or 1½ hours (high), plus 15 minutes (high) Makes: 6 servings

2	pounds turkey breast tenderloins
8	ounces fresh mushrooms, quartered
⅓	cup water
1	teaspoon salt
½	teaspoon dried dillweed, crushed
¼	teaspoon black pepper
¾	cup fat-free half-and-half
2	tablespoons cornstarch
4	ounces smoked salmon (not lox-style), skinned and flaked
¼	cup sliced green onions (2)

1 Cut turkey into 1-inch pieces. In a 3½- or 4-quart slow cooker combine turkey and mushrooms. Stir in water, salt, dillweed, and pepper.

2 Cover and cook on low-heat setting for 3½ hours or on high-heat setting for 1½ hours.

3 If using low-heat setting, turn to high-heat setting. In a small bowl combine half-and-half and cornstarch. Stir into mixture in cooker. Cover and cook for 15 minutes more. Stir in salmon and green onions.

Nutrition Facts per serving: 227 cal., 2 g total fat (0 g sat. fat), 104 mg chol., 628 mg sodium, 7 g carbo., 0 g fiber, 42 g pro.
Daily Values: 1% vit. A, 1% vit. C, 4% calcium, 13% iron
Exchanges: 1 Vegetable, 5½ Very Lean Meat

spicy turkey thighs

A touch of cayenne pepper adds just enough spice to spark these meaty turkey thighs; the cranberry juice helps round out the flavors.

Prep: 15 minutes **Cook:** 5 to 6 hours (low) or 2½ to 3 hours (high), plus 15 minutes (high) **Makes:** 8 servings

4	pounds turkey thighs, skinned
½	teaspoon salt
¼	teaspoon black pepper
½	cup chopped onion (1 medium)
½	cup cranberry juice
2	tablespoons Dijon-style mustard
⅛ to ¼	teaspoon cayenne pepper
2	tablespoons cornstarch
2	tablespoons cold water

1 In a 4- to 5-quart slow cooker place turkey. Sprinkle turkey with salt and black pepper. Top with onion. In a small bowl whisk together cranberry juice, mustard, and cayenne pepper. Pour over mixture in cooker.

2 Cover and cook on low-heat setting for 5 to 6 hours or on high-heat setting for 2½ to 3 hours.

3 Transfer turkey to a serving platter, reserving cooking liquid. Cover turkey with foil to keep warm.

4 If using low-heat setting, turn to high-heat setting. In a small bowl combine cornstarch and water. Stir into liquid in cooker. Cover and cook about 15 minutes more or until thickened. Spoon sauce over turkey.

Nutrition Facts per serving: 183 cal., 4 g total fat (1 g sat. fat), 116 mg chol.,
335 mg sodium, 6 g carbo., 0 g fiber, 30 g pro.
Daily Values: 10% vit. C, 3% calcium, 14% iron
Exchanges: ½ Other Carbo., 4 Very Lean Meat

6 to 10 grams of carbs

pumpkin-sage soup

This creamy, delicious soup makes a perfect starter at your next dinner party or holiday gathering.

Prep: 15 minutes Cook: 6 to 8 hours (low) or 3 to 4 hours (high) Makes: 8 side-dish servings

3	14-ounce cans reduced-sodium chicken broth
1	15-ounce can pumpkin
2/3	cup sliced leeks (2 medium)
2	teaspoons ground sage
1/8	teaspoon salt
1/8	teaspoon black pepper
1	cup fat-free half-and-half
	Shredded Parmesan cheese (optional)

1 In a 3½-quart slow cooker combine broth, pumpkin, leeks, sage, salt, and pepper.

2 Cover and cook on low-heat setting for 6 to 8 hours or on high-heat setting for 3 to 4 hours. Stir in half-and-half. If desired, sprinkle each serving with Parmesan cheese.

Nutrition Facts per serving: 53 cal., 0 g total fat (0 g sat. fat), 0 mg chol., 388 mg sodium, 9 g carbo., 2 g fiber, 3 g pro.
Daily Values: 168% vit. A, 5% vit. C, 4% calcium, 5% iron
Exchanges: ½ Vegetable, ½ Starch

eggplant-zucchini parmesan

When your garden's bounty includes eggplant and zucchini, this is the perfect recipe for you.

Prep: 20 minutes Cook: 4 to 5 hours (low) or 2 to 2 ½ hours (high) Makes: 8 side-dish servings

1	medium eggplant, peeled and cut into 1-inch cubes
1	medium zucchini, cut into 1-inch cubes
1	medium onion, cut into thin wedges
1½	cups light spaghetti sauce
⅓	cup shredded Parmesan cheese
	Shredded Parmesan cheese (optional)

1 In a 3½- or 4-quart slow cooker combine eggplant, zucchini, onion, spaghetti sauce, and the ⅓ cup Parmesan cheese.

2 Cover and cook on low-heat setting for 4 to 5 hours or on high-heat setting for 2 to 2½ hours. If desired, sprinkle each serving with additional Parmesan cheese.

Nutrition Facts per serving: 55 cal., 1 g total fat (1 g sat. fat), 2 mg chol., 210 mg sodium, 9 g carbo., 3 g fiber, 3 g pro.
Daily Values: 4% vit. A, 17% vit. C, 6% calcium, 3% iron
Exchanges: 1 Vegetable, ½ Other Carbo.

curried vegetables

Whenever you see the word "curry," think "lots of flavor, not a lot of effort." You see, curry powder blends up to 20 herbs and spices for a deep, intriguing taste.

Prep: 15 minutes Cook: 5 to 6 hours (low) or 2½ to 3 hours (high), plus 15 minutes (high) Makes: 8 to 10 side-dish servings

1	medium eggplant, peeled and cut into 1-inch cubes
1	medium zucchini, cut into 1-inch cubes
1	medium onion, cut into thin wedges
1	cup sliced fresh mushrooms
1	clove garlic, minced
½	cup reduced-sodium chicken broth
1	tablespoon curry powder
½	teaspoon salt
¼	teaspoon black pepper
1	tablespoon cornstarch
1	tablespoon cold water

1 In a 3½- or 4-quart slow cooker combine eggplant, zucchini, onion, mushrooms, and garlic. In a small bowl combine chicken broth, curry powder, salt, and pepper. Pour over vegetables in cooker.

2 Cover and cook on low-heat setting for 5 to 6 hours or on high-heat setting for 2½ to 3 hours.

3 Transfer vegetables to a serving dish, reserving cooking liquid. Cover vegetables with foil to keep warm.

4 If using low-heat setting, turn to high-heat setting. In a small bowl combine cornstarch and water. Stir into liquid in cooker. Cover and cook about 15 minutes more or until thickened. Spoon sauce over vegetables and toss to coat.

Nutrition Facts per serving: 30 cal., 0 g total fat (0 g sat. fat), 0 mg chol., 186 mg sodium, 6 g carbo., 2 g fiber, 1 g pro.
Daily Values: 1% vit. A, 10% vit. C, 2% calcium, 3% iron
Exchanges: 1 Vegetable

chapter three

11 to 15

grams of carbs

jerk beef roast

You'll enjoy the combination of spicy-sweet flavors that the Jamaican jerk seasoning gives the roast—chiles, thyme, cinnamon, ginger, allspice, and cloves.

Prep: 30 minutes Cook: 8 to 10 hours (low) or 4 to 5 hours (high) Makes: 6 servings

1	2- to 2½-pound boneless beef chuck pot roast
¾	cup water
¼	cup raisins
¼	cup steak sauce
3	tablespoons balsamic vinegar
2	tablespoons sugar (optional)
2	tablespoons quick-cooking tapioca
1	teaspoon cracked black pepper
1	teaspoon Jamaican jerk seasoning
2	cloves garlic, minced
	Hot cooked brown rice (optional)

1 Trim fat from meat. If necessary, cut meat to fit into a 3½- or 4-quart slow cooker. Place meat in the cooker. In a medium bowl combine water, raisins, steak sauce, balsamic vinegar, sugar (if desired), tapioca, pepper, Jamaican jerk seasoning, and garlic. Pour mixture over roast.

2 Cover and cook on low-heat setting for 8 to 10 hours or on high-heat setting for 4 to 5 hours. Remove meat from cooker. Skim fat from sauce. If desired, serve meat and sauce with hot cooked rice.

Nutrition Facts per serving: 237 cal., 6 g total fat (2 g sat. fat), 89 mg chol., 309 mg sodium, 12 g carbo., 1 g fiber, 33 g pro.
Daily Values: 2% vit. A, 4% vit. C, 2% calcium, 23% iron
Exchanges: 1 Other Carbo., 4 Lean Meat

11 to 15 grams of carbs

home-style beef and vegetables

You can spoon this savory beef and veggie dish over whole wheat noodles if you like, but it's equally good on its own.

Prep: 20 minutes **Cook:** 8 to 9 hours (low) or 4 to 4½ hours (high), plus 30 minutes (high) **Makes:** 8 servings

	Nonstick cooking spray
1	3- to 3½-pound boneless beef chuck pot roast
1	0.6-ounce envelope dry Italian salad dressing mix
3	tablespoons quick-cooking tapioca
1	14-ounce can beef broth seasoned with onion
1	16-ounce package frozen Italian vegetables (zucchini, carrots, cauliflower, lima beans, Italian beans)

1 Coat a 3½- or 4-quart slow cooker with cooking spray. Trim fat from meat. Coat a large skillet with cooking spray. Cook meat in hot skillet over medium heat until brown on all sides. Place meat in prepared cooker. Sprinkle with salad dressing mix and tapioca. Add beef broth.

2 Cover and cook on low-heat setting for 8 to 9 hours or on high-heat setting for 4 to 4½ hours.

3 If using low-heat setting, turn to high-heat setting. Add frozen vegetables to cooker. Cover and cook about 30 minutes more or until vegetables are tender.

Nutrition Facts per serving: 338 cal., 8 g total fat (3 g sat. fat), 134 mg chol., 787 mg sodium, 11 g carbo., 2 g fiber, 50 g pro.
Daily Values: 46% vit. A, 9% vit. C, 3% calcium, 32% iron
Exchanges: 1 Vegetable, ½ Starch, 6½ Very Lean Meat, 1 Fat

11 to 15 grams of carbs

curried pot roast

A combination of ginger, curry, and turmeric takes this spicy roast beyond the ordinary. Serve with gravy made from the cooking juices.

Prep: 35 minutes Cook: 8 to 10 hours (low) or 4 to 5 hours (high), plus 10 minutes Makes: 6 to 8 servings

1	2½-pound boneless beef chuck pot roast
1	teaspoon ground ginger
1	teaspoon curry powder
1	teaspoon ground turmeric
½	teaspoon salt
¼	teaspoon black pepper
2	cups chopped onions (2 large)
6	medium carrots, cut into 1-inch pieces
2	cloves garlic, minced
½	teaspoon dried thyme, crushed
1	14½-ounce can diced tomatoes, undrained
½	cup reduced-sodium beef broth
1	bay leaf
½	cup cold water
2	tablespoons cornstarch

1 Trim fat from meat. In a small bowl combine ginger, curry powder, turmeric, salt, and pepper. Sprinkle ginger mixture over meat; rub in with your fingers. In a 3 ½- or 4-quart slow cooker place onions, carrots, and garlic. Place meat on top of the vegetables in cooker. Sprinkle with thyme. Add undrained tomatoes, beef broth, and bay leaf.

2 Cover and cook on low-heat setting for 8 to 10 hours or on high-heat setting for 4 to 5 hours. Remove and discard bay leaf.

3 Transfer meat and vegetables to a serving platter, reserving cooking liquid. Cover meat and vegetables with foil to keep warm.

4 For gravy, pour cooking liquid into a glass measuring cup. Skim off fat. Measure 1½ cups liquid (add water, if necessary, to make 1½ cups). Pour liquid into a small saucepan. In a small bowl combine water and cornstarch. Stir into liquid in saucepan. Cook and stir over medium heat until thickened and bubbly. Cook and stir for 2 minutes more. Serve meat and vegetables with gravy.

Nutrition Facts per serving: 236 cal., 5 g total fat (2 g sat. fat), 84 mg chol., 386 mg sodium, 14 g carbo., 2 g fiber, 31 g pro.
Daily Values: 99% vit. A, 18% vit. C, 6% calcium, 24% iron
Exchanges: 2½ Vegetable, 3½ Very Lean Meat

italian beef soup

Fennel may look like an awkward and potbellied cousin to celery, but its flavors are much more refined and fragrant. It brings a subtle licorice-like note to recipes.

Prep: 25 minutes Cook: 10 to 11 hours (low) or 5 to 5½ hours (high) Stand: 15 minutes Makes: 8 servings

1	2- to 2½-pound boneless beef chuck pot roast
¼	teaspoon black pepper
1	tablespoon olive oil or cooking oil
2	14-ounce cans reduced-sodium beef broth
1	26-ounce jar light spaghetti sauce
2	small fennel bulbs, trimmed and thinly sliced
2	medium zucchini, halved lengthwise and thinly sliced (2½ cups)
½	cup shredded Parmesan cheese (2 ounces) (optional)

1 Trim fat from meat. Cut the meat into 1-inch pieces. Sprinkle meat with pepper. In a large nonstick skillet cook the meat, half at a time, in hot oil over medium heat until brown. Drain off fat. Place meat in a 4- to 5-quart slow cooker. Stir in beef broth, spaghetti sauce, and fennel.

2 Cover and cook on low-heat setting for 10 to 11 hours or on high-heat setting for 5 to 5½ hours.

3 Stir in zucchini. Turn off heat. Cover and let stand for 15 minutes before serving. If desired, top each serving with Parmesan cheese.

Nutrition Facts per serving: 209 cal., 5 g total fat (1 g sat. fat), 67 mg chol., 565 mg sodium, 12 g carbo., 3 g fiber, 27 g pro.
Daily Values: 6% vit. A, 29% vit. C, 4% calcium, 19% iron
Exchanges: 1 Vegetable, ½ Other Carbo., 3½ Very Lean Meat, 1 Fat

11 to 15 grams of carbs

fireside beef stew

The name says it all—and even if you don't have a fireplace, this is exactly the kind of heartwarming stew that will warm you on a winter's night. Pictured on the front cover.

11 to 15 grams of carbs

Prep: 25 minutes Cook: 8 to 10 hours (low) or 4 to 5 hours (high), plus 15 minutes (high) Makes: 6 servings

1¹/₂	pounds boneless beef chuck pot roast
1	pound butternut squash, peeled, seeded, and cut into 1-inch pieces (about 2¹/₂ cups)
2	small onions, cut into wedges
2	cloves garlic, minced
1	14-ounce can reduced-sodium beef broth
1	8-ounce can tomato sauce
2	tablespoons Worcestershire sauce
1	teaspoon dry mustard
¹/₄	teaspoon black pepper
¹/₈	teaspoon ground allspice
4	teaspoons cornstarch
2	tablespoons cold water
1	9-ounce package frozen Italian green beans

1 Trim fat from meat. Cut meat into 1-inch pieces. Place meat in a 3¹/₂- to 4¹/₂-quart slow cooker. Add squash, onions, and garlic. Stir in beef broth, tomato sauce, Worcestershire sauce, mustard, pepper, and allspice.

2 Cover and cook on low-heat setting for 8 to 10 hours or on high-heat setting for 4 to 5 hours.

3 If using low-heat setting, turn to high-heat setting. In a small bowl combine cornstarch and water. Stir cornstarch mixture and green beans into mixture in cooker. Cover and cook about 15 minutes more or until thickened.

Nutrition Facts per serving: 206 cal., 4 g total fat (1 g sat. fat), 67 mg chol., 440 mg sodium, 15 g carbo., 3 g fiber, 27 g pro.
Daily Values: 18% vit. A, 21% vit. C, 5% calcium, 23% iron
Exchanges: 1¹/₂ Vegetable, ¹/₂ Starch, 2¹/₂ Lean Meat

paprika beef stew

You'll want to use paprika at its peak of color and freshness, so if yours has been on the shelf for more than six months, get a new batch. Paprika keeps best in the refrigerator.

Prep: 20 minutes Cook: 8 to 9 hours (low) or 4 to 4½ hours (high) Makes: 6 servings (6 cups)

2	pounds boneless beef chuck pot roast
1½	cups chopped onions (3 medium)
1	14-ounce can reduced-sodium beef broth
1½	cups water
1	6-ounce can tomato paste
3	cloves garlic, minced
1	tablespoon paprika
1	tablespoon caraway seeds
2	teaspoons dried marjoram, crushed
¼	teaspoon black pepper
2	cups coarsely chopped green and/or red sweet peppers (2 large)
½	cup light dairy sour cream

1 Trim fat from meat. Cut meat into ¾-inch pieces. In a 3½-quart slow cooker combine meat, onions, beef broth, water, tomato paste, garlic, paprika, caraway seeds, marjoram, and black pepper.

2 Cover and cook on low-heat setting for 8 to 9 hours or on high-heat setting for 4 to 4½ hours. Stir in sweet peppers the last 45 minutes of cooking. Top each serving with sour cream.

Nutrition Facts per serving: 280 cal., 8 g total fat (3 g sat. fat), 96 mg chol., 259 mg sodium, 15 g carbo., 3 g fiber, 37 g pro.
Daily Values: 16% vit. A, 70% vit. C, 8% calcium, 31% iron
Exchanges: 2½ Vegetable, 4½ Lean Meat

11 to 15 grams of carbs

burgundy beef stew

Burgundy wines are made from Pinot Noir grapes, so if you don't want to splurge for a real Burgundy wine from France, simply choose a good Pinot Noir from California.

11 to 15 grams of carbs

Prep: 20 minutes Cook: 10 to 12 hours (low) or 5 to 6 hours (high) Makes: 6 servings

2	pounds boneless beef chuck pot roast
1/2	teaspoon salt
1/4	teaspoon black pepper
2	tablespoons cooking oil (optional)
2	tablespoons quick-cooking tapioca
6	medium carrots, cut into 1-inch pieces
1	9-ounce package frozen cut green beans
1/2	of a 16-ounce package (2 cups) frozen small whole onions
2	cloves garlic, minced
1	14-ounce can reduced-sodium beef broth
1	cup Burgundy wine
4	slices bacon, crisp-cooked, drained, and crumbled

1 Trim fat from meat. Cut meat into 1-inch pieces. Sprinkle meat with salt and pepper. If desired, in a large skillet cook meat, half at a time, in hot oil over medium heat until brown. Drain off fat.

2 Place meat in a 3½- or 4-quart slow cooker. Sprinkle with tapioca. Stir in carrots, green beans, onions, and garlic. Pour beef broth and Burgundy over mixture in cooker.

3 Cover and cook on low-heat setting for 10 to 12 hours or on high-heat setting for 5 to 6 hours. Sprinkle each serving with crumbled bacon.

Nutrition Facts per serving: 312 cal., 8 g total fat (3 g sat. fat), 95 mg chol., 682 mg sodium, 15 g carbo., 4 g fiber, 36 g pro.
Daily Values: 134% vit. A, 9% vit. C, 8% calcium, 25% iron
Exchanges: 3 Vegetable, 4 Lean Meat, ½ Fat

beefy vegetable soup

Here's a dinner solution when you're hungry for the beefy taste of steak, but you don't want all 12 ounces. This alternative is lighter but just as satisfying.

Prep: 25 minutes Cook: 9 to 10 hours (low) or 4½ to 5 hours (high), plus 15 minutes (high) Makes: 6 servings

1½	pounds beef stew meat
1	tablespoon cooking oil
3	cups sliced fresh mushrooms (8 ounces)
1	cup frozen baby lima beans
1	cup chopped onion (2 medium)
1½	teaspoons ground chipotle chile pepper or chili powder
1	teaspoon dried oregano, crushed
¼	teaspoon salt
2	14-ounce cans reduced-sodium beef broth
1	cup water
1	tablespoon cornstarch
1	tablespoon cold water

1 Trim fat from meat. Cut meat into ½-inch pieces. In a large nonstick skillet brown meat, half at a time, in hot oil over medium heat. Drain off fat.

2 In a 3½- or 4-quart slow cooker layer mushrooms, lima beans, and onion. Add meat, chipotle pepper, oregano, and salt. Pour beef broth and the 1 cup water over all.

3 Cover and cook on low-heat setting for 9 to 10 hours or on high-heat setting for 4½ to 5 hours.

4 If using low-heat setting, turn to high-heat setting. In a small bowl combine cornstarch and water. Stir into mixture in cooker. Cover and cook about 15 minutes more or until slightly thickened.

Nutrition Facts per serving: 234 cal., 8 g total fat (2 g sat. fat), 67 mg chol., 537 mg sodium, 13 g carbo., 3 g fiber, 29 g pro.
Daily Values: 6% vit. A, 7% vit. C, 3% calcium, 22% iron
Exchanges: 1 Vegetable, ½ Starch, 3½ Lean Meat

11 to 15 grams of carbs

mediterranean beef ragout

Gremolata—a garnish consisting of parsley, lemon, and garlic—is typically served on Osso Bucco, a classic Italian veal stew. Here it dresses up a beef stew.

Prep: 25 minutes Cook: 7 to 9 hours (low) or 3½ to 4½ hours (high), plus 30 minutes (high) Makes: 6 servings

1½	pounds beef stew meat, trimmed and cut into 1-inch cubes
1	tablespoon olive oil
2	medium onions, cut into wedges
3	medium carrots, cut into ½-inch slices
1	14½-ounce can diced tomatoes, undrained
½	cup reduced-sodium beef broth
2	cloves garlic, minced
1½	teaspoons dried thyme, crushed
¼	teaspoon salt
¼	teaspoon black pepper
1	medium zucchini, halved lengthwise and cut into ¼-inch slices
6	ounces fresh green beans, cut into 2-inch pieces (1¾ cups)
1	recipe Gremolata

1 In a large nonstick skillet cook meat, half at a time, in hot oil over medium heat until brown. Drain off fat. Place meat in a 3½- or 4-quart slow cooker. Add onions and carrots. In a medium bowl combine undrained tomatoes, beef broth, garlic, thyme, salt, and pepper. Pour over meat and vegetables in cooker.

2 Cover and cook on low-heat setting for 7 to 9 hours or on high-heat setting for 3½ to 4½ hours.

3 If using low-heat setting, turn to high-heat setting. Stir in zucchini and green beans. Cover and cook for 30 minutes more. Top each serving with Gremolata.

Gremolata: In a small bowl combine ¼ cup snipped fresh parsley; 1 tablespoon finely shredded lemon peel; and 2 cloves garlic, minced.

Nutrition Facts per serving: 221 cal., 7 g total fat (2 g sat. fat), 67 mg chol., 349 mg sodium, 13 g carbo., 3 g fiber, 26 g pro.
Daily Values: 76% vit. A, 38% vit. C, 8% calcium, 23% iron
Exchanges: 2½ Vegetable, 3 Lean Meat

beef and cabbage stew

At first glance, beef and cabbage seem like an unlikely combination. But you'll love the way their flavors get bolder and richer when simmered all day in a beer-spiked broth.

Prep: 10 minutes Cook: 6 to 7 hours (low) or 3 to 3½ hours (high),
plus 15 minutes (high) Makes: 4 servings (about 7 cups)

1	pound beef stew meat
4	cups shredded cabbage
1	envelope (½ of a 2.2-ounce package) onion soup mix
2	cups water
1	12-ounce can light beer
¾	cup reduced-sodium beef broth
3	tablespoons cornstarch
3	tablespoons cold water

1 Trim fat from meat. Cut meat into 1-inch pieces. In a 3½- or 4-quart slow cooker place meat and cabbage; sprinkle with soup mix. Add the 2 cups water, the beer, and broth.

2 Cover and cook on low-heat setting for 6 to 7 hours or on high-heat setting for 3 to 3½ hours.

3 If using low-heat setting, turn to high-heat setting. In a small bowl combine cornstarch and the 3 tablespoons water. Stir into mixture in cooker. Cover and cook about 15 minutes more or until slightly thickened.

Nutrition Facts per serving: 226 cal., 4 g total fat (1 g sat. fat), 67 mg chol., 808 mg sodium, 15 g carbo., 2 g fiber, 26 g pro.
Daily Values: 2% vit. A, 38% vit. C, 5% calcium, 18% iron
Exchanges: 1½ Vegetable, ½ Other Carbo., 3 Lean Meat

11 to 15 grams of carbs

steak with mushrooms

If you're a meat and potatoes type and you can't imagine having one without the other, cook a package of frozen mashed potatoes to serve with this saucy round steak.

Prep: 10 minutes Cook: 8 to 10 hours (low) or 4 to 5 hours (high) Makes: 4 servings

1	pound boneless beef round steak, cut 1 inch thick
2	medium onions, sliced
2	4½-ounce jars whole mushrooms, drained
1	12-ounce jar beef gravy
¼	cup dry red wine

11 to 15 grams of carbs

1 Trim fat from meat. Cut meat into 4 serving-size pieces. Place onion in a 3½- or 4-quart slow cooker. Arrange mushrooms over onions. Add meat. In a small bowl combine gravy and wine. Pour over mixture in cooker.

2 Cover and cook on low-heat setting for 8 to 10 hours or on high-heat setting for 4 to 5 hours.

Note: For a 5- to 6-quart cooker, recipe may be doubled.

Nutrition Facts per serving: 220 cal., 4 g total fat (2 g sat. fat), 51 mg chol., 814 mg sodium, 11 g carbo., 3 g fiber, 31 g pro.
Daily Values: 3% vit. A, 3% calcium, 20% iron
Exchanges: 1 Vegetable, ½ Other Carbo., 4 Very Lean Meat, ½ Fat

creamy tomato-sauced round steak

This is the satisfying round steak fix-up that moms have been serving families for decades. Try it for a home-style weeknight supper.

Prep: 20 minutes Cook: 8 to 10 hours (low) or 4 to 5 hours (high), plus 15 minutes (high) Makes: 6 servings

2	pounds boneless beef top round steak, cut 1 inch thick
	Black pepper
1	tablespoon cooking oil
1	large onion, sliced and separated into rings
1	14½-ounce can diced tomatoes, undrained
1	10¾-ounce can reduced-fat and reduced-sodium condensed cream of mushroom soup
1	teaspoon dried thyme, crushed
1	teaspoon Worcestershire sauce
⅛	teaspoon garlic powder
2	tablespoons cornstarch
2	tablespoons cold water
9	ounces dried whole wheat pasta, cooked and drained

1 Cut meat into 6 serving-size pieces; sprinkle with pepper. In a large skillet cook meat, half at a time, in hot oil over medium heat until brown on both sides. Drain off fat.

2 Place onion in a 3½- to 5-quart slow cooker. Add meat. In a bowl combine undrained tomatoes, mushroom soup, thyme, Worcestershire sauce, and garlic powder. Pour over mixture in cooker.

3 Cover and cook on low-heat setting for 8 to 10 hours or on high-heat setting for 4 to 5 hours.

4 Transfer meat to a serving platter, reserving cooking liquid. Cover meat with foil to keep warm.

5 If using low-heat setting, turn to high-heat setting. For sauce, in a small bowl combine cornstarch and water. Stir into liquid in cooker. Cover and cook about 15 minutes more or until thickened. Serve meat and sauce over hot cooked pasta.

Nutrition Facts per serving: 277 cal., 8 g total fat (2 g sat. fat), 87 mg chol., 506 mg sodium, 13 g carbo., 1 g fiber, 35 g pro.
Daily Values: 1% vit. A, 17% vit. C, 4% calcium, 22% iron
Exchanges: 1 Vegetable, ½ Starch, 4 Lean Meat

11 to 15 grams of carbs

gingered beef and vegetable stew

If you have ginger left over from this boldly flavored stew, place the unpeeled piece in a freezer bag and store in the freezer; you can grate or slice the ginger while it's frozen.

Prep: 25 minutes **Cook:** 7 to 8 hours, (low) or 3½ to 4 hours (high), plus 15 minutes (high) **Makes:** 8 servings

2½	pounds boneless beef round steak
	Nonstick cooking spray
1	tablespoon cooking oil
2	medium carrots, bias-sliced into ½-inch pieces
¾	cup chopped red sweet pepper (1 medium)
⅔	cup sliced leeks (2 medium)
1¼	cups water
3	tablespoons reduced-sodium soy sauce
1	tablespoon grated fresh ginger
3	cloves garlic, minced
1½	teaspoons instant beef bouillon granules
⅛	to ¼ teaspoon cayenne pepper
2	tablespoons cornstarch
2	tablespoons cold water
1	10-ounce package frozen sugar snap pea pods, thawed
½	cup sliced green onions (4)

1 Trim fat from meat. Cut meat into 1-inch pieces. Coat a 3½- or 4-quart slow cooker with cooking spray. Coat a large skillet with cooking spray. Brown half of the meat in hot skillet over medium heat. Remove meat from skillet. Add oil to skillet. Brown remaining meat in hot oil. Drain off fat. Place meat, carrots, sweet pepper, and leeks in slow cooker. In a medium bowl combine the 1¼ cups water, soy sauce, ginger, garlic, bouillon granules, and cayenne pepper. Pour over mixture in cooker.

2 Cover and cook on low-heat setting for 7 to 8 hours or on high-heat setting for 3½ to 4 hours.

3 If using low-heat setting, turn to high-heat setting. In a small bowl combine cornstarch and water. Stir cornstarch mixture and frozen pea pods into mixture in cooker. Cover and cook about 15 minutes more or until sauce is thickened and pea pods are tender, stirring once. Stir in green onions.

Nutrition Facts per serving: 280 cal., 10 g total fat (3 g sat. fat), 81 mg chol., 464 mg sodium, 12 g carbo., 2 g fiber, 33 g pro.
Daily Values: 55% vit. A, 68% vit. C, 5% calcium, 25% iron
Exchanges: 2 Vegetable, 4 Lean Meat

mushroom steak diane stew

Heavenly news! The flavors of steak Diane, a classic French dish, translate well to this hearty stew that cooks up perfectly in the slow cooker.

Prep: 20 minutes Cook: 8 to 10 hours (low) or 4 to 5 hours (high) Makes: 6 servings

1½	pounds boneless beef round steak
2	medium onions, cut into thin wedges
3	cups sliced fresh button mushrooms (8 ounces)
1	10¾-ounce can condensed golden mushroom soup
¼	cup tomato paste
2	teaspoons Worcestershire sauce
1	teaspoon dry mustard
½	teaspoon cracked black pepper
3	cups hot cooked whole wheat noodles or pasta (optional)

1 Trim fat from meat. Cut meat into 1-inch pieces. Place onions in a 3½- or 4-quart slow cooker. Top with mushrooms and meat. In a medium bowl combine soup, tomato paste, Worcestershire sauce, dry mustard, and pepper. Pour over mixture in cooker.

2 Cover and cook on low-heat setting for 8 to 10 hours or on high-heat setting for 4 to 5 hours. If desired, serve over hot cooked noodles.

Nutrition Facts per serving: 222 cal., 7 g total fat (2 g sat. fat), 66 mg chol., 475 mg sodium, 11 g carbo., 2 g fiber, 28 g pro.
Daily Values: 6% vit. A, 6% vit. C, 1% calcium, 20% iron
Exchanges: 1 Vegetable, ½ Other Carbo., 3½ Very Lean Meat, 1 Fat

11 to 15 grams of carbs

cajun pork

The deep South is known for hot weather and even hotter food. This pork stew bears only mild Cajun flavor—a good introduction for folks new to the flavor.

Prep: 20 minutes Cook: 6 to 7 hours (low) or 3 to 3½ hours (high),
plus 30 minutes (high) Makes: 6 to 8 servings

2½	**to 3 pounds boneless pork shoulder**
	Nonstick cooking spray
2	**medium yellow sweet peppers, cut into 1-inch pieces**
1	**tablespoon Cajun seasoning**
1	**14½-ounce can diced tomatoes with green pepper and onion, undrained**
1	**16-ounce package frozen cut okra**
	Bottled hot pepper sauce (optional)

1 Trim fat from meat. Cut meat into 1-inch pieces. Coat a large skillet with cooking spray. Cook meat, half at a time, in hot skillet over medium heat until brown. Drain off fat. In a 3½- or 4-quart slow cooker place meat and sweet peppers. Sprinkle with Cajun seasoning. Top with undrained tomatoes.

2 Cover and cook on low-heat setting for 6 to 7 hours or on high-heat setting for 3 to 3½ hours.

3 If using low-heat setting, turn to high-heat setting. Stir in frozen okra. Cover and cook for 30 minutes more. If desired, pass hot pepper sauce.

Nutrition Facts per serving: 233 cal., 8 g total fat (3 g sat. fat), 77 mg chol., 444 mg sodium, 15 g carbo., 4 g fiber, 25 g pro.
Daily Values: 10% vit. A, 187% vit. C, 10% calcium, 14% iron
Exchanges: 2 Vegetable, 3 Lean Meat

cherry-and port-sauced pork

Pork shoulder roast—sometimes called Boston butt—is a wonderful cut of meat. The streaks of fat melt away during cooking, bringing rich, bold flavors to the dish.

Prep: 30 minutes Cook: 7 to 8 hours (low) or 3½ to 4 hours (high), plus 15 minutes (high) Makes: 6 servings

1	2½-pound boneless pork shoulder roast
½	cup dried tart cherries (4 ounces)
1	8-ounce can tomato sauce
½	cup chopped onion (1 medium)
½	cup port wine
½	cup water
1	tablespoon Worcestershire sauce
1	teaspoon dried marjoram, crushed
½	teaspoon dried oregano, crushed
2	cloves garlic, minced
2	tablespoons cornstarch
2	tablespoons cold water
6	ounces dried whole wheat pasta, cooked and drained (optional)

1 Trim fat from meat. Cut meat into 1-inch pieces. In a 3½- or 4-quart slow cooker place pork and cherries. In a small bowl combine tomato sauce, onion, port, the ½ cup water, Worcestershire sauce, marjoram, oregano, and garlic. Pour over meat mixture.

2 Cover and cook on low-heat setting for 7 to 8 hours or on high-heat setting for 3½ to 4 hours.

3 If using low-heat setting, turn to high-heat setting. In a small bowl combine cornstarch and water. Stir into mixture in cooker. Cover and cook about 15 minutes more or until thickened. If desired, serve over hot cooked pasta.

Nutrition Facts per serving: 347 cal., 11 g total fat (4 g sat. fat), 122 mg chol., 364 mg sodium, 15 g carbo., 1 g fiber, 38 g pro.
Daily Values: 1% vit. A, 4% vit. C, 2% calcium, 19% iron
Exchanges: 1 Other Carbo., 5 Lean Meat

11 to 15 grams of carbs

pork and edamame soup

Eat this Asian-influenced soup with good nutrition in mind. Green soybeans (edamame) are good sources of soy, which may reduce the risk of some types of cancer.

Prep: 30 minutes Cook: 8 to 10 hours (low) or 4 to 5 hours (high) Makes: 4 to 5 servings

1	2- to 2½-pound boneless pork shoulder roast
1	tablespoon cooking oil
2	14-ounce cans reduced-sodium chicken broth
1	8-ounce can sliced water chestnuts, drained
6	cloves garlic, minced
2	tablespoons reduced-sodium soy sauce
1	tablespoon hoisin sauce
2	teaspoons grated fresh ginger
¼	to ½ teaspoon crushed red pepper
1	12-ounce package frozen green soybeans (edamame)
1	medium red sweet pepper, cut into bite-size strips

1 Trim fat from meat. Cut meat into 1-inch pieces. In a large nonstick skillet brown meat, half at a time, in hot oil over medium heat. Drain off fat. Place meat in a 3½- or 4-quart slow cooker. Stir in chicken broth, water chestnuts, garlic, soy sauce, hoisin sauce, ginger, and crushed red pepper.

2 Cover and cook on low-heat setting for 8 to 10 hours or on high-heat setting for 4 to 5 hours, adding the soybeans and sweet pepper the last 30 minutes of cooking. Skim off fat.

Nutrition Facts per serving: 344 cal., 15 g total fat (4 g sat. fat), 98 mg chol.,
675 mg sodium, 12 g carbo., 3 g fiber, 39 g pro.
Daily Values: 13% vit. A, 86% vit. C, 14% calcium, 22% iron
Exchanges: 1 Starch, 5 Lean Meat

pork and red pepper soup

Balsamic vinegar and roasted red peppers add an Italian angle to this utterly up-to-date soup. Both were once hard-to-find ingredients that are now widely available.

Prep: 25 minutes Cook: 6 to 8 hours (low) or 3 to 4 hours (high), plus 15 minutes (high) Makes: 6 servings

1½	**pounds boneless pork shoulder**
2	**14-ounce cans reduced-sodium beef broth**
1	**14½-ounce can diced tomatoes with basil, oregano, and garlic; undrained**
1	**12-ounce jar roasted red sweet peppers, drained and cut into bite-size strips**
½	**cup chopped onion (1 medium)**
2	**tablespoons balsamic vinegar**
¼	**teaspoon black pepper**
2	**medium zucchini, halved lengthwise and cut into ¼-inch slices**

1 Trim fat from meat. Cut meat into 1-inch pieces. In a 3½- or 4-quart slow cooker combine meat, beef broth, undrained tomatoes, roasted sweet peppers, onion, vinegar, and black pepper.

2 Cover and cook on low-heat setting for 6 to 8 hours or on high-heat setting for 3 to 4 hours.

3 If using low-heat setting, turn to high-heat setting. Stir in zucchini. Cover and cook about 15 minutes more or until zucchini is crisp-tender.

Nutrition Facts per serving: 219 cal., 7 g total fat (2 g sat. fat), 73 mg chol., 696 mg sodium, 13 g carbo., 2 g fiber, 26 g pro.
Daily Values: 10% vit. A, 194% vit. C, 6% calcium, 17% iron
Exchanges: 2½ Vegetable, 3 Lean Meat

11 to 15 grams of carbs

chile verde

Mexico's famous pork shoulder braise simmers up beautifully in the slow cooker. Serve this colorful dish with a bright, vinaigrette-tossed salad topped with sparkling orange slices.

Prep: 40 minutes Cook: 6 to 8 hours (low) or 3 to 4 hours (high), plus 15 minutes (high) Makes: 6 servings

1	teaspoon ground cumin
½	teaspoon salt
¼	teaspoon black pepper
1½	pounds boneless pork shoulder, cut into 1-inch pieces
	Nonstick cooking spray
1	tablespoon olive oil
1	pound fresh tomatillos, husks removed and chopped (about 4 cups)
1	cup chopped onion (1 large)
1	teaspoon finely shredded lime peel
2	tablespoons lime juice
4	cloves garlic, minced
¾	cup chopped yellow or red sweet pepper (1 medium)
1	8-ounce carton light dairy sour cream
2	tablespoons snipped fresh cilantro

1 In a bowl combine cumin, salt, and pepper. Set aside. Trim fat from meat. Sprinkle cumin mixture over meat. Coat a large skillet with cooking spray. Cook half of the meat in hot skillet over medium heat until brown. Remove meat from skillet. Add oil to skillet. Brown remaining meat in hot oil. Drain off fat. Place meat in a 3½- to 4½-quart slow cooker. Add tomatillos, onion, lime peel, lime juice, and garlic. Stir to combine.

2 Cover and cook on low-heat setting for 6 to 8 hours or on high-heat setting for 3 to 4 hours.

3 If using low-heat setting, turn to high-heat setting. Add sweet peppers to mixture in cooker. Cover and cook for 15 minutes more. Meanwhile, in a small bowl combine sour cream and cilantro. Serve sour cream mixture with chile.

Nutrition Facts per serving: 270 cal., 13 g total fat (4 g sat. fat), 86 mg chol.,
316 mg sodium, 12 g carbo., 1 g fiber, 26 g pro.
Daily Values: 8% vit. A, 115% vit. C, 10% calcium, 10% iron
Exchanges: 2½ Vegetable, 3 Lean Meat, 1 Fat

asian ribs

If you're one of those people who count the ingredients in a recipe and turn the page if it's too long, do yourself a favor and try this recipe anyway. It's full of spicy, aromatic flavors.

Prep: 15 minutes Cook: 8 to 10 hours (low) or 4 to 5 hours (high), plus 15 minutes (high) Makes: 10 servings

1	tablespoon purchased five-spice powder or Homemade Five-Spice Powder*
1	tablespoon grated fresh ginger
2	cloves garlic, minced
1	teaspoon toasted sesame oil
1/8	teaspoon cayenne pepper
3	pounds boneless pork country-style ribs
1	16-ounce can whole, unpitted purple plums
1/4	cup hoisin sauce
2	tablespoons rice vinegar
1	tablespoon reduced-sodium soy sauce
1	tablespoon dry sherry or orange juice
1	tablespoon cornstarch

1 In a small bowl combine five-spice powder, ginger, garlic, sesame oil, ½ teaspoon black pepper, ¼ teaspoon salt, and cayenne pepper. If necessary, cut ribs to fit into a 3½- to 4½-quart slow cooker. Rub spice mixture into ribs with your fingers. Place ribs in cooker. Drain and pit plums. In a food processor or blender combine plums, hoisin sauce, rice vinegar, soy sauce, and sherry. Cover and process or blend until smooth. Pour over ribs in cooker.

2 Cover and cook on low-heat setting for 8 to 10 hours or on high-heat setting for 4 to 5 hours.

3 If using low-heat setting, turn to high-heat setting. In a small bowl combine cornstarch and 1 tablespoon water. Stir into meat mixture in cooker. Cover and cook about 15 minutes more or until sauce is thickened. Transfer ribs to a serving platter. Strain sauce; skim off fat. Serve sauce over ribs.

Nutrition Facts per serving: 264 cal., 11 g total fat (4 g sat. fat), 86 mg chol.,
299 mg sodium, 11 g carbo., 1 g fiber, 27 g pro.
Daily Values: 3% vit. A, 3% vit. C, 5% calcium, 12% iron
Exchanges: 1 Other Carbo., 4 Lean Meat

*Homemade Five-Spice Powder: In a blender combine 3 tablespoons ground cinnamon; 2 teaspoons anise seeds or 6 star anise; 1½ teaspoons fennel seeds; 1½ teaspoons whole Szechwan peppers or whole black peppercorns; and ¾ teaspoon ground cloves. Cover and blend until powdery. Store mixture in a covered container. Makes about ⅓ cup.

spiced lamb with curried slaw

This main dish comes with a side-dish bonus: a crisp, refreshing slaw that contrasts with the complex flavors of the lamb.

Prep: 30 minutes Cook: 10 to 12 hours (low) or 5 to 6 hours (high) Makes: 6 servings

1	2½- to 3-pound boneless lamb shoulder roast
1	medium onion, cut into thin wedges
¼	teaspoon black pepper
¼	cup reduced-sodium beef broth
¼	cup reduced-sugar apricot jam
¼	cup reduced-sodium soy sauce
1	teaspoon curry powder
1	teaspoon finely shredded lemon peel
½	teaspoon ground cinnamon
¼	teaspoon cayenne pepper
½	cup low-fat mayonnaise dressing
3	tablespoons fat-free half-and-half
½	teaspoon curry powder
5	cups shredded cabbage or one 10-ounce package shredded cabbage with carrot (coleslaw mix)

1 Trim fat from meat. If necessary, cut meat to fit into a 3½- or 4-quart slow cooker. Place onion in cooker. Add meat. Sprinkle with black pepper. In a small bowl combine beef broth, jam, soy sauce, the 1 teaspoon curry powder, the lemon peel, cinnamon, and cayenne pepper. Pour over meat.

2 Cover and cook on low-heat setting for 10 to 12 hours or on high-heat setting for 5 to 6 hours.

3 Meanwhile, for curried slaw, in a large bowl combine mayonnaise, half-and-half, and the ½ teaspoon curry powder. Add cabbage; stir until coated. Cover and chill for up to 12 hours.

4 Remove meat and onion from cooker, reserving cooking liquid. Using two forks, pull meat apart into shreds. Transfer meat and onion to a serving bowl. Skim fat from the reserved liquid. Drizzle meat with enough of the cooking liquid to moisten. Serve with curried slaw.

Nutrition Facts per serving: 316 cal., 11 g total fat (3 g sat. fat), 119 mg chol.,
724 mg sodium, 14 g carbo., 2 g fiber, 40 g pro.
Daily Values: 3% vit. A, 40% vit. C, 7% calcium, 23% iron
Exchanges: 1 Vegetable, ½ Other Carbo., 5 Lean Meat

lemon-mustard lamb roast

Spoon golden mustard-and-lemon-flavor gravy over tender lamb and roasted vegetables.

Prep: 25 minutes Cook: 8 to 10 hours (low) or 4 to 5 hours (high),
plus 45 minutes (high) Makes: 6 to 8 servings

¹⁄₂	teaspoon lemon-pepper seasoning
¹⁄₂	teaspoon dry mustard
1	2- to 2¹⁄₂-pound boneless lamb shoulder roast
	Nonstick cooking spray
1¹⁄₂	cups tiny whole carrots
1	cup reduced-sodium chicken broth
¹⁄₄	cup Dijon-style mustard
¹⁄₄	teaspoon finely shredded lemon peel
1	tablespoon lemon juice
¹⁄₂	teaspoon dried rosemary, crushed
¹⁄₄	teaspoon black pepper
2	cloves garlic, minced
1	8- or 9-ounce package frozen artichoke hearts, thawed
2	tablespoons cornstarch
2	tablespoons cold water

1 In a small bowl combine lemon-pepper seasoning and dry mustard. Trim fat from meat. Sprinkle mustard mixture evenly over meat; rub in with your fingers. If necessary, cut meat to fit into a 3¹⁄₂- or 4-quart slow cooker. Coat a large skillet with cooking spray. Cook meat in hot skillet over medium-high heat until brown on all sides. Drain off fat. Place carrots in cooker; add meat. In a small bowl combine chicken broth, mustard, lemon peel, lemon juice, rosemary, pepper, and garlic. Pour over meat in cooker.

2 Cover and cook on low-heat setting for 8 to 10 hours or on high-heat setting for 4 to 5 hours.

3 If using low-heat setting, turn to high-heat setting. Stir in artichoke hearts. Cover and cook for 30 minutes more. Transfer meat and vegetables to a serving platter, reserving cooking liquid. If present, remove string or netting from meat. Cover meat and vegetables with foil to keep warm.

4 For gravy, skim fat from cooking liquid. In a small bowl combine cornstarch and water. Stir into liquid in cooker. Cover and cook about 15 minutes more or until thickened. Serve meat and vegetables with gravy.

Nutrition Facts per serving: 242 cal., 7 g total fat (2 g sat. fat), 95 mg chol., 576 mg sodium, 11 g carbo., 3 g fiber, 34 g pro.
Daily Values: 67% vit. A, 9% vit. C, 7% calcium, 18% iron
Exchanges: 2 Vegetable, 4 Lean Meat

11 to 15 grams of carbs

garam masala lamb

Garam masala is a blend of ground, dry-roasted spices that brings the warming effect to Indian recipes. Garam is the Indian word for "warm."

Prep: 20 minutes Cook: 8 to 10 hours (low) or 4 to 5 hours (high), plus 15 minutes (high) Makes: 6 servings

2	pounds boneless lamb shoulder roast
2	medium onions, cut into thin wedges
2	cups sliced fresh mushrooms
2	teaspoons garam masala
2	teaspoons grated fresh ginger
1/2	teaspoon salt
1/4	teaspoon black pepper
2	cloves garlic, minced
1/3	cup reduced-sodium beef broth
1	8-ounce carton plain low-fat yogurt
2	tablespoons cornstarch
2	medium yellow summer squash or zucchini, quartered lengthwise and sliced (2½ cups)

1 Trim fat from meat. Cut meat into 1½-inch pieces. In a 3½- or 4-quart slow cooker place meat, onions, and mushrooms. Sprinkle with garam masala, ginger, salt, pepper, and garlic. Add beef broth.

2 Cover and cook on low-heat setting for 8 to 10 hours or on high-heat setting for 4 to 5 hours.

3 If using low-heat setting, turn to high-heat setting. In a small bowl combine yogurt and cornstarch. Stir yogurt mixture and summer squash into cooker. Cover and cook about 15 minutes more or until sauce is slightly thickened.

Nutrition Facts per serving: 253 cal., 8 g total fat (3 g sat. fat), 97 mg chol., 353 mg sodium, 11 g carbo., 1 g fiber, 34 g pro.
Daily Values: 2% vit. A, 17% vit. C, 11% calcium, 19% iron
Exchanges: 2 Vegetable, 4 Lean Meat

brown rice risotto with lamb

Curry adds intrigue to this colorful main dish. Round out the meal with a salad of fresh spinach, cucumber, and tomato.

Prep: 15 minutes Cook: 8 to 9 hours (low), 4 to 4½ hours (high), plus 5 minutes (standing) Makes: 6 servings

1	2- to 2½-pound boneless lamb shoulder roast
1	tablespoon cooking oil
2½	cups hot-style vegetable juice
1	cup uncooked regular brown rice
1	teaspoon curry powder
¼	teaspoon salt
2	medium carrots, diced
¾	cup chopped green sweet pepper (1 medium)

1 Trim fat from meat. If necessary, cut meat to fit into a 3½- or 4-quart slow cooker. In a large skillet cook meat in hot oil until brown on all sides. In the slow cooker combine vegetable juice, uncooked rice, curry powder, and salt. Add carrots. Add meat.

2 Cover and cook on low-heat setting for 8 to 9 hours or on high-heat setting for 4 to 4½ hours.

3 Add the sweet pepper to the cooker. Cover and let stand 5 to 10 minutes.

Nutrition Facts per serving: 299 cal., 12 g total fat (3 g sat. fat), 99 mg chol., 537 mg sodium, 15 g carbo., 2 g fiber, 32 g pro.
Daily Values: 122% vit. A, 53% vit. C, 4% calcium, 18% iron
Exchanges: ½ Vegetable, 1 Starch, 4 Lean Meat

11 to 15 grams of carbs

115

savory lamb soup

Save some steps! Baby-cut carrots come perfectly sized and already peeled, as do the frozen small onions. Hence, you can skip the peeling and chopping duties for this recipe.

Prep: 20 minutes Cook: 10 to 12 hours (low) or 5 to 6 hours (high) Makes: 6 servings

1½	pounds lean lamb stew meat
1	tablespoon cooking oil
2	14-ounce cans reduced-sodium beef broth
3	cups frozen cut green beans
2	cups tiny whole carrots
1½	cups frozen small whole onions
2	teaspoons dried thyme, crushed
½	teaspoon garlic powder
¼	teaspoon black pepper
½	cup dry white wine
	Snipped fresh parsley (optional)

1 Trim fat from meat. Cut meat into 1-inch pieces. In a large skillet cook meat, half at a time, in hot oil over medium heat until brown. Drain off fat. Transfer meat to a 4- to 5-quart slow cooker. Stir in beef broth, green beans, carrots, onions, thyme, garlic powder, and pepper.

2 Cover and cook on low-heat setting for 10 to 12 hours or on high-heat setting for 5 to 6 hours. If necessary, skim off fat. Stir in wine. If desired, sprinkle each serving with snipped parsley.

Nutrition Facts per serving: 234 cal., 7 g total fat (2 g sat. fat), 71 mg chol., 368 mg sodium, 13 g carbo., 4 g fiber, 26 g pro.
Daily Values: 138% vit. A, 23% vit. C, 10% calcium, 18% iron
Exchanges: 2½ Vegetable, 3 Lean Meat

mediterranean lamb shanks

Pesto sauce captures the essence of the Mediterranean sun and its summer garden. If you like, serve the lamb sprinkled with shredded lemon peel and snipped parsley.

Prep: 10 minutes Cook: 7 to 9 hours (low) or 3½ to 4½ hours (high) Makes: 6 servings

1	16-ounce package frozen Italian vegetables (zucchini, carrots, cauliflower, lima beans, Italian beans)
1	14½-ounce can no-salt-added diced tomatoes, undrained
1	teaspoon dried basil, crushed
1	14-ounce can reduced-sodium chicken broth
3	to 3½ pounds meaty lamb shanks
⅓	cup purchased refrigerated basil pesto

1 In a 5- to 6-quart slow cooker combine frozen vegetables, undrained tomatoes, dried basil, and chicken broth. Top with lamb shanks. Spoon pesto over lamb shanks.

2 Cover and cook on low-heat setting for 7 to 9 hours or on high-heat setting for 3½ to 4½ hours. Using a slotted spoon transfer lamb shanks and vegetables to a serving platter; discard cooking liquid.

Nutrition Facts per serving: 247 cal., 11 g total fat (1 g sat. fat), 65 mg chol.,
387 mg sodium, 11 g carbo., 3 g fiber, 23 g pro.
Daily Values: 51% vit. A, 17% vit. C, 4% calcium, 11% iron
Exchanges: 2 Vegetable, 3 Lean Meat, ½ Fat

11 to 15 grams of carbs

spicy lamb shanks

Lamb shanks are an underutilized and wonderfully flavorful cut of lamb. Ideal for the slow cooker, the lamb literally falls off the bone in this warming supper for chilly spring days.

Prep: 25 minutes Cook: 8 to 9 hours (low) or 4 to 4 ½ hours (high), plus 10 minutes Makes: 4 to 6 servings

2	large oranges
5	medium carrots, cut into 2-inch pieces
1½	cups frozen small whole onions
4	large cloves garlic, thinly sliced
4	meaty lamb shanks (about 4 pounds), cut into 3- to 4-inch pieces
6	inches stick cinnamon, broken into 1-inch pieces
1¼	cups reduced-sodium beef broth
1½	teaspoons ground cardamom
1	teaspoon ground cumin
½	teaspoon ground turmeric
½	teaspoon black pepper
2	tablespoons cold water
4	teaspoons cornstarch
⅓	cup pitted kalamata or other black olives, halved (optional)
1	tablespoon snipped fresh cilantro (optional)

1 Using a vegetable peeler, remove the orange part of the peel from one of the oranges. Cut peel into thin strips (to yield about ¼ cup). Squeeze juice from both oranges to make about ⅔ cup. Set aside.

2 In a 5- to 6-quart slow cooker place carrots, onions, and garlic. Add orange peel strips, meat, and stick cinnamon. In a small bowl combine the reserved orange juice, beef broth, cardamom, cumin, turmeric, and pepper. Pour over mixture in cooker.

3 Cover and cook on low-heat setting for 8 to 9 hours or on high-heat setting for 4 to 4½ hours.

4 Transfer meat and vegetables to a serving platter, reserving cooking liquid. Cover meat and vegetables with foil to keep warm. Remove stick cinnamon.

5 For sauce, pour cooking liquid into a glass measuring cup; skim off fat. Measure 1½ cups of the cooking liquid. Pour the liquid into a small saucepan. In a small bowl combine water and cornstarch. Stir into liquid in saucepan. Cook and stir over medium heat until thickened and bubbly. Cook and stir for 2 minutes more. Serve meat and vegetables with sauce. If desired, sprinkle with olives and cilantro.

Nutrition Facts per serving: 207 cal., 4 g total fat (1 g sat. fat), 85 mg chol., 428 mg sodium, 15 g carbo., 3 g fiber, 28 g pro.
Daily Values: 111% vit. A, 40% vit. C, 9% calcium, 16% iron
Exchanges: 2½ Vegetable, 3 Lean Meat

greek lamb shanks

Lamb shanks are popular in trendy bistros. But why pay top dollar? Braise up these beauties in your slow cooker with Greek touches for dine-out tastes at dine-at-home prices.

Prep: 15 minutes Cook: 7 to 9 hours (low) or 3½ to 4½ hours (high) Makes: 6 servings

1	tablespoon olive oil
4	cloves garlic, minced
2	teaspoons finely shredded lemon peel
2	teaspoons dried oregano or marjoram, crushed
¼	teaspoon salt
¼	teaspoon crushed red pepper
4	meaty lamb shanks (4 to 5 pounds)
1	14½-ounce can black or white soybeans or one 15-ounce can black beans, rinsed and drained
1⅓	cups chopped, seeded roma tomatoes (4 medium)
1	large onion, cut into thin wedges
¼	cup pitted kalamata olives, halved
½	cup dry white wine or reduced-sodium chicken broth
2	tablespoons lemon juice
2	ounces feta cheese or goat cheese (chèvre), crumbled (optional)
	Snipped fresh parsley (optional)

1 In a small bowl combine olive oil, garlic, lemon peel, oregano, salt, and crushed red pepper. Rub oil mixture into meat with your fingers. In a 4½- to 6-quart slow cooker combine soybeans, tomatoes, onion, and olives. Add meat. Pour wine and lemon juice over all.

2 Cover and cook on low-heat setting for 7 to 9 hours or on high-heat setting for 3½ to 4½ hours.

3 Transfer lamb shanks and vegetables to a serving platter. Discard cooking liquid. Cut lamb shanks into 6 servings. If desired, sprinkle with cheese and parsley.

Nutrition Facts per serving: 282 cal., 10 g total fat (2 g sat. fat), 85 mg chol., 280 mg sodium, 12 g carbo., 6 g fiber, 33 g pro.
Daily Values: 16% vit. A, 21% vit. C, 8% calcium, 24% iron
Exchanges: 1 Starch, 4 Lean Meat

11 to 15 grams of carbs

saffron chicken and sausage

Saffron threads—the dried stigmas of the crocus flower—are traditionally used in Spanish paella. They are fairly expensive, so substitute ground turmeric if you wish.

Prep: 30 minutes Cook: 5 to 6 hours (low) or 2½ to 3 hours (high),
Stand: 5 minutes Makes: 6 servings

2½	to 3 pounds meaty chicken pieces (breast halves, thighs, and drumsticks), skinned
1	tablespoon cooking oil
8	ounces cooked smoked turkey sausage, halved lengthwise and sliced
1	large onion, sliced
3	cloves garlic, minced
2	tablespoons snipped fresh thyme or 2 teaspoons dried thyme, crushed
¼	teaspoon black pepper
⅛	teaspoon thread saffron or ¼ teaspoon ground turmeric
1	14-ounce can reduced-sodium chicken broth
½	cup water
2	cups chopped tomatoes (4 medium)
2	yellow or green sweet peppers, cut into very thin bite-size strips

1 In a large nonstick skillet cook chicken, half at a time, in hot oil over medium heat until brown on all sides. Drain off fat. In a 3½- to 5-quart slow cooker place chicken, sausage, and onion. Sprinkle with garlic, dried thyme (if using), black pepper, and saffron. Add chicken broth and water to mixture in cooker.

2 Cover and cook on low-heat setting for 5 to 6 hours or on high-heat setting for 2½ to 3 hours.

3 Stir in the tomatoes, sweet peppers, and if using, fresh thyme. Cover and let stand for 5 minutes.

Nutrition Facts per serving: 231 cal., 8 g total fat (2 g sat. fat), 89 mg chol., 565 mg sodium, 11 g carbo., 2 g fiber, 28 g pro.
Daily Values: 14% vit. A, 211% vit. C, 4% calcium, 11% iron
Exchanges: 2 Vegetable, 3½ Lean Meat

spicy chicken with peppers and olives

Spicy red pepper spaghetti sauce is the tastiest choice for this recipe. If you can't find it, use your favorite variety of pasta sauce.

Prep: 20 minutes **Cook:** 6 to 7 hours (low) or 3 to 3½ hours (high) **Makes:** 6 servings

2½ to 3	pounds meaty chicken pieces (breast halves, thighs, and drumsticks), skinned
	Salt and black pepper
½	cup coarsely chopped yellow sweet pepper (1 small)
⅓	cup sliced, pitted ripe olives and/or pimiento-stuffed green olives
1	26-ounce jar meatless spaghetti sauce

---

1 Place chicken in a 3½- or 4-quart slow cooker. Sprinkle chicken lightly with salt and black pepper. Add sweet pepper and olives to cooker. Pour spaghetti sauce over mixture in cooker.

2 Cover and cook on low-heat setting for 6 to 7 hours or on high-heat setting for 3 to 3½ hours.

Nutrition Facts per serving: 181 cal., 5 g total fat (2 g sat. fat), 68 mg chol., 704 mg sodium, 14 g carbo., 2 g fiber, 21 g pro.
Daily Values: 7% vit. A, 94% vit. C, 5% calcium, 13% iron
Exchanges: 1½ Vegetable, ½ Other Carbo., 2½ Lean Meat

11 to 15 grams of carbs

chicken merlot with mushrooms

To ensure proper doneness, always place ingredients in your crockery cooker in the order listed in the recipe.

11 to 15 grams of carbs

Prep: 25 minutes Cook: 5 to 6 hours (low) or 2½ to 3 hours (high), plus 15 minutes (high) Makes: 6 servings

3	cups sliced fresh mushrooms (8 ounces)
1	cup chopped onion (1 large)
2	cloves garlic, minced
2½	to 3 pounds meaty chicken pieces (breast halves, thighs, and drumsticks), skinned
¾	cup reduced-sodium chicken broth
1	6-ounce can tomato paste
¼	cup Merlot or other dry red wine or chicken broth
1½	teaspoons dried basil, crushed
½	teaspoon salt
¼	teaspoon black pepper
2	tablespoons cornstarch
2	tablespoons cold water
3	tablespoons shredded Parmesan cheese

---

1 In a 3½- to 5-quart slow cooker place mushrooms, onion, and garlic. Add chicken. In a medium bowl combine chicken broth, tomato paste, wine, basil, salt, and pepper. Pour over chicken in cooker.

2 Cover and cook on low-heat setting for 5 to 6 hours or on high-heat setting for 2½ to 3 hours.

3 Transfer chicken to a serving platter, reserving cooking liquid. Cover chicken with foil to keep warm.

4 If using low-heat setting, turn to high-heat setting. In a small bowl combine cornstarch and water. Stir into liquid in cooker. Cover and cook about 15 minutes more or until thickened. Spoon sauce over chicken. Sprinkle with Parmesan cheese.

Nutrition Facts per serving: 249 cal., 8 g total fat (4 g sat. fat), 75 mg chol., 639 mg sodium, 13 g carbo., 2 g fiber, 30 g pro.
Daily Values: 4% vit. A, 15% vit. C, 24% calcium, 11% iron
Exchanges: 2½ Vegetable, 3½ Lean Meat

cassoulet

Look for herbes de Provence in the spice aisle of most supermarkets. It is a fragrant blend of spices—typically basil, fennel seed, lavender, marjoram, rosemary, savory, and thyme.

Prep: 25 minutes Cook: 8 to 10 hours (low) or 4 to 5 hours (high) Makes: 6 servings

6	ounces cooked smoked turkey sausage, halved lengthwise and cut into $1/2$-inch slices
1	15-ounce can black soybeans*, rinsed and drained
1	$14^1/_2$-ounce can no-salt-added stewed tomatoes, undrained and cut up
1	cup chopped celery (2 stalks)
$3/4$	cup chopped red or yellow sweet pepper (1 medium)
1	medium onion, cut into thin wedges
$1/4$	cup dry red wine
3	cloves garlic, minced
1	tablespoon dried herbes de Provence, crushed
$1/2$	teaspoon salt
3	pounds meaty chicken pieces (breast halves, thighs, drumsticks), skinned
	Salt and black pepper

11 to 15 grams of carbs

1 In a $4^1/_2$- to 6-quart slow cooker combine sausage, beans, undrained tomatoes, celery, sweet pepper, onion, wine, garlic, herbes de Provence, and the $1/2$ teaspoon salt. Stir gently to mix. Place chicken on top. Sprinkle chicken lightly with additional salt and black pepper.

2 Cover and cook on low-heat setting for 8 to 10 hours or on high-heat setting for 4 to 5 hours.

3 Remove chicken from cooker. Spoon bean mixture into shallow serving bowls; top with chicken.

*Note: If you like, substitute one 15-ounce can black beans, rinsed and drained, for the black soy beans and omit the $1/2$ teaspoon salt.

Nutrition Facts per serving: 285 cal., 9 g total fat (2 g sat. fat), 95 mg chol., 444 mg sodium, 14 g carbo., 6 g fiber, 36 g pro.
Daily Values: 22% vit. A, 78% vit. C, 9% calcium, 19% iron
Exchanges: $1^1/_2$ Vegetable, $1/2$ Starch, 4 Lean Meat

basil-cream chicken thighs

In this luscious recipe, cream cheese adds extra richness to already-creamy Alfredo sauce.

Prep: 20 minutes Cook: 5 to 6 hours (low) or 2½ to 3 hours (high) Makes: 6 servings

2½	pounds chicken thighs, skinned
¼	teaspoon black pepper
2	10-ounce containers refrigerated light Alfredo sauce
¼	cup water
2	teaspoons dried basil, crushed
1	16-ounce package frozen broccoli, cauliflower, and carrots
3	ounces fat-free cream cheese, cubed
	Hot cooked whole wheat pasta (optional)

---

1 Place chicken in a 3½- or 4-quart slow cooker. Sprinkle with pepper. In a small bowl combine Alfredo sauce, water, and basil. Pour over chicken in cooker. Top with frozen vegetables.

2 Cover and cook on low-heat setting for 5 to 6 hours or on high-heat setting for 2½ to 3 hours. Using a slotted spoon, transfer chicken and vegetables to a serving platter. Add cream cheese to sauce in slow cooker; stir until smooth. Serve sauce over chicken and vegetables. If desired, serve with hot cooked pasta.

Nutrition Facts per serving: 267 cal., 12 g total fat (7 g sat. fat), 93 mg chol.,
759 mg sodium, 13 g carbo., 2 g fiber, 23 g pro.
Daily Values: 41% vit. A, 26% vit. C, 17% calcium, 6% iron
Exchanges: ½ Vegetable, ½ Other Carbo., 3 Lean Meat, 1 Fat

11 to 15 grams of carbs

apricot chicken

Apricot and mustard flavors come together for this chicken dish. Soak up the flavorful juices by serving with brown rice.

Prep: 25 minutes **Cook:** 8 to 9 hours (low) or 4 to 4 ½ hours (high) **Makes:** 8 servings

2½	pounds skinless, boneless chicken thighs
1	tablespoon cooking oil
2	cups frozen small whole onions, thawed
4	medium carrots, bias-cut into ½-inch slices
	Salt and black pepper
½	cup chicken broth
⅓	cup reduced-sugar apricot preserves
2	tablespoons quick-cooking tapioca
1	to 2 tablespoons Dijon-style mustard
⅛	teaspoon ground allspice
	Hot cooked brown rice (optional)

1 In a very large skillet cook chicken, half at a time, in hot oil over medium heat until brown on both sides. (Add more oil, if necessary.) Drain off fat. Set aside.

2 In a 3½- or 4-quart slow cooker combine onions and carrots. Top with chicken. Sprinkle chicken with salt and pepper. In a small bowl combine chicken broth, apricot preserves, tapioca, mustard, and allspice. Pour over mixture in cooker.

3 Cover and cook on low-heat setting for 8 to 9 hours or on high-heat setting for 4 to 4½ hours. Serve chicken and vegetables with some of the cooking liquid. If desired, serve with hot cooked rice.

Nutrition Facts per serving: 246 cal., 8 g total fat (3 g sat. fat), 113 mg chol., 217 mg sodium, 12 g carbo., 2 g fiber, 29 g pro.
Daily Values: 67% vit. A, 13% vit. C, 4% calcium, 9% iron
Exchanges: ½ Vegetable, ½ Other Carbo., 4 Very Lean Meat, 1½ Fat

11 to 15 grams of carbs

italian chicken with white beans

Americans have just recently discovered the creamy richness white kidney beans bring to cooking, but Italians have been savoring the legumes for ages. Serve in shallow bowls.

Prep: 20 minutes Cook: 6 to 7 hours (low) or 3 to 3 ½ hours (high)
Stand: 10 minutes Makes: 8 servings

1	cup chopped onion (1 large)
1	cup chopped carrots (2 medium)
½	cup thinly sliced celery (1 stalk)
3	cloves garlic, minced
2	pounds skinless, boneless chicken thighs
¼	teaspoon salt
⅛	teaspoon black pepper
1	14½-ounce can diced tomatoes, undrained
½	cup reduced-sodium chicken broth
½	cup dry white wine
1½	teaspoons dried Italian seasoning, crushed
1	15- or 19-ounce can white kidney (cannellini) beans, rinsed and drained
½	cup grated Parmesan cheese (2 ounces)

1 In a 3½- or 4-quart slow cooker combine onion, carrots, celery, and garlic. Add chicken; sprinkle with salt and pepper. In a medium bowl combine undrained tomatoes, chicken broth, wine, and Italian seasoning. Pour over mixture in cooker.

2 Cover and cook on low-heat setting for 6 to 7 hours or on high-heat setting for 3 to 3½ hours. Turn off cooker. Stir beans into chicken mixture in cooker. Cover and let stand for 10 minutes.

3 Using a slotted spoon, transfer chicken and vegetables to serving bowls, reserving cooking liquid. Drizzle chicken and vegetables with enough of the liquid to moisten. Sprinkle each serving with Parmesan cheese.

Nutrition Facts per serving: 231 cal., 6 g total fat (2 g sat. fat), 95 mg chol., 447 mg sodium, 14 g carbo., 4 g fiber, 29 g pro.
Daily Values: 35% vit. A, 19% vit. C, 12% calcium, 12% iron
Exchanges: 1½ Vegetable, 3 Lean Meat, ½ Fat

11 to 15 grams of carbs

mediterranean chicken

Tender chicken pieces and vegetable chunks draw attention to this Mediterranean-flavored meal. Serve with crusty bread and a tossed green salad.

Prep: 25 minutes Cook: 7 to 8 hours (low) or 3½ to 4 hours (high), plus 15 minutes (high) Makes: 6 servings

2	cups sliced fresh mushrooms
1	14½-ounce can no-salt-added diced tomatoes, drained
1	2¼-ounce can sliced, pitted ripe olives, drained
2	to 2½ pounds chicken thighs and/or drumsticks, skinned
1	tablespoon dried Italian seasoning, crushed
¼	teaspoon salt
¼	teaspoon black pepper
1	cup reduced-sodium chicken broth
¼	cup dry white wine
3	tablespoons cornstarch
3	tablespoons cold water
1	10-ounce package frozen artichoke hearts, thawed
⅓	cup grated Parmesan cheese (optional)

1 In a 3½- or 4-quart slow cooker combine mushrooms, tomatoes, and olives. Add chicken. Sprinkle with Italian seasoning, salt, and pepper. Add chicken broth and wine to mixture in cooker.

2 Cover and cook on low-heat setting for 7 to 8 hours or on high-heat setting for 3½ to 4 hours.

3 Transfer chicken to a serving platter, reserving cooking liquid. Cover chicken with foil to keep warm.

4 If using low-heat setting, turn to high-heat setting. In a small bowl combine cornstarch and water. Stir into mixture in cooker. Add artichokes. Cover and cook for 15 to 30 minutes more or until thickened and artichokes are tender. If desired, sprinkle each serving with Parmesan cheese.

Nutrition Facts per serving: 184 cal., 5 g total fat (1 g sat. fat), 71 mg chol., 404 mg sodium, 13 g carbo., 5 g fiber, 20 g pro.
Daily Values: 8% vit. A, 14% vit. C, 6% calcium, 12% iron
Exchanges: 1 Vegetable, ½ Other Carbo., 2½ Very Lean Meat, ½ Fat

11 to 15 grams of carbs

honey-mustard sauced chicken

Mustard ranks as one of the all-time-great fat-free flavor-boosters. Here, it joins forces with apple juice, lemon juice, and seasonings—for a tangy (and unbelievably simple) sauce.

Prep: 30 minutes Cook: 5 to 6 hours (low) or 2½ to 3 hours (high),
plus 15 minutes (high) Makes: 8 to 10 servings

3	pounds chicken thighs and/or legs, skinned
	Salt and black pepper
¼	cup honey mustard
¾	cup apple juice
½	of a 16-ounce package shredded cabbage with carrot (coleslaw mix) (about 4 cups)
1	cup chopped Granny Smith apples
½	cup sliced green onions (4)
¼	cup snipped fresh parsley
2	tablespoons olive oil
2	tablespoons honey mustard
1	tablespoon lemon juice
¼	teaspoon salt
⅛	teaspoon cayenne pepper
2	tablespoons cornstarch
2	tablespoons cold water

1 Sprinkle chicken with salt and pepper. Brush chicken with the ¼ cup honey mustard.

2 Place apple juice in a 3½- or 4-quart slow cooker. Add chicken to cooker. Cover and cook on low-heat setting for 5 to 6 hours or on high-heat setting for 2½ to 3 hours.

3 Meanwhile, for salad in a large bowl combine shredded cabbage mixture, apples, green onions, and parsley. In a screw-top jar combine olive oil, the 2 tablespoons honey mustard, the lemon juice, the ¼ teaspoon salt, and the cayenne pepper. Add to cabbage mixture; toss to coat. Cover and chill until ready to serve.

4 Transfer chicken to a serving platter, reserving cooking liquid. Cover chicken with foil to keep warm. Strain cooking liquid; return to cooker. If using low-heat setting, turn to high-heat setting. Combine cornstarch and water. Add to liquid in cooker. Cover and cook 15 minutes more or until thickened. Serve sauce with chicken and salad.

Nutrition Facts per serving: 203 cal., 7 g total fat (1 g sat. fat), 80 mg chol., 199 mg sodium, 13 g carbo., 1 g fiber, 20 g pro.
Daily Values: 16% vit. A, 29% vit. C, 3% calcium, 7% iron
Exchanges: ½ Vegetable, ½ Fruit, 2½ Very Lean Meat, 1½ Fat

coq au vin stew

Never mind traditional pairings. Beefy onion soup mix and red wine combine with chicken for a succulent stew that's luscious on a cold night.

Prep: 20 minutes Cook: 5 to 6 hours (low) or 2½ to 3 hours (high) Makes: 4 servings

	Nonstick cooking spray
3	pounds chicken thighs, skinned
1	envelope (½ of a 2.2-ounce package) beefy onion soup mix
1½	cups frozen small whole onions
2	cups fresh button or wild mushrooms, quartered
½	cup dry red wine

1 Lightly coat a large nonstick skillet with cooking spray. Cook chicken, several pieces at a time, in hot skillet over medium heat until brown on both sides. Drain off fat. Place chicken in a 3½- or 4-quart slow cooker. Sprinkle chicken with soup mix. Add onions and mushrooms. Pour wine over mixture in cooker.

2 Cover and cook on low-heat setting for 5 to 6 hours or on high-heat setting for 2½ to 3 hours.

Nutrition Facts per serving: 305 cal., 8 g total fat (2 g sat. fat), 161 mg chol., 759 mg sodium, 12 g carbo., 2 g fiber, 41 g pro.
Daily Values: 2% vit. A, 14% vit. C, 8% calcium, 14% iron
Exchanges: 1 Vegetable, ½ Other Carbo., 5½ Very Lean Meat, 1 Fat

11 to 15 grams of carbs

herbed chicken and mushrooms

This fuss-free recipe is ideal for casual entertaining. Rent some videos or arrange to play games, and invite some friends for dinner and entertainment.

Prep: 25 minutes **Cook:** 7 to 8 hours (low) or 3½ to 4 hours (high) **Makes:** 6 servings

5	cups sliced assorted fresh mushrooms, such as shiitake, button, crimini, and oyster
½	cup chopped onion (1 medium)
½	cup chopped carrot (1 medium)
¼	cup dried tomato pieces (not oil-packed)
¾	cup reduced-sodium chicken broth
¼	cup dry white wine or reduced-sodium chicken broth
3	tablespoons quick-cooking tapioca
1	teaspoon dried thyme, crushed
½	teaspoon dried basil, crushed
½	teaspoon garlic salt
¼	to ½ teaspoon black pepper
3	pounds chicken thighs or drumsticks, skinned
4½	cups hot cooked whole wheat or spinach linguine or fettuccine, or hot cooked brown rice (optional)

1 In a 4- to 5-quart slow cooker combine mushrooms, onion, carrot, and dried tomato pieces. Add chicken broth and wine. Sprinkle with tapioca, thyme, basil, garlic salt, and pepper. Add chicken pieces.

2 Cover and cook on low-heat setting for 7 to 8 hours or on high-heat setting for 3½ to 4 hours.

3 Transfer chicken and vegetables to a serving platter. Spoon some cooking liquid over the top. If desired, serve with hot cooked pasta.

Nutrition Facts per serving: 219 cal., 6 g total fat (1 g sat. fat), 107 mg chol., 299 mg sodium, 11 g carbo., 1 g fiber, 29 g pro.
Daily Values: 27% vit. A, 3% vit. C, 3% calcium, 12% iron
Exchanges: 1 Vegetable, ½ Other Carbo., 3½ Very Lean Meat, 1 Fat

thai-style coconut chicken soup

Coconut milk—a popular ingredient in Thai cooking—adds a nice undertone of coconut flavor to this soup.

Prep: 30 minutes Cook: 5 to 6 hours (low) or 2½ to 3 hours (high)
Stand: 5 minutes Makes: 6 servings

1	pound skinless, boneless chicken breasts or thighs
4	cups reduced-sodium chicken broth
2	medium carrots, bias-sliced into ¼-inch pieces (1 cup)
1	cup chopped onion (1 large)
2	tablespoons grated fresh ginger
3	cloves garlic, minced
1	teaspoon finely shredded lemon peel
¼	teaspoon crushed red pepper
1	15-ounce can unsweetened light coconut milk
2	medium red, yellow, and/or green sweet peppers, cut into ½-inch pieces
1	15-ounce can straw mushrooms or two 6-ounce jars button mushrooms, drained
¼	cup snipped fresh cilantro
⅓	cup chopped roasted peanuts (optional)

1 Cut chicken into ¾-inch pieces. In a 3½- to 4½-quart slow cooker combine chicken, chicken broth, carrots, onion, ginger, garlic, lemon peel, and crushed red pepper.

2 Cover and cook on low-heat setting for 5 to 6 hours or on high-heat setting for 2½ to 3 hours.

3 Skim off fat. Stir coconut milk, sweet peppers, mushrooms, and cilantro into mixture in cooker. Cover and let stand for 5 to 10 minutes. If desired, sprinkle each serving with peanuts.

Nutrition Facts per serving: 186 cal., 5 g total fat (3 g sat. fat), 44 mg chol., 603 mg sodium, 13 g carbo., 3 g fiber, 21 g pro.
Daily Values: 72% vit. A, 115% vit. C, 3% calcium, 11% iron
Exchanges: 1 Vegetable, ½ Other Carbo., 2½ Very Lean Meat, ½ Fat

chinese chicken salad

Many restaurants serve a version of an Asian Chicken Salad, but tonight, you can drive past them knowing that a fresh-tasting home-cooked version is ready and waiting at home.

Prep: 15 minutes Cook: 5 to 6 hours (low) or 2½ to 3 hours (high) Makes: 6 to 8 servings

2	pounds chicken thighs, skinned
	Black pepper
1	cup chopped celery (2 stalks)
½	cup chopped onion (1 medium)
2	cloves garlic, minced
½	cup hoisin sauce
3	tablespoons reduced-sodium soy sauce
2	tablespoons grated fresh ginger
1	tablespoon dry sherry
2	teaspoons Oriental chili sauce
1	teaspoon toasted sesame oil
¼	cup rice vinegar
8	cups shredded romaine
1	cup shredded carrots (2 medium)
½	cup unsalted dry-roasted cashews (optional)
2	tablespoons snipped fresh cilantro

1 Sprinkle chicken with pepper. In a 3- to 4-quart slow cooker place chicken, celery, onion, and garlic. In a small bowl combine hoisin sauce, soy sauce, ginger, sherry, chili sauce, and sesame oil. Pour over mixture in slow cooker. Stir to coat.

2 Cover and cook on low-heat setting for 5 to 6 hours or on high-heat setting for 2½ to 3 hours.

3 Remove chicken from cooker, reserving ½ cup of the cooking liquid. When chicken is cool enough to handle, remove chicken from bones. Using two forks, pull chicken apart into shreds.

4 For dressing, in a screw-top jar combine the reserved ½ cup cooking liquid and the rice vinegar. Cover and shake until combined; set aside.

5 In a large salad bowl combine chicken, romaine, carrots, cashews (if desired), and cilantro. Just before serving, shake dressing and drizzle over salad. Toss to coat.

Nutrition Facts per serving: 191 cal., 5 g total fat (1 g sat. fat), 71 mg chol., 682 mg sodium, 14 g carbo., 3 g fiber, 20 g pro.
Daily Values: 144% vit. A, 37% vit. C, 8% calcium, 10% iron
Exchanges: 1½ Vegetable, ½ Other Carbo., 2½ Lean Meat

cashew chicken

As easy as carry-out, this savory dish is a fun way to celebrate the Chinese New Year—or any red-letter day.

Prep: 15 minutes Cook: 6 to 8 hours (low) or 3 to 4 hours (high) Makes: 6 servings

1	10³/₄-ounce can condensed golden mushroom soup
2	tablespoons soy sauce
¹/₂	teaspoon ground ginger
1¹/₂	pounds chicken tenders
1	cup sliced fresh mushrooms or one 4-ounce can sliced mushrooms, drained
1	cup sliced celery (2 stalks)
1	cup shredded carrots (2 medium)
1	8-ounce can sliced water chestnuts, drained
¹/₂	cup cashews
	Hot cooked brown rice (optional)

1 In a 3¹/₂- or 4-quart slow cooker combine mushroom soup, soy sauce, and ginger. Stir in chicken, mushrooms, celery, carrots, and water chestnuts.

2 Cover and cook on low-heat setting for 6 to 8 hours or on high-heat setting for 3 to 4 hours.

3 Stir cashews into chicken mixture. If desired, serve over hot cooked rice.

Nutrition Facts per serving: 251 cal., 9 g total fat (2 g sat. fat), 67 mg chol., 847 mg sodium, 15 g carbo., 2 g fiber, 31 g pro.
Daily Values: 52% vit. A, 3% vit. C, 4% calcium, 12% iron
Exchanges: 1¹/₂ Vegetable, ¹/₂ Starch, 4 Very Lean Meat, 1 Fat

11 to 15 grams of carbs

texas turkey bonanza

The Lime Sour Cream is optional but is a perfect addition to this black-eyed pea and turkey dish. On the fly? Use dairy sour cream without adding lime.

11 to 15 grams of carbs

Prep: 20 minutes **Cook:** 8 to 10 hours (low) or 4 to 5 hours (high), plus 30 minutes (high) **Makes:** 6 servings

2	cups dry black-eyed peas
1	pound turkey or pork tenderloins
1	to 3 fresh jalapeño chile peppers, seeded and quartered lengthwise*
1½	teaspoons dried leaf sage, crushed
1	teaspoon salt
2	medium yellow summer squash, quartered lengthwise and cut into ½-inch pieces
½	cup finely chopped red onion (1 medium)
⅓	cup snipped fresh cilantro
1	recipe Lime Sour Cream or dairy sour cream (optional)
	Finely chopped fresh jalapeño chile pepper (optional)

1 Sort through black-eyed peas to remove any pebbles or other foreign matter. Rinse peas. In a large saucepan combine peas and 5 cups water. Bring to boiling; reduce heat. Cook, uncovered, for 10 minutes. Remove from heat. Drain and rinse peas; set aside. Cut turkey into ½-inch pieces; set aside. In a 4- or 4½-quart slow cooker combine peas, 3 cups water, the quartered jalapeño peppers, sage, and salt. Top with turkey.

2 Cover and cook on low-heat setting for 8 to 10 hours or on high-heat setting for 4 to 5 hours.

3 If using low-heat setting, turn to high-heat setting. Stir squash into mixture in cooker. Cover and cook for 30 minutes more. Sprinkle each serving with red onion and cilantro. If desired, top with Lime Sour Cream and chopped jalapeño pepper.

*Note: Because hot chile peppers, such as jalapeños, contain volatile oils that can burn your skin and eyes, avoid direct contact with chiles as much as possible. When working with chile peppers, wear plastic or rubber gloves. If your bare hands do touch the chile peppers, wash your hands well with soap and water.

Nutrition Facts per serving: 145 cal., 1 g total fat (0 g sat. fat), 47 mg chol., 437 mg sodium, 12 g carbo., 3 g fiber, 20 g pro.
Daily Values: 8% vit. A, 18% vit. C, 9% calcium, 8% iron
Exchanges: 1 Vegetable, ½ Starch, 2½ Very Lean Meat

Lime Sour Cream: In a small bowl combine ½ cup light dairy sour cream, ½ teaspoon finely shredded lime peel, and 1 tablespoon lime juice. Cover and chill until ready to serve.

turkey thighs in barbecue sauce

Who needs a grill for barbecue? These shapely, saucy thighs keep their form during slow-heat cooking and can hold their own among other grilled turkey dishes.

Prep: 15 minutes Cook: 10 to 12 hours (low) or 5 to 6 hours (high) Makes: 4 to 6 servings

1/2	cup ketchup
2	tablespoons heat-stable granular sugar substitute
1	tablespoon quick-cooking tapioca
1	tablespoon vinegar
1	teaspoon Worcestershire sauce
1/4	teaspoon ground cinnamon
1/4	teaspoon crushed red pepper
2	to 2 1/2 pounds turkey thighs (about 2 thighs) or meaty chicken pieces (breast halves, thighs, and drumsticks), skinned
	Hot cooked brown rice (optional)

1 In a 3½- or 4-quart slow cooker combine ketchup, sugar substitute, tapioca, vinegar, Worcestershire sauce, cinnamon, and crushed red pepper. Place turkey, meaty side down, on ketchup mixture.

2 Cover and cook on low-heat setting for 10 to 12 hours or high-heat setting for 5 to 6 hours.

3 Transfer turkey to a serving platter. Pour cooking liquid into a small bowl. Skim off fat. Serve turkey with cooking liquid and, if desired, hot cooked rice.

Nutrition Facts per serving: 225 cal., 6 g total fat (2 g sat. fat), 100 mg chol., 444 mg sodium, 12 g carbo., 1 g fiber, 30 g pro.
Daily Values: 3% calcium, 15% iron
Exchanges: 1 Other Carbo., 4 Very Lean Meat, ½ Fat

11 to 15 grams of carbs

clam chowder

Turn your slow cooker into a "chaudière"—that's the French term for the large pot in which fishermen simmered hearty seafood stews, such as clam chowder.

Prep: 25 minutes Cook: 4½ to 5 hours (low) or 2 to 2½ hours (high),
plus 30 minutes (high) Makes: 8 servings (about 8 cups)

3	cups chopped celery (6 stalks)
1½	cups chopped onions (3 medium)
1	cup chopped carrots (2 medium)
2	8-ounce bottles clam juice
1	14-ounce can reduced-sodium chicken broth
1½	teaspoons dried thyme, crushed
½	teaspoon salt
½	teaspoon coarsely ground black pepper
1	cup fat-free half-and-half
2	tablespoons cornstarch
2	6½-ounce cans chopped clams, drained
2	tablespoons dry sherry (optional)
4	slices turkey bacon, crisp-cooked, drained, and crumbled
	Chopped green onions (optional)

1 In a 3- to 4-quart slow cooker combine celery, onions, carrots, clam juice, chicken broth, thyme, salt, and pepper.

2 Cover and cook on low-heat setting for 4½ to 5 hours or on high-heat setting for 2 to 2½ hours.

3 If using low-heat setting, turn to high-heat setting. In a small bowl combine half-and-half and cornstarch. Stir half-and-half mixture, clams, and if desired, sherry into the vegetable mixture. Cover and cook for 30 minutes more. Sprinkle each serving with crumbled bacon and, if desired, green onions.

Nutrition Facts per serving: 144 cal., 2 g total fat (0 g sat. fat), 38 mg chol., 309 mg sodium, 14 g carbo., 2 g fiber, 15 g pro.
Daily Values: 44% vit. A, 24% vit. C, 10% calcium, 75% iron
Exchanges: 2½ Vegetable, 1½ Very Lean Meat, ½ Fat

cioppino

Cioppino may sound like a classic from the Old Country, but it was actually created in San Francisco. Basically, it's a dish of fish and seafood in a tomato-sparked stew.

Prep: 25 minutes **Cook:** 4 to 5 hours (low) or 2 to 2½ hours (high), plus 15 minutes (high) **Makes:** 6 to 8 servings

1	pound fresh or frozen cod fillets or halibut steaks
8	ounces fresh or frozen shrimp, peeled and deveined
1	28-ounce can fire-roasted crushed tomatoes, undrained
1¾	cups water
¾	cup chopped yellow or green sweet pepper (1 medium)
½	cup dry white wine
½	cup finely chopped onion (1 medium)
4	cloves garlic, minced
2	teaspoons dried Italian seasoning, crushed
¼	teaspoon salt
1	10-ounce can whole baby clams, drained
	Lemon wedges
	Snipped fresh basil

1 Thaw fish and shrimp, if frozen. Pat dry with paper towels. Cut fish into bite-size pieces. Cover and chill until needed.

2 In a 3½- or 4-quart slow cooker combine undrained tomatoes, water, sweet pepper, wine, onion, garlic, Italian seasoning, and salt.

3 Cover and cook on low-heat setting for 4 to 5 hours or on high-heat setting for 2 to 2½ hours.

4 If using low-heat setting, turn to high-heat setting. Add reserved fish and shrimp to tomato mixture in cooker. Cover and cook about 15 minutes more or until shrimp turn opaque. Stir in clams. Garnish each serving with lemon wedges and basil.

Nutrition Facts per serving: 213 cal., 2 g total fat (0 g sat. fat), 112 mg chol., 610 mg sodium, 13 g carbo., 1 g fiber, 31 g pro.
Daily Values: 17% vit. A, 137% vit. C, 10% calcium, 64% iron
Exchanges: 2½ Vegetable, 3½ Very Lean Meat, ½ Fat

11 to 15 grams of carbs

garden bounty tomato soup

The bounty here is fresh veggies—tomatoes plus your choice of carrots, celery, sweet peppers, fennel, and onion. What a terrific way to use up your farmer's market harvest!

Prep: 25 minutes Cook: 6 to 8 hours (low) or 3 to 4 hours (high) Makes: 8 to 10 side-dish servings (9 cups)

2	pounds roma tomatoes, chopped
2	14-ounce cans beef broth
2	cups finely chopped vegetables (carrot, celery, sweet pepper, fennel, and/or onion)
1	6-ounce can tomato paste
1	to 2 teaspoons sugar or heat-stable granular sugar substitute

1 In a 3½- or 4-quart slow cooker combine tomatoes, beef broth, vegetables, tomato paste, and sugar.

2 Cover and cook on low-heat setting for 6 to 8 hours or on high-heat setting for 3 to 4 hours.

Nutrition Facts per serving: 56 cal., 0 g total fat (0 g sat. fat), 0 mg chol., 221 mg sodium, 11 g carbo., 3 g fiber, 3 g pro.
Daily Values: 92% vit. A, 33% vit. C, 2% calcium, 4% iron
Exchanges: 2 Vegetable

11 to 15 grams of carbs

curried pumpkin and eggplant soup

Popular in the flavorful cooking of the Mediterranean, Middle East, and India, garbanzo beans add nuttiness, heft, and total satisfaction to meatless dishes such as this one.

Prep: 15 minutes Cook: 6 to 8 hours (low) or 3 to 4 hours (high) Makes: 8 side-dish servings

1	medium eggplant, cut into ½-inch cubes (5 cups)
3	cups cubed, seeded, and peeled pumpkin or butternut squash
1	15-ounce can garbanzo beans (chickpeas), rinsed and drained
1	14½-ounce can no-salt-added diced tomatoes, undrained
2	teaspoons grated fresh ginger
2	teaspoons curry powder
½	teaspoon ground coriander
⅛	teaspoon cayenne pepper
4	cups reduced-sodium chicken broth
1	8-ounce can tomato sauce
½	cup dry-roasted cashews (optional)

1 In a 4- to 5-quart slow cooker combine eggplant, pumpkin, garbanzo beans, and undrained tomatoes. Sprinkle with ginger, curry powder, coriander, and cayenne pepper. In a medium bowl combine chicken broth and tomato sauce. Pour over vegetable mixture in cooker.

2 Cover and cook on low-heat setting for 6 to 8 hours or on high-heat setting for 3 to 4 hours. If desired, sprinkle each serving with cashews.

Nutrition Facts per serving: 78 cal., 1 g total fat (0 g sat. fat), 0 mg chol., 483 mg sodium, 14 g carbo., 4 g fiber, 4 g pro.
Daily Values: 53% vit. A, 11% vit. C, 3% calcium, 6% iron
Exchanges: 1 Vegetable, ½ Starch

triple-onion, garlic, and tomato soup

Add even more of an Italian twist to this soup by topping steaming bowls with the optional proscuitto.

Prep: 20 minutes Cook: 10 to 12 hours (low) or 5 to 6 hours (high) Makes: 6 side-dish servings

2	14-ounce cans reduced-sodium beef broth
1	14½-ounce can no-salt-added stewed tomatoes, undrained
1	large sweet onion (such as Vidalia or Walla Walla), quartered and cut into thin slices
½	cup water
¼	cup coarsely chopped shallots (2 medium)
2	tablespoons no-salt-added tomato paste
1	teaspoon bottled minced roasted garlic
⅓	cup sliced green onions (3)
⅓	cup finely shredded fresh basil
⅓	cup finely shredded Romano or Parmesan cheese
⅓	cup finely shredded proscuitto (optional)

1 In a 3½- or 4-quart slow cooker combine beef broth, undrained tomatoes, onion, water, shallots, tomato paste, and roasted garlic.

2 Cover and cook on low-heat setting for 10 to 12 hours or on high-heat setting for 5 to 6 hours. Sprinkle each serving with green onions, basil, Romano cheese, and, if desired, proscuitto.

Nutrition Facts per serving: 73 cal., 1 g total fat (1 g sat. fat), 5 mg chol.,
312 mg sodium, 11 g carbo., 2 g fiber, 4 g pro.
Daily Values: 11% vit. A, 22% vit. C, 9% calcium, 7% iron
Exchanges: 2½ Vegetable

french onion soup

This recipe simplifies the French bistro classic—just combine everything in the slow cooker, then top off individual servings with croutons and shredded cheese.

Prep: 15 minutes Cook: 9 to 10 hours (low) or 4½ to 5 hours (high) Makes: 6 side-dish servings

3	14-ounce cans reduced-sodium beef broth
4	to 6 large onions, thinly sliced
2	cloves garlic, minced
1	teaspoon Worcestershire sauce
⅛	teaspoon black pepper
½	cup shredded Swiss or Gruyère cheese (2 ounces)
	Whole Wheat Croutons (optional)

---

1 In a 3½- or 4-quart slow cooker combine beef broth, onions, garlic, Worcestershire sauce, and pepper.

2 Cover and cook on low-heat setting for 9 to 10 hours or on high-heat setting for 4½ to 5 hours. Ladle soup into bowls. Sprinkle with cheese and, if desired, Whole Wheat Croutons.

Nutrition Facts per serving: 95 cal., 3 g total fat (2 g sat. fat), 9 mg chol., 503 mg sodium, 13 g carbo., 2 g fiber, 5 g pro.
Daily Values: 2% vit. A, 10% vit. C, 10% calcium, 2% iron
Exchanges: 1 Vegetable, ½ Other Carbo., ½ Medium-Fat Meat

Whole Wheat Croutons: Cut four slices of whole wheat bread into cubes. Place bread cubes in a 15×10×1-inch baking pan. Lightly coat cubes with nonstick cooking spray. Bake in a 300°F oven for 10 to 15 minutes or until bread is dry and crisp, tossing once or twice.

curried winter vegetable soup

If you have an immersion blender, use it to puree the soup in the slow cooker instead of the blender or food processor.

Prep: 30 minutes Cook: 6 to 8 hours (low) or 3 to 4 hours (high) Makes: 8 to 10 side-dish servings

4	**cups chopped peeled celeriac (2 pounds)**
3	**cups chopped peeled butternut squash (1 pound)**
½	**cup chopped onion (1 medium)**
2	**cloves garlic, minced**
2	**14-ounce cans reduced-sodium chicken broth**
2	**tablespoons dry sherry**
1	**tablespoon grated fresh ginger**
2	**teaspoons curry powder**
½	**cup fat-free half-and-half**
	Sliced green onions

1 In a 3½- or 4-quart slow cooker combine celeriac, squash, onion, and garlic. Add chicken broth, sherry, ginger, and curry powder.

2 Cover and cook on low-heat setting for 6 to 8 hours or on high-heat setting for 3 to 4 hours.

3 Remove vegetable mixture from cooker. Place half of the mixture in a blender or food processor. Cover and blend or process until smooth. Return to cooker. Repeat with remaining mixture. Stir in half-and-half; heat through, if necessary. Sprinkle each serving with sliced green onions.

Nutrition Facts per serving: 68 cal., 0 g total fat (0 g sat. fat), 0 mg chol., 281 mg sodium, 13 g carbo., 2 g fiber, 3 g pro.
Daily Values: 9% vit. A, 15% vit. C, 6% calcium, 5% iron
Exchanges: 1 Vegetable, ½ Starch

alfredo green beans

This saucy side dish is perfect for your next potluck—or holidays when your oven is busy.

Prep: 15 minutes Cook: 5 to 6 hours (low) or 2½ to 3 hours (high) Makes: 8 side-dish servings

	Nonstick cooking spray
2	9-ounce packages or one 20-ounce package frozen cut green beans (about 5 cups)
1½	cups chopped red sweet pepper (2 medium)
1	10-ounce container refrigerated light Alfredo sauce
1	cup chopped onion (1 large)
1	8-ounce can sliced water chestnuts, drained
¼	teaspoon garlic salt
½	cup Parmesan-flavored croutons, slightly crushed (optional)

1 Lightly coat a 3½- or 4-quart slow cooker with cooking spray. In a large bowl combine green beans, sweet pepper, Alfredo sauce, onion, water chestnuts, and garlic salt. Spoon bean mixture into prepared slow cooker.

2 Cover and cook on low-heat setting for 5 to 6 hours or on high-heat setting for 2½ to 3 hours. Serve with slotted spoon. If desired, sprinkle each serving with croutons.

Nutrition Facts per serving: 117 cal., 5 g total fat (3 g sat. fat), 16 mg chol., 358 mg sodium, 14 g carbo., 3 g fiber, 4 g pro.
Daily Values: 28% vit. A, 80% vit. C, 8% calcium, 2% iron
Exchanges: 1 Vegetable, ½ Other Carbo., 1 Fat

11 to 15 grams of carbs

caraway cabbage in cream

Caraway and cabbage are a classic flavor combo. Now, fix them up in your slow cooker for a side dish that complements roasted meats.

Prep: 10 minutes **Cook:** 6 hours (low) or 3 hours (high) **Makes:** 8 side-dish servings

1	cup reduced-sodium chicken broth
2	tablespoons quick-cooking tapioca
2	teaspoons caraway seeds, crushed
1/2	teaspoon salt
1/4	teaspoon black pepper
12	cups coarsely chopped red cabbage (1 large head)
1/2	cup fat-free half-and-half
2	tablespoons prepared horseradish

1 In a small bowl combine chicken broth, tapioca, caraway seeds, salt, and pepper. Pour broth mixture into a 4- to 5-quart slow cooker. Add cabbage. Toss to coat.

2 Cover and cook on low-heat setting for 6 hours or on high-heat setting for 3 hours. Stir half-and-half and horseradish into mixture in cooker until coated.

Nutrition Facts per serving: 58 cal., 0 g total fat (0 g sat. fat), 0 mg chol., 272 mg sodium, 12 g carbo., 3 g fiber, 2 g pro.
Daily Values: 23% vit. A, 102% vit. C, 6% calcium, 5% iron
Exchanges: 1½ Vegetable, ½ Other Carbo.

11 to 15 grams of carbs

italian-style zucchini

If you like Eggplant Parmesan, here's a way to stretch your enjoyment. Apply the same basic idea to zucchini for a zesty side dish.

Prep: 15 minutes Cook: 4 to 5 hours (low) or 2 to 2½ hours (high),
plus 15 minutes (high) Makes: 8 to 10 side-dish servings

2½	to 3 pounds zucchini and/or yellow summer squash, halved or quartered lengthwise and cut into 1-inch pieces
2	14½-ounce cans no-salt-added stewed tomatoes, drained
1	teaspoon dried basil, crushed
2	cloves garlic, minced
1	tablespoon cornstarch
1	tablespoon cold water
½	cup shredded part-skim mozzarella cheese (2 ounces)

1 In a 3½- or 4-quart slow cooker place squash. In a large bowl combine tomatoes, basil, and garlic. Stir into squash in cooker.

2 Cover and cook on low-heat setting for 4 to 5 hours or on high-heat setting for 2 to 2½ hours.

3 If using low-heat setting, turn to high-heat setting. In a small bowl combine cornstarch and water. Stir into mixture in cooker. Cover and cook about 15 minutes more or until thickened. Transfer to a serving dish. Sprinkle with cheese.

Nutrition Facts per serving: 73 cal., 1 g total fat (1 g sat. fat), 3 mg chol., 178 mg sodium, 13 g carbo., 3 g fiber, 5 g pro.
Daily Values: 7% vit. A, 51% vit. C, 8% calcium, 4% iron
Exchanges: 3 Vegetable

turnip and parsnip gratin

Hearty root vegetables cook to perfection in the slow cooker, while blue cheese and bacon intensify the flavors!

Prep: 25 minutes Cook: 6 to 8 hours (low) or 3 to 4 hours (high) Makes: 8 to 10 side-dish servings

2	pounds turnips, peeled and cut into bite-size pieces
2	medium parsnips, peeled and cut into bite-size pieces
2	medium onions, cut into thin wedges
1	10³/₄-ounce can reduced-fat and reduced-sodium condensed cream of mushroom soup
¹/₂	cup crumbled blue cheese (2 ounces)
¹/₄	cup reduced-sodium chicken broth
1	teaspoon dried thyme, crushed
¹/₂	teaspoon black pepper
3	slices reduced-sodium bacon, crisp-cooked, drained, and crumbled (optional)

1 In a 3¹/₂- to 4¹/₂-quart slow cooker combine turnips, parsnips, and onions. In a small bowl combine mushroom soup, blue cheese, chicken broth, thyme, and pepper. Stir into vegetables in cooker.

2 Cover and cook on low-heat setting for 6 to 8 hours or on high-heat setting for 3 to 4 hours. If desired, sprinkle each serving with bacon.

Nutrition Facts per serving: 86 cal., 2 g total fat (1 g sat. fat), 5 mg chol., 269 mg sodium, 14 g carbo., 3 g fiber, 3 g pro.
Daily Values: 2% vit. A, 28% vit. C, 7% calcium, 3% iron
Exchanges: 1 Vegetable, ¹/₂ Starch, ¹/₂ Fat

chapter four

16 to 20
grams of carbs

beef roast with tomato-wine gravy

Sure to become an autumn favorite, this recipe highlights some of the produce you'll find at farmers' markets during the peak of the season.

Prep: 30 minutes Cook: 10 to 12 hours (low) or 5 to 6 hours (high) Makes: 6 servings

1	2- to 2½-pound boneless beef chuck pot roast
	Nonstick cooking spray
2	medium turnips, peeled and cut into 1-inch pieces (2 cups)
3	medium carrots, cut into ½-inch pieces (1½ cups)
1	15-ounce can tomato sauce
¼	cup dry red wine or reduced-sodium beef broth
3	tablespoons quick-cooking tapioca
¼	teaspoon salt
⅛	teaspoon ground allspice
⅛	teaspoon black pepper
1	pound winter squash, peeled, seeded, and cut into thin wedges or 1½-inch pieces (2 cups)

1 Trim fat from meat. If necessary, cut meat to fit into a 3½- to 6-quart slow cooker. Lightly coat a large skillet with cooking spray. Cook meat in hot skillet over medium heat until brown on all sides; set aside. Place turnips and carrots in cooker. In a medium bowl combine tomato sauce, red wine, tapioca, salt, allspice, and pepper. Pour over vegetables in cooker. Place meat in cooker. Place squash on top of meat.

2 Cover and cook on low-heat setting for 10 to 12 hours or on high-heat setting for 5 to 6 hours.

3 Transfer roast and vegetables to a serving platter. Skim fat from gravy. Serve meat and vegetables with gravy.

Nutrition Facts per serving: 273 cal., 6 g total fat (2 g sat. fat), 89 mg chol., 575 mg sodium, 19 g carbo., 3 g fiber, 34 g pro.
Daily Values: 80% vit. A, 22% vit. C, 5% calcium, 26% iron
Exchanges: 2 Vegetable, ½ Starch, 3½ Lean Meat

16 to 20 grams of carbs

148

saucy pot roast

This recipe is the epitome of comfort food and will have your family asking for seconds.

Prep: 25 minutes Cook: 10 to 12 hours (low) or 4 to 5 hours (high) Makes: 6 to 8 servings

1	2- to 2½-pound boneless beef chuck pot roast
1	tablespoon cooking oil
1	cup coarsely chopped carrots (2 medium)
1	cup sliced celery (2 stalks)
1	medium onion, sliced
2	cloves garlic, minced
1	tablespoon quick-cooking tapioca
1	14½-ounce can Italian-style stewed tomatoes, undrained
1	6-ounce can Italian-style tomato paste
½	teaspoon salt
¼	teaspoon black pepper
1	bay leaf

---

1 Trim fat from meat. If necessary, cut meat to fit into a 3½- or 4-quart slow cooker. In a large skillet cook meat in hot oil over medium heat until brown on all sides. Drain off fat. Place carrots, celery, onion, and garlic in cooker. Sprinkle tapioca over vegetables. Place meat on top of vegetables. In a medium bowl combine undrained tomatoes, tomato paste, salt, pepper, and bay leaf. Pour over mixture in cooker.

2 Cover and cook on low-heat setting for 10 to 12 hours or on high-setting for 4 to 5 hours.

3 Transfer meat to a serving platter. Skim fat from sauce. Remove and discard bay leaf. Drizzle some of the sauce over meat. Pass remaining sauce.

Nutrition Facts per serving: 289 cal., 9 g total fat (2 g sat. fat), 89 mg chol., 710 mg sodium, 16 g carbo., 3 g fiber, 34 g pro.
Daily Values: 46% vit. A, 14% vit. C, 5% calcium, 27% iron
Exchanges: 1 Vegetable, 1 Other Carbo., 4½ Very Lean Meat, 1 Fat

16 to 20 grams of carbs

pot roast with chipotle-fruit sauce

Dried fruit provides a hint of sweetness to balance the spice in this palate pleaser.

Prep: 15 minutes Cook: 10 to 11 hours (low) or 5 to 5 ½ hours (high),
plus 10 minutes Makes: 8 servings

1	3-pound boneless beef chuck pot roast
2	teaspoons garlic pepper seasoning
1	7-ounce package dried mixed fruit
1	tablespoon finely chopped chipotle peppers in adobo sauce
½	cup water
1	tablespoon cold water
2	teaspoons cornstarch

1 Trim fat from meat. Sprinkle both sides of meat with garlic pepper seasoning. If necessary, cut the roast to fit into a 3½- or 4-quart slow cooker. Place meat in the cooker. Add fruit and chipotle peppers. Pour the ½ cup water over all.

2 Cover and cook on low-heat setting for 10 to 11 hours or on high-heat setting for 5 to 5½ hours. Transfer meat and fruit to a serving platter. Cover to keep warm.

3 Transfer cooking liquid to a large measuring cup; skim fat. In a medium saucepan combine the 1 tablespoon water and the cornstarch; add cooking liquid. Cook and stir until thickened and bubbly; cook and stir for 2 minutes more. Thinly slice meat. To serve, spoon sauce over sliced meat and fruit.

Nutrition Facts per serving: 275 cal., 6 g total fat (2 g sat. fat), 101 mg chol.,
378 mg sodium, 17 g carbo., 1 g fiber, 37 g pro.
Daily Values: 2% vit. C, 2% calcium, 27% iron
Exchanges: 1 Fruit, 5 Very Lean Meat, 1 Fat

16 to 20 grams of carbs

easy italian beef

Purchased spaghetti sauce simplifies the prep time for this beef dinner. If you like, sop up the sauce with low-carb pasta.

Prep: 25 minutes Cook: 9 to 10 hours (low) or 4 ½ to 5 hours (high), plus 1 hour (high) Makes: 6 to 8 servings

1	2-pound boneless beef chuck pot roast
2	medium onions, cut into 1-inch pieces
1	large red sweet pepper, cut into 3/4-inch pieces
1 2/3	cups light spaghetti sauce
1 1/2	pounds zucchini, cut into 3/4-inch chunks
	Black pepper

---

1 Trim fat from meat. Cut meat into 1-inch pieces. In a 3½- or 4-quart slow cooker place meat, onions, and sweet pepper. Add spaghetti sauce.

2 Cover and cook on low-heat setting for 9 to 10 hours or on high-heat setting for 4½ to 5 hours.

3 If using low-heat setting, turn to high-heat setting. Add zucchini; cook for 1 hour more. Season to taste with black pepper.

Nutrition Facts per serving: 256 cal., 6 g total fat (2 g sat. fat), 89 mg chol., 327 mg sodium, 16 g carbo., 3 g fiber, 35 g pro.
Daily Values: 19% vit. A, 111% vit. C, 4% calcium, 25% iron
Exchanges: 3 Vegetable, 3½ Lean Meat

16 to 20 grams of carbs

beefy borscht

Most of us know Borscht as a ruby-hued beet soup. This version is more brown than red because it's made with beef chuck that adds an excellent flavor.

Prep: 15 minutes Cook: 8 to 10 hours (low) or 4 to 5 hours (high) Makes: 6 main-dish servings

12	ounces boneless beef chuck pot roast
4	cups water
1	16-ounce jar sweet and sour red cabbage, undrained
1	15- to 16-ounce can diced beets, drained
1	envelope (1/2 of a 2.2-ounce package) onion soup mix
1/2	cup light dairy sour cream

1 Trim fat from meat. Cut meat into 1/2-inch pieces. In a 3 1/2- or 4-quart slow cooker place meat, water, undrained cabbage, beets, and soup mix.

2 Cover and cook on low-heat setting for 8 to 10 hours or on high-heat setting for 4 to 5 hours. Top each serving with sour cream.

Nutrition Facts per serving: 174 cal., 4 g total fat (2 g sat. fat), 40 mg chol., 935 mg sodium, 20 g carbo., 3 g fiber, 14 g pro.
Daily Values: 3% vit. A, 3% vit. C, 5% calcium, 12% iron
Exchanges: 1 Vegetable, 1 Other Carbo., 2 Very Lean Meat, 1/2 Fat

16 to 20 grams of carbs

beef and onions over broccoli

Cooking with condensed soup is convenient and brings a comforting sense of mother's kitchen. Adding a little cream cheese and sour cream makes this dish rich and satisfying.

Prep: 25 minutes Cook: 8 to 10 hours (low) or 4 to 5 hours (high)
Stand: 10 minutes Makes: 8 servings

2	pounds boneless beef chuck pot roast
1½	cups thinly sliced onions
1	4½-ounce jar sliced mushrooms, drained
¼	teaspoon black pepper
1	10¾-ounce can reduced-fat and reduced-sodium condensed cream of mushroom soup
1	10¾-ounce can reduced-fat and reduced-sodium condensed cream of celery soup
1	8-ounce package reduced-fat cream cheese (Neufchâtel), cut up and softened
1	8-ounce carton light dairy sour cream
6	cups hot steamed broccoli

1 Trim fat from meat. Cut meat into 1-inch pieces. In a 3½- or 4-quart slow cooker place meat and onions. Top with mushrooms. Sprinkle with pepper. Add mushroom soup and celery soup to cooker.

2 Cover and cook on low-heat setting for 8 to 10 hours or on high-heat setting for 4 to 5 hours. Turn off heat. Stir in cream cheese and sour cream. Cover and let stand for 10 minutes; stir until cheese is melted and sauce is smooth. Serve over hot broccoli.

Nutrition Facts per serving: 347 cal., 15 g total fat (8 g sat. fat), 101 mg chol., 597 mg sodium, 20 g carbo., 5 g fiber, 33 g pro.
Daily Values: 57% vit. A, 128% vit. C, 16% calcium, 22% iron
Exchanges: 1 Vegetable, 1 Starch, 4 Lean Meat, ½ Fat

16 to 20 grams of carbs

provençal beef stew

Perfect for a cozy dinner with friends, all this stew needs is some whole grain bread, olives, and a hearty red wine.

Prep: 20 minutes **Cook:** 10 to 12 hours (low) or 5 to 6 hours (high), plus 30 minutes **Makes:** 6 servings

1½	pounds boneless beef chuck pot roast
8	tiny new potatoes
1	pound small carrots with tops, peeled and trimmed, or one 16-ounce package peeled baby carrots
1	large onion, cut into wedges
½	cup pitted green or ripe olives
1	cup beef broth
1	tablespoon quick-cooking tapioca
1	teaspoon dried herbes de Provence, crushed
¼	teaspoon salt
¼	teaspoon cracked black pepper
4	to 6 cloves garlic, minced
¼	cup dry red wine
	Snipped fresh parsley (optional)
	Capers (optional)

1 Trim fat from meat. Cut meat into 2-inch pieces. Set aside. Remove a narrow strip of peel from around the middle of each new potato. In a 3½- or 4-quart slow cooker place potatoes, carrots, onion, and olives. Add meat. In a small bowl combine beef broth, tapioca, herbes de Provence, salt, pepper, and garlic. Pour over mixture in cooker.

2 Cover and cook on low-heat setting for 10 to 12 hours or on high-heat setting for 5 to 6 hours. Stir in wine. Cover and cook for 30 minutes more. If desired, sprinkle each serving with parsley and capers.

Nutrition Facts per serving: 242 cal., 6 g total fat (2 g sat. fat), 67 mg chol., 399 mg sodium, 19 g carbo., 4 g fiber, 27 g pro.
Daily Values: 165% vit. A, 18% vit. C, 6% calcium, 22% iron
Exchanges: 1 Vegetable, 1 Starch, 3 Very Lean Meat, 1 Fat

16 to 20 grams of carbs

mushroom beef stew

Wine, garlic, and mustard add zest to this tangy dish. Any variety of mushrooms you have on hand will work in this recipe.

Prep: 25 minutes Cook: 9 to 10 hours (low) or 4 ½ to 5 hours (high), plus 15 minutes (high) Makes: 8 servings

2	pounds boneless beef chuck pot roast
8	ounces portobello mushrooms, cut into 1-inch pieces
8	ounces shiitake mushrooms or button mushrooms, stemmed and halved
1	cup chopped onion (1 large)
2	tablespoons Dijon-style mustard
4	cloves garlic, minced
½	teaspoon salt
½	teaspoon black pepper
1	14-ounce can reduced-sodium beef broth
½	cup dry red wine
1	8-ounce carton light dairy sour cream
2	tablespoons cornstarch
1	tablespoon snipped fresh chives

1 Trim fat from meat. Cut meat into 1-inch pieces. In a 4½- to 5½-quart slow cooker combine beef, mushrooms, onion, mustard, garlic, salt, and pepper. Stir in beef broth and wine.

2 Cover and cook on low-heat setting for 9 to 10 hours or on high-heat setting for 4½ to 5 hours.

3 If using low-heat setting, turn to high-heat setting. In a small bowl combine sour cream and cornstarch. Stir ½ cup of the hot cooking liquid into the sour cream mixture. Return all of the sour cream mixture to the slow cooker; stir well. Cover and cook about 15 minutes more or until thickened. Top each serving with chives.

Nutrition Facts per serving: 313 cal., 9 g total fat (4 g sat. fat), 102 mg chol.,
566 mg sodium, 16 g carbo., 2 g fiber, 38 g pro.
Daily Values: 5% vit. A, 5% vit. C, 10% calcium, 25% iron
Exchanges: 2 Vegetable, ½ Other Carbo., 4½ Lean Meat

16 to 20 grams of carbs

spicy steak and beans

Queso fresco (KAY-so FRESK-o) means "fresh cheese" in Spanish. Look for it in large supermarkets and Mexican food stores.

Prep: 25 minutes Cook: 7 to 9 hours (low) or 3 ½ to 4 ½ hours (high),
plus 30 minutes (high) Makes: 6 servings

1½	pounds beef flank steak
1	10-ounce can chopped tomatoes with green chile peppers, undrained
½	cup chopped onion (1 medium)
2	cloves garlic, minced
1	tablespoon snipped fresh oregano or 1 teaspoon dried oregano, crushed
1	teaspoon chili powder
1	teaspoon ground cumin
¼	teaspoon salt
¼	teaspoon black pepper
2	small green, red, and/or yellow sweet peppers, cut into strips
1	15-ounce can pinto beans, rinsed and drained
	Hot cooked brown rice (optional)
	Crumbled queso fresco or feta cheese (optional)

1 Trim fat from meat. Place meat in a 3½- or 4-quart slow cooker. In a bowl stir together undrained tomatoes, onion, garlic, dried oregano (if using), chili powder, cumin, salt, and black pepper. Pour over meat.

2 Cover and cook on low-heat setting for 7 to 9 hours or on high-heat setting for 3½ to 4½ hours.

3 If using low-heat setting, turn to high-heat setting. Stir in sweet pepper strips and pinto beans. Cover and cook for 30 minutes. Remove meat; cool slightly. Shred or thinly slice meat across the grain. Stir fresh oregano (if using) into bean mixture.

4 If desired, spoon rice into soup bowls. Arrange meat on top of rice. Spoon bean mixture over meat. If desired, sprinkle with cheese.

Nutrition Facts per serving: 262 cal., 8 g total fat (3 g sat. fat), 45 mg chol., 452 mg sodium, 17 g carbo., 4 g fiber, 29 g pro.
Daily Values: 9% vit. A, 37% vit. C, 8% calcium, 18% iron
Exchanges: 1 Vegetable, 1 Starch, 3½ Very Lean Meat, 1 Fat

16 to 20 grams of carbs

sweet and sour beef stew

Sweet and sour sauce adds a whole new dimension to this beef stew. Start off the meal with purchased egg rolls.

Prep: 10 minutes Cook: 10 to 11 hours (low) or 5 to 5½ hours (high) Makes: 6 to 8 servings

1½	pounds beef stew meat
1	16-ounce package frozen stew vegetables (3 cups)
2	10¾-ounce cans condensed beefy mushroom soup
½	cup water
½	cup bottled sweet and sour sauce
⅛	to ¼ teaspoon cayenne pepper

1 Trim fat from meat. Cut meat into 1-inch pieces. In a 3½- or 4-quart slow cooker place meat and frozen vegetables. Stir in beefy mushroom soup, water, sweet and sour sauce, and cayenne pepper.

2 Cover and cook on low-heat setting for 10 to 11 hours or on high-heat setting for 5 to 5½ hours.

Nutrition Facts per serving: 289 cal., 9 g total fat (3 g sat. fat), 62 mg chol., 898 mg sodium, 19 g carbo., 2 g fiber, 30 g pro.
Daily Values: 74% vit. A, 4% vit. C, 1% calcium, 16% iron
Exchanges: 1 Vegetable, 1 Other Carbo., 4 Lean Meat

16 to 20 grams of carbs

beef with broccoli

Brimming with all the flavors and fixings of a traditional stir-fry, this easy beef-and-veggie combo is draped in a sauce that begins with an envelope of gravy mix.

Prep: 20 minutes   Cook: 8 to 10 hours (low) or 4 to 5 hours (high), plus 15 minutes (high)   Makes: 6 servings

6	medium carrots, cut into 1-inch pieces
2	medium onions, cut into wedges
1½	pounds beef round steak, cut into ½-inch strips
1	tablespoon minced fresh ginger
2	cloves garlic, minced
½	cup water
2	tablespoons reduced-sodium soy sauce
1	¾-ounce envelope beef gravy mix
4	cups broccoli florets

1 In a 3½- or 4-quart slow cooker place carrots, onions, meat, ginger, and garlic. In a small bowl combine water, soy sauce, and beef gravy mix. Pour over meat and vegetables.

2 Cover and cook on low-heat setting for 8 to 10 hours or on high-heat setting for 4 to 5 hours.

3 If using low-heat setting, turn to high-heat setting. Stir in broccoli. Cover and cook about 15 minutes more or until broccoli is crisp-tender.

Nutrition Facts per serving: 213 cal., 3 g total fat (1 g sat. fat), 64 mg chol., 507 mg sodium, 16 g carbo., 5 g fiber, 29 g pro.
Daily Values: 401% vit. A, 103% vit. C, 6% calcium, 19% iron
Exchanges: 2 Vegetable, ½ Other Carbo., 3½ Very Lean Meat

16 to 20 grams of carbs

italian wedding soup

Italian wedding soup derives its name from the blissful union of meats and greens. Its many versions are based on local availability of ingredients.

Prep: 30 minutes Cook: 8 to 10 hours (low) or 4 to 5 hours (high), plus 15 minutes (high) Makes: 8 servings

1	large onion
1	egg, slightly beaten
1/4	cup fine dry bread crumbs
3	oil-packed dried tomatoes, finely chopped
2	teaspoons dried Italian seasoning, crushed
1	pound lean ground beef
2	teaspoons olive oil
1	large fennel bulb
4	14-ounce cans chicken broth
1/2	teaspoon ground white pepper
6	cloves garlic, thinly sliced
1/2	cup dried orzo pasta (rosamarina)
5	cups shredded fresh spinach

1 Finely chop one-third of the onion; thinly slice remaining onion. In a medium bowl combine the chopped onion, egg, bread crumbs, dried tomatoes, and 1 teaspoon of the Italian seasoning. Add ground beef; mix well. Shape into 12 meatballs. In a large skillet brown meatballs in hot oil over medium heat. Drain off fat. Transfer meatballs to a 4½- to 5½-quart slow cooker. Add the sliced onion.

2 Cut off and discard upper stalks of fennel. If desired, save some of the feathery leaves for garnish. Remove any wilted outer layers; cut off a thin slice from fennel base. Cut fennel into thin wedges. Stir fennel, chicken broth, white pepper, garlic, and remaining 1 teaspoon Italian seasoning into mixture in cooker.

3 Cover and cook on low-heat setting for 8 to 10 hours or on high-heat setting for 4 to 5 hours.

4 If using low-heat setting, turn to high-heat setting. Gently stir in orzo. Cover and cook about 15 minutes more or until orzo is tender. Stir in spinach. If desired, garnish each serving with reserved fennel leaves.

Nutrition Facts per serving: 200 cal., 8 g total fat (3 g sat. fat), 62 mg chol., 618 mg sodium, 16 g carbo., 2 g fiber, 15 g pro.
Daily Values: 36% vit. A, 18% vit. C, 6% calcium, 14% iron
Exchanges: 1 Vegetable, ½ Starch, 2 Lean Meat, ½ Fat

16 to 20 grams of carbs

cranberry-mustard pork roast

Onion soup mix has long been a favorite ingredient for time-pressed cooks. Combined with cranberry-orange relish and mustard, the trio brings a windfall of flavor to a pork roast.

Prep: 20 minutes Cook: 5 to 6 hours (low) or 2 ½ to 3 hours (high) Makes: 8 servings

1	2½- to 3-pound boneless pork sirloin or shoulder roast
1	tablespoon cooking oil
1	10-ounce package frozen cranberry-orange sauce, thawed
1	envelope (½ of a 2.2-ounce package) onion soup mix
2	tablespoons Dijon-style mustard
2	tablespoons water

1 Trim fat from meat. If necessary, cut meat to fit into a 3½- or 4-quart slow cooker. In a large skillet cook meat in hot oil over medium heat until brown on all sides. Drain off fat. Place meat in cooker. In a medium bowl combine cranberry-orange sauce, soup mix, mustard, and water. Pour over meat in cooker.

2 Cover and cook on low-heat setting for 5 to 6 hours or on high-heat setting for 2½ to 3 hours.

3 Remove meat from cooker, reserving juices. If present, remove string or netting from meat. Cut meat into slices. Skim fat from cooking liquid. Serve meat with cooking liquid.

Nutrition Facts per serving: 293 cal., 9 g total fat (3 g sat. fat), 89 mg chol., 480 mg sodium, 18 g carbo., 2 g fiber, 30 g pro.
Daily Values: 12% vit. C, 2% calcium, 7% iron
Exchanges: 1 Other Carbo., 4 Lean Meat

16 to 20 grams of carbs

peruvian peanut soup

Chipotle peppers are simply dried, smoked jalapeños. For those with a more sensitive palate, stick to one pepper at a time. The heat can build quickly.

Prep: 40 minutes Cook: 7 to 8 hours (low) or 3½ to 4 hours (high) Makes: 8 servings

1	pound boneless pork shoulder
1	pound skinless, boneless chicken thighs, cut into 1-inch pieces
	Nonstick cooking spray
1	tablespoon cooking oil (optional)
2	medium parsnips, peeled and cut into ½-inch chunks
1	to 2 chipotle peppers in adobo sauce, finely chopped
3	cloves garlic, minced
2	bay leaves
3	14-ounce cans reduced-sodium chicken broth
²/₃	cup reduced-fat creamy peanut butter
¼	cup snipped fresh cilantro

1 Trim fat from meat. Cut meat and chicken into 1-inch pieces. Lightly coat an extra large nonstick skillet with cooking spray; heat skillet over medium-high heat. Cook pork in hot skillet until brown. Place pork in a 4- to 4½-quart slow cooker. If necessary add the cooking oil to skillet. Cook chicken in skillet until no longer pink. Place chicken in cooker. Add parsnips, chipotle pepper, garlic, and bay leaves. Pour chicken broth over mixture in cooker

2 Cover and cook on low-heat setting for 7 to 8 hours or on high-heat setting for 3½ to 4 hours.

3 Skim off fat. Remove and discard bay leaves. Stir in peanut butter until combined. Top each serving with fresh cilantro.

Nutrition Facts per serving: 311 cal., 14 g total fat (4 g sat. fat), 82 mg chol., 582 mg sodium, 16 g carbo., 3 g fiber, 31 g pro.
Daily Values: 4% vit. A, 14% vit. C, 3% calcium, 11% iron
Exchanges: 1 Other Carbo., 4 Lean Meat, ½ Fat

16 to 20 grams of carbs

ribs and sauerkraut

Sauerkraut and onions join the classic apple-and-pork combo for a luscious sweet-salty sensation. Pair this with new potatoes or slices of rye bread.

Prep: 20 minutes Cook: 6 to 7 hours (low) or 3 to 3 ½ hours (high) Makes: 6 to 8 servings

1	14-ounce can sauerkraut, drained
1	large sweet onion, sliced
2	cups sliced peeled tart cooking apples (2 medium)
2	pounds boneless pork country-style ribs
1	cup apple juice

1 In a 4- or 4½-quart slow cooker place sauerkraut, onion, and apples. Top with meat. Pour apple juice over mixture in cooker.

2 Cover and cook on low-heat setting for 6 to 7 hours or on high-heat setting for 3 to 3½ hours. Serve with a slotted spoon; discard cooking liquid.

Nutrition Facts per serving: 312 cal., 12 g total fat (4 g sat. fat), 96 mg chol., 541 mg sodium, 19 g carbo., 4 g fiber, 30 g pro.
Daily Values: 1% vit. A, 28% vit. C, 7% calcium, 16% iron
Exchanges: 1 Vegetable, 1 Fruit, 4 Lean Meat

16 to 20 grams of carbs

tomato-sauced pork ribs

The sauce for these scrumptious ribs contains hot pepper sauce for extra kick.

Prep: 20 minutes Cook: 8 to 10 hours (low) or 4 to 5 hours (high) Makes: 6 servings

1	28-ounce can crushed tomatoes, undrained
1	cup chopped celery (2 stalks)
3/4	cup chopped green sweet pepper (1 medium)
1/2	cup chopped onion (1 medium)
2	tablespoons quick-cooking tapioca
1 1/2	teaspoons snipped fresh basil or 1/2 teaspoon dried basil, crushed
1/2	teaspoon salt
1/4	teaspoon black pepper
1/4	teaspoon bottled hot pepper sauce
1	clove garlic, minced
2	pounds boneless pork country-style ribs

---

1 In a 3½- or 4-quart slow cooker combine undrained tomatoes, celery, sweet pepper, onion, tapioca, dried basil (if using), salt, black pepper, hot pepper sauce, and garlic. Add ribs, stirring to coat ribs with tomato mixture.

2 Cover and cook on low-heat setting for 8 to 10 hours or on high-heat setting for 4 to 5 hours.

3 Transfer ribs to a serving platter, reserving cooking liquid. Skim fat from sauce. If using fresh basil, stir into sauce. Spoon some of the sauce over meat. Pass remaining sauce.

Nutrition Facts per serving: 303 cal., 12 g total fat (4 g sat. fat), 96 mg chol., 489 mg sodium, 16 g carbo., 3 g fiber, 32 g pro.
Daily Values: 15% vit. A, 47% vit. C, 7% calcium, 22% iron
Exchanges: 1½ Vegetable, ½ Other Carbo., 4 Lean Meat

16 to 20 grams of carbs

sage, pork, and squash stew

Poblano chiles are mild to medium-hot, with complex flavor. Look for them at Mexican markets and large supermarkets. For richer flavor, choose poblanos that are dark in color.

Prep: 30 minutes Cook: 8 to 9 hours (low) or 4 to 4 ½ hours (high), plus 15 minutes (high) Makes: 6 servings

1½	**pounds lean pork stew meat**
1	**tablespoon cooking oil**
1	**medium butternut squash, peeled, seeded, and cut into 2-inch pieces**
4	**medium parsnips, cut into ½-inch slices (3 cups)**
2	**medium poblano peppers, seeded and chopped***
½	**cup chopped onion (1 medium)**
1	**teaspoon dried sage, crushed**
1	**teaspoon dried thyme, crushed**
¼	**teaspoon salt**
¼	**teaspoon black pepper**
2	**cloves garlic, minced**
2	**14-ounce cans reduced-sodium chicken broth**
2	**tablespoons cornstarch**
2	**tablespoons cold water**

1 Trim fat from meat. In a large nonstick skillet cook meat, half at a time, in hot oil over medium heat until brown. Drain off fat. Set aside. In a 4- to 5-quart slow cooker place squash, parsnips, poblano peppers, and onion. Add meat. Sprinkle with sage, thyme, salt, black pepper, and garlic. Pour chicken broth over mixture in cooker.

2 Cover and cook on low-heat setting for 8 to 9 hours or on high-heat setting for 4 to 4½ hours.

3 If using low-heat setting, turn to high-heat setting. In a small bowl combine cornstarch and water. Stir into mixture in cooker. Cover and cook about 15 minutes more or until thickened.

*Note: Because hot chile peppers, such as poblanos, contain volatile oils that can burn your skin and eyes, avoid direct contact with chiles as much as possible. When working with chile peppers, wear plastic or rubber gloves. If your bare hands do touch the chile peppers, wash your hands well with soap and water.

Nutrition Facts per serving: 273 cal., 9 g total fat (3 g sat. fat), 71 mg chol., 478 mg sodium, 20 g carbo., 3 g fiber, 27 g pro.
Daily Values: 21% vit. A, 196% vit. C, 6% calcium, 15% iron
Exchanges: 1 Vegetable, 1 Starch, 3 Lean Meat

16 to 20 grams of carbs

mushroom-sauced pork chops

Mushroom soup and canned mushrooms give a double dose of earthy flavor to this comforting food.

Prep: 15 minutes Cook: 8 to 9 hours (low) or 4 to 4½ hours (high) Makes: 4 servings

4	pork loin chops (with bone), cut ¾-inch thick
1	tablespoon cooking oil
1	small onion, thinly sliced
2	tablespoons quick-cooking tapioca
1	10¾-ounce can reduced-fat and reduced-sodium condensed cream of mushroom soup
½	cup apple juice
1	4-ounce can sliced mushrooms, drained
2	teaspoons Worcestershire sauce
¾	teaspoon dried thyme, crushed
¼	teaspoon garlic powder
2	cups hot cooked brown rice (optional)

1 Trim fat from chops. In a large skillet cook chops in hot oil over medium heat until brown on both sides. Drain off fat. Place onion in a 3½- or 4-quart slow cooker. Add chops. Crush tapioca with a mortar and pestle. In a bowl combine tapioca, mushroom soup, apple juice, mushrooms, Worcestershire sauce, thyme, and garlic powder. Pour over chops in cooker.

2 Cover and cook on low-heat setting for 8 to 9 hours or on high-heat setting for 4 to to 4 ½ hours. If desired, serve with hot cooked rice.

For a 5- or 6-quart slow cooker: Use 6 pork loin chops. Leave remaining ingredient amounts the same and prepare as above. If serving with rice, increase to 3 cups hot cooked brown rice. Makes 6 servings.

Nutrition Facts per serving: 252 cal., 10 g total fat (2 g sat. fat), 50 mg chol.,
502 mg sodium, 18 g carbo., 1 g fiber, 21 g pro.
Daily Values: 1% vit. A, 2% vit. C, 3% calcium, 9% iron
Exchanges: 1 Other Carbo., 2½ Very Lean Meat, 2 Fat

16 to 20 grams of carbs

pork chops with winter squash

Orange marmalade and mustard team up for a glistening, piquant sauce to coat the chops and winter squash slices. Steam green beans or asparagus to serve alongside.

Prep: 20 minutes Cook: 5 to 6 hours (low) or 2½ to 3 hours (high) Makes: 6 servings

2	small or medium acorn squash (1½ to 2 pounds)
1	large onion, halved and sliced
6	pork chops (with bone), cut ¾-inch thick
½	cup reduced-sodium chicken broth
⅓	cup reduced-sugar orange marmalade
1	tablespoon Dijon-style mustard
1	teaspoon dried marjoram or thyme, crushed
¼	teaspoon black pepper
2	tablespoons cornstarch
2	tablespoons cold water

1 Cut squash in half lengthwise. Remove and discard seeds and membranes. Cut each squash half into 3 wedges. In a 5- to 6-quart slow cooker place squash and onion. Trim fat from chops. Place chops in cooker. In a small bowl combine chicken broth, marmalade, mustard, marjoram, and pepper. Pour over mixture in cooker.

2 Cover and cook on low-heat setting for 5 to 6 hours or on high-heat setting for 2½ to 3 hours.

3 Transfer chops and vegetables to a serving platter, reserving cooking liquid. Cover chops and vegetables with foil to keep warm.

4 For sauce, strain cooking liquid into a glass measuring cup. Skim off fat. Measure 1¾ cups liquid (add water, if necessary, to make 1¾ cups). Pour liquid into a medium saucepan. In a small bowl combine cornstarch and water. Stir into liquid in saucepan. Cook and stir over medium heat until thickened and bubbly. Cook and stir for 2 minutes more. Serve chops and vegetables with sauce.

Nutrition Facts per serving: 283 cal., 8 g total fat (3 g sat. fat), 78 mg chol., 176 mg sodium, 18 g carbo., 2 g fiber, 33 g pro.
Daily Values: 21% vit. A, 17% vit. C, 6% calcium, 11% iron
Exchanges: 1 Starch, 4 Lean Meat

16 to 20 grams of carbs

orange-dijon pork chops

Serve these marmalade-glazed chops with steamed broccoli.

Prep: 15 minutes Cook: 6 to 7 hours (low) or 3 to 3½ hours (high) Makes: 6 servings

6	boneless pork loin chops, cut 1 inch thick
	Salt and black pepper
½	teaspoon dried thyme, crushed
1	cup reduced-sugar orange marmalade
⅓	cup Dijon-style mustard
¼	cup water

1 Trim fat from chops. Sprinkle both sides of chops lightly with salt and pepper. Place chops in a 3½- or 4-quart slow cooker; sprinkle with thyme. In a small bowl combine orange marmalade and mustard. For glaze, remove 2 tablespoons of the mixture for the glaze; cover and chill until needed. Combine remaining marmalade mixture and water. Pour over chops.

2 Cover and cook on low-heat setting for 6 to 7 hours or on high-heat setting for 3 to 3½ hours. Transfer chops to a serving platter; discard cooking liquid. Spread reserved marmalade glaze over chops.

Nutrition Facts per serving: 323 cal., 10 g total fat (3 g sat. fat), 107 mg chol.,
501 mg sodium, 19 g carbo., 0 g fiber, 38 g pro.
Daily Values: 1% vit. A, 3% vit. C, 4% calcium, 11% iron
Exchanges: 1 Other Carbo., 5 Very Lean Meat, 2 Fat

16 to 20 grams of carbs

southwest pork chops

Pork chops from a slow cooker? Yes! Slow cookers are versatile as well as convenient. Four ingredients are all you need for this tasty dish.

Prep: 15 minutes   **Cook:** 5 hours (low) or 2½ hours (high), plus 30 minutes (high)   **Makes:** 6 servings

6	pork rib chops (with bone), cut ¾ inch thick
1	15-ounce can Mexican-style or Tex-Mex-style chili beans
1¼	cups bottled salsa
1	cup fresh or frozen whole kernel corn*
	Hot cooked brown rice (optional)
	Snipped fresh cilantro (optional)

---

1 Trim fat from the chops. Place chops in a 3½- or 4-quart slow cooker. Add chili beans and salsa.

2 Cover and cook on low-heat setting for 5 hours or on high-heat setting for 2½ hours.

3 If using low-heat setting, turn to high-heat setting. Stir in corn. Cover and cook for 30 minutes more. If desired, serve over hot cooked rice and sprinkle with cilantro.

For all-day cooking: Substitute 8 boneless pork chops for the 6 rib chops. (When cooked this long, chops with bone may leave bony fragments in the cooked mixture.) Cover and cook on low-heat setting for 9½ hours. Turn to high-heat setting. Stir in corn. Cover and cook for 30 minutes more.

*Note: 2 medium ears of fresh corn equal about 1 cup of whole kernel corn.

Nutrition Facts per serving: 265 cal., 7 g total fat (2 g sat. fat), 77 mg chol., 715 mg sodium, 19 g carbo., 4 g fiber, 32 g pro.
Daily Values: 5% vit. A, 13% vit. C, 6% calcium, 15% iron
Exchanges: 1½ Starch, 4 Very Lean Meat

16 to 20 grams of carbs

curried lamb and vegetable soup

This fascinating soup is topped with a delightfully cooling yogurt, cucumber, and lime mixture. The topper is patterned after raita, a classic Indian condiment.

Prep: 30 minutes Cook: 9 to 10 hours (low) or 4½ to 5 hours (high),
plus 5 minutes (standing) Makes: 8 servings (10 cups)

1	tablespoon curry powder
1	teaspoon ground cumin
½	teaspoon salt
¼	teaspoon black pepper
2½	to 3 pounds lamb stew meat
1	14½-ounce can diced tomatoes, undrained
2	cups coarsely chopped celeriac
2	cups cauliflower florets
1	medium onion, cut into thick wedges
⅔	cup coarsely chopped cooking apple (1 medium)
1	cup unsweetened light coconut milk
½	cup frozen peas
1	8-ounce carton plain lowfat yogurt
½	cup chopped, seeded cucumber
1	tablespoon lime juice

1 In a small bowl combine curry powder, cumin, salt, and pepper. Set aside. Trim fat from meat. Cut meat into 1-inch pieces. Sprinkle spice mixture over meat. Place meat in a 4½- to 6-quart slow cooker. Add undrained tomatoes, celeriac, cauliflower, onion, and apple.

2 Cover and cook on low-heat setting for 9 to 10 hours or on high-heat setting for 4½ to 5 hours. Turn off the cooker. Stir in coconut milk and peas. Cover and let stand for 5 to 10 minutes or until heated through.

3 Meanwhile, in a small bowl combine yogurt, cucumber, and lime juice. Top each serving with a dollop of yogurt mixture.

Nutrition Facts per serving: 270 cal., 8 g total fat (3 g sat. fat), 91 mg chol., 413 mg sodium, 16 g carbo., 3 g fiber, 32 g pro.
Daily Values: 5% vit. A, 42% vit. C, 12% calcium, 22% iron
Exchanges: 1½ Vegetable, ½ Starch, 3½ Lean Meat

16 to 20 grams of carbs

lamb and barley vegetable soup

Look for lean lamb at the supermarket or buy extra (2½ pounds) and trim it yourself. Beef and pork make delicious substitutes.

Prep: 25 minutes Cook: 6 to 8 hours (low) or 3 to 4 hours (high) Makes: 8 servings

1½	pounds lamb stew meat, cut into 1-inch pieces
2	cups sliced fresh mushrooms
½	cup regular barley
1	cup chopped onion (1 large)
1	medium carrot, cut into ½-inch pieces
1	large parsnip, peeled and cut into ½-inch pieces
1	14½-ounce can Italian-style stewed tomatoes, undrained
2	cloves garlic, minced
1	teaspoon dried marjoram, crushed
½	teaspoon salt
¼	teaspoon black pepper
1	bay leaf
4	cups reduced-sodium beef broth

1 In a 3½- to 6-quart slow cooker place meat, mushrooms, barley, onion, carrot, parsnip, undrained tomatoes, garlic, marjoram, salt, pepper, and bay leaf. Pour broth over all.

2 Cover and cook on low-heat setting for 6 to 8 hours or on high-heat setting for 3 to 4 hours. Remove and discard bay leaf.

Nutrition Facts per serving: 205 cal., 5 g total fat (1 g sat. fat), 54 mg chol., 540 mg sodium, 19 g carbo., 4 g fiber, 21 g pro.
Daily Values: 17% vit. A, 7% vit. C, 4% calcium, 14% iron
Exchanges: 1 Vegetable, 1 Starch, 2 Lean Meat

16 to 20 grams of carbs

lamb korma

The flavors of India emerge when you mix lamb with garam masala. You'll find garam masala—an Indian spice mix—at ethnic grocery stores and many supermarkets.

Prep: 15 minutes Cook: 8 to 10 hours (low) or 4 to 5 hours (high) Makes: 6 servings

2	pounds lean boneless lamb
1	tablespoon garam masala
3	cups cubed, peeled potatoes (about 1 pound)
1/4	teaspoon salt
1/4	teaspoon black pepper
1	14 1/2-ounce can diced tomatoes with garlic and onion, undrained
1/4	cup water
3/4	cup plain low-fat yogurt (optional)

1 Trim fat from meat. Cut meat into 1-inch pieces. Sprinkle meat with garam masala. Place potatoes in a 3 1/2- or 4-quart slow cooker. Add meat. Sprinkle with salt and pepper. Pour undrained tomatoes and water over mixture in cooker.

2 Cover and cook on low-heat setting for 8 to 10 hours or on high-heat setting for 4 to 5 hours. If desired, top each serving with yogurt.

Nutrition Facts per serving: 282 cal., 8 g total fat (3 g sat. fat), 97 mg chol., 538 mg sodium, 18 g carbo., 1 g fiber, 33 g pro.
Daily Values: 32% vit. C, 4% calcium, 23% iron
Exchanges: 1 Starch, 4 Lean Meat

16 to 20 grams of carbs

lamb stew with mint

Pearl barley adds a slightly chewy texture to this stew. "Pearl" refers to the polishing process of the hulled grain. It is sold in regular and quick-cooking forms.

Prep: 20 minutes Cook: 8 to 10 hours (low) or 4 to 5 hours (high) Makes: 6 servings

1½	pounds lamb stew meat
2	tablespoons cooking oil
½	cup chopped onion (1 medium)
4	cloves garlic, minced
2½	cups reduced-sodium chicken broth
1	14½-ounce can diced tomatoes, undrained
½	cup regular barley
¼	cup dry white wine (optional)
2	tablespoons snipped fresh dill or 1½ teaspoons dried dill, crushed
½	teaspoon salt
¼	teaspoon black pepper
1½	7-ounce jars roasted red sweet peppers, drained and thinly sliced (about 1½ cups)
¼	cup snipped fresh mint

16 to 20 grams of carbs

1 Trim fat from meat. Cut meat into 1-inch pieces. In a large nonstick skillet cook half of the meat in hot oil over medium heat until brown. Transfer meat to a 3½- to 5-quart slow cooker. Cook remaining meat, the onion, and garlic in hot skillet until meat is brown and onion is tender. Drain off fat. Add meat mixture to meat in cooker.

2 Stir in chicken broth, undrained tomatoes, barley, wine (if desired), dried dill (if using), salt, and black pepper.

3 Cover and cook on low-heat setting for 8 to 10 hours or on high-heat setting for 4 to 5 hours. Just before serving, stir in the roasted peppers, fresh mint, and if using, the fresh dill.

Nutrition Facts per serving: 276 cal., 10 g total fat (2 g sat. fat), 72 mg chol.,
621 mg sodium, 20 g carbo., 4 g fiber, 27 g pro.
Daily Values: 190% vit. C, 5% calcium, 23% iron
Exchanges: 1 Vegetable, 1 Starch, 3 Lean Meat

thai chicken and vegetable soup

Look for lemongrass in the produce aisle of most supermarkets or your local Asian market. If you can't find it, substitute an equal amount of lemon peel.

Prep: 30 minutes Cook: 7 to 8 hours (low) or 3½ to 4 hours (high)
Stand: 15 minutes Makes: 6 servings

1½	pounds skinless, boneless chicken thighs
3	cups cauliflower florets
2	cups bias-sliced carrots (4 medium)
¾	cup chopped onions (1½ medium)
1	8-ounce can bamboo shoots, drained
3	tablespoons finely chopped lemongrass
3	tablespoons grated fresh ginger
4	cloves garlic, minced
½	teaspoon crushed red pepper
2	14-ounce cans reduced-sodium chicken broth
1	15-ounce can unsweetened light coconut milk
2	cups fresh snow peas, halved
3	serrano chile peppers, seeded and chopped*
1	tablespoon finely shredded lime peel

1 Cut chicken into 1-inch pieces. In a 4- to 5-quart slow cooker combine chicken, cauliflower, carrots, onions, bamboo shoots, lemongrass, ginger, garlic, and crushed red pepper. Pour chicken broth over mixture in cooker.

2 Cover and cook on low-heat setting for 7 to 8 hours or on high-heat setting for 3½ to 4 hours.

3 Stir in coconut milk, snow peas, serrano peppers, and lime peel. Cover and let stand for 15 minutes.

*Note: Because hot chile peppers, such as serranos, contain volatile oils that can burn your skin and eyes, avoid direct contact with chiles as much as possible. When working with chile peppers, wear plastic or rubber gloves. If your bare hands do touch the chile peppers, wash your hands well with soap and water.

Nutrition Facts per serving: 260 cal., 9 g total fat (4 g sat. fat), 91 mg chol., 460 mg sodium, 16 g carbo., 4 g fiber, 27 g pro.
Daily Values: 91% vit. A, 57% vit. C, 6% calcium, 14% iron
Exchanges: 1½ Vegetable, ½ Other Carbo., 3½ Very Lean Meat, 1½ Fat

16 to 20 grams of carbs

tangy pineapple chicken

When testing this recipe, our taste panel really enjoyed the pleasant sweetness and tang from the pineapple chunks.

Prep: 35 minutes Cook: 5 to 6 hours (low) or 2½ to 3 hours (high) Makes: 6 servings

2	pounds skinless, boneless chicken thighs
1	tablespoon cooking oil
1	20-ounce can pineapple tidbits (juice pack), drained
1	cup chopped red sweet pepper (1 large)
½	cup bottled barbecue sauce
¼	cup bottled low-calorie Italian salad dressing
2	teaspoons dried oregano, crushed

1 Cut chicken into 1-inch strips. In a large skillet cook chicken, half at a time, in hot oil over medium heat until brown. Drain off fat. Place chicken in a 3½- or 4-quart slow cooker. Top with pineapple and sweet pepper. In a small bowl combine barbecue sauce, salad dressing, and oregano. Pour over mixture in cooker.

2 Cover and cook on low-heat setting for 5 to 6 hours or on high-heat setting for 2½ to 3 hours.

Nutrition Facts per serving: 285 cal., 9 g total fat (2 g sat. fat), 126 mg chol.,
412 mg sodium, 20 g carbo., 2 g fiber, 31 g pro.
Daily Values: 18% vit. A, 96% vit. C, 4% calcium, 13% iron
Exchanges: ½ Fruit, 1 Other Carbo., 4 Lean Meat

16 to 20 grams of carbs

chicken and white bean stew

Refrigerated light Alfredo sauce gives this chicken and bean stew an amazing creaminess.

Prep: 35 minutes Cook: 4 to 5 hours (low) or 2 to 2½ hours (high) Makes: 8 servings

2	pounds skinless, boneless chicken thighs
2	teaspoons ground cumin
⅛	teaspoon black pepper
1	tablespoon olive oil
2	10-ounce packages refrigerated light alfredo sauce
1	15- to 15½-ounce can Great Northern or white kidney (canellini) beans, rinsed and drained
1	cup reduced-sodium chicken broth
½	cup chopped onion (1 medium)
1	4-ounce can diced green chile peppers
4	cloves garlic, minced
¼	cup shredded Monterey Jack cheese (1 ounce) (optional)

1 Cut chicken into 1-inch pieces. Sprinkle chicken with cumin and pepper. In a large skillet cook chicken, half at a time, in hot oil over medium heat until brown. Place chicken in a 3½- or 4-quart slow cooker. Stir in alfredo sauce, beans, chicken broth, onion, chile peppers, and garlic.

2 Cover and cook on low-heat setting for 4 to 5 hours or on high-heat setting for 2 to 2½ hours. If desired, sprinkle each serving with cheese.

Nutrition Facts per serving: 360 cal., 16 g total fat (8 g sat. fat), 122 mg chol.,
918 mg sodium, 20 g carbo., 3 g fiber, 31 g pro.
Daily Values: 17% vit. A, 14% vit. C, 17% calcium, 10% iron
Exchanges: 1½ Starch, 4 Lean Meat, ½ Fat

16 to 20 grams of carbs

cacciatore-style drumsticks

Like the stovetop version, this one is brimming with onions, mushrooms, and tomatoes perfectly seasoned with herbs.

Prep: 25 minutes Cook: 5 to 6 hours (low) or 2½ to 3 hours (high), plus 20 minutes (high) Makes: 6 servings

2	cups sliced fresh mushrooms
1	cup chopped carrots (2 medium)
2	medium onions, cut into wedges
1	green, yellow, or red sweet pepper, cut into strips
12	chicken drumsticks, skinned (about 3½ pounds)
½	cup reduced-sodium chicken broth
¼	teaspoon black pepper
1	14½-ounce can diced tomatoes with basil, oregano, and garlic; undrained
⅓	cup tomato paste
2	tablespoons cornstarch
	Hot cooked brown rice (optional)

---

1 In a 5- to 6-quart slow cooker combine mushrooms, carrots, onions, and sweet pepper. Add chicken. Pour chicken broth over mixture in cooker. Sprinkle with black pepper.

2 Cover and cook on low-heat setting for 5 to 6 hours or on high-heat setting for 2½ to 3 hours.

3 If using low-heat setting, turn to high-heat setting. In a bowl combine undrained tomatoes, tomato paste, and cornstarch. Stir into mixture in cooker. Cover and cook about 20 minutes more or until thickened. If desired, serve with hot cooked rice.

Nutrition Facts per serving: 251 cal., 6 g total fat (1 g sat. fat), 114 mg chol., 531 mg sodium, 16 g carbo., 2 g fiber, 34 g pro.
Daily Values: 55% vit. A, 39% vit. C, 7% calcium, 17% iron
Exchanges: 1½ Vegetable, ½ Other Carbo., 4 Very Lean Meat, 1 Fat

16 to 20 grams of carbs

jambalaya-style chicken and shrimp

Hot cooked rice makes a perfect accompaniment to this Cajun-inspired dish. Pass hot sauce at the table for those who want a little extra heat.

Prep: 30 minutes Cook: 6 to 8 hours (low) or 3 to 4 hours (high), plus 30 minutes (high) Makes: 6 servings

1	pound skinless, boneless chicken thighs
4	ounces cooked smoked turkey sausage
1½	cups chopped red, yellow, or green sweet pepper (2 medium)
1	cup thinly sliced celery (2 stalks)
1	cup chopped onion (1 large)
1	14½-ounce can no-salt-added diced tomatoes, undrained
1	10-ounce can chopped tomatoes and green chile peppers, undrained
2	tablespoons quick-cooking tapioca
1	teaspoon dried basil, crushed
¼	teaspoon cayenne pepper
4	ounces frozen peeled and deveined medium shrimp, thawed
2	cups frozen cut okra
	Hot cooked brown rice (optional)

1 Cut chicken into bite-size pieces. Halve sausage lengthwise and cut into ½-inch slices. In a 3½- or 4-quart slow cooker combine chicken, sausage, sweet pepper, celery, and onion. Stir in undrained tomatoes, tapioca, basil, and cayenne pepper.

2 Cover and cook on low-heat setting for 6 to 8 hours or on high-heat setting for 3 to 4 hours.

3 If using low-heat setting, turn to high-heat setting. Stir in shrimp and okra. Cover and cook about 30 minutes more or until shrimp turn opaque. If desired, serve with hot cooked rice.

Nutrition Facts per serving: 209 cal., 5 g total fat (1 g sat. fat), 102 mg chol., 421 mg sodium, 16 g carbo., 4 g fiber, 24 g pro.
Daily Values: 35% vit. A, 120% vit. C, 10% calcium, 12% iron
Exchanges: 2 Vegetable, 3 Very Lean Meat, 1 Fat

16 to 20 grams of carbs

spinach, chicken, and wild rice soup

A crisp green salad topped with citrus slices and your favorite vinaigrette would round out this meal nicely.

Prep: 15 minutes **Cook:** 7 to 8 hours (low) or 3½ to 4 hours (high) **Makes:** 6 servings

3	cups water
1	14-ounce can chicken broth
1	10¾-ounce can condensed cream of chicken soup
⅔	cup uncooked wild rice, rinsed and drained
½	teaspoon dried thyme, crushed
¼	teaspoon black pepper
3	cups chopped cooked chicken or turkey
2	cups shredded fresh spinach

1 In a 3½- or 4-quart slow cooker combine water, chicken broth, chicken soup, wild rice, thyme, and pepper.

2 Cover and cook on low-heat setting for 7 to 8 hours or on high-heat setting for 3½ to 4 hours. Just before serving, stir in chicken and spinach.

Nutrition Facts per serving: 235 cal., 6 g total fat (1 g sat. fat), 67 mg chol., 449 mg sodium, 19 g carbo., 1 g fiber, 25 g pro.
Daily Values: 20% vit. A, 5% vit. C, 3% calcium, 9% iron
Exchanges: ½ Vegetable, 1 Starch, 3 Very Lean Meat, 1 Fat

16 to 20 grams of carbs

mushroom, turkey, and rice soup

When you know the morning will be hectic, cut up the turkey and vegetables the night before and refrigerate them in separate plastic bags.

Prep: 25 minutes Cook: 8 to 10 hours (low) or 4 to 5 hours (high) Stand: 5 minutes Makes: 6 servings

1	pound turkey breast tenderloins or skinless, boneless chicken breast halves
2	cups sliced fresh shiitake or button mushrooms
1½	cups sliced bok choy
2	medium carrots, cut into thin bite-size strips
½	cup chopped onion (1 medium)
2	14-ounce cans reduced-sodium chicken broth
2	tablespoons reduced-sodium soy sauce
1	tablespoon toasted sesame oil (optional)
2	teaspoons grated fresh ginger
4	cloves garlic, minced
1	cup uncooked instant white rice

1 Cut turkey into 1-inch pieces. Set aside. In a 3½- or 4-quart slow cooker place mushrooms, bok choy, carrots, and onion. Add turkey. In a medium bowl combine chicken broth, soy sauce, sesame oil (if desired), ginger, and garlic. Pour over mixture in cooker.

2 Cover and cook on low-heat setting for 8 to 10 hours or on high-heat setting for 4 to 5 hours. Turn off cooker. Stir in rice. Cover and let stand for 5 to 10 minutes or until rice is tender.

Note: This recipe may be doubled for a 5- or 6- quart cooker.

Nutrition Facts per serving: 186 cal., 2 g total fat (0 g sat. fat), 45 mg chol., 570 mg sodium, 19 g carbo., 1 g fiber, 22 g pro.
Daily Values: 60% vit. A, 17% vit. C, 5% calcium, 11% iron
Exchanges: 1 Vegetable, 1 Starch, 2½ Very Lean Meat

16 to 20 grams of carbs

hearty turkey soup

Dried Italian seasoning is a fragrant blend of basil, oregano, rosemary, fennel seed, and sometimes garlic powder and cayenne pepper.

Prep: 30 minutes Cook: 5 to 6 hours (low) or 2 ½ to 3 hours (high) Makes: 4 or 5 servings

1	pound uncooked ground turkey or chicken
1	cup chopped celery (2 stalks)
½	cup thinly sliced carrot (1 medium)
½	cup chopped onion (1 medium)
1	clove garlic, minced
3	cups tomato juice
2	cups frozen French-cut green beans
1	cup sliced fresh mushrooms
½	cup chopped tomato (1 medium)
2	teaspoons dried Italian seasoning, crushed
1½	teaspoons Worcestershire sauce
¼	teaspoon black pepper
1	bay leaf

1 In a large skillet cook turkey, celery, carrot, onion, and garlic over medium heat until turkey is no longer pink. Drain off fat. Transfer turkey mixture to a 3½- or 4-quart slow cooker. Stir in tomato juice, frozen green beans, mushrooms, tomato, Italian seasoning, Worcestershire sauce, pepper, and bay leaf.

2 Cover and cook on low-heat setting for 5 to 6 hours or on high-heat setting for 2½ to 3 hours. Remove and discard bay leaf.

Nutrition Facts per serving: 256 cal., 10 g total fat (3 g sat. fat), 90 mg chol., 636 mg sodium, 19 g carbo., 4 g fiber, 34 g pro.
Daily Values: 62% vit. A, 79% vit. C, 10% calcium, 20% iron
Exchanges: 4 Vegetable, 2½ Lean Meat, ½ Fat

16 to 20 grams of carbs

turkey brats in beer

Not grilling season? These turkey brats cook up perfectly in the slow cooker. They take on just a bit of heat from the jalapeño peppers.

Prep: 10 minutes Cook: 5 to 6 hours (low) or 2½ to 3 hours (high) Makes: 12 servings

12	uncooked turkey bratwurst (about 3 pounds)
4	jalapeño chile peppers, stemmed and sliced crosswise* (about 1 cup)
1	12-ounce can light beer
12	whole wheat hot dog buns
	Dijon-style, coarse-grain, or other mustard (optional)

---

1 Pierce bratwurst with a fork. In a large skillet cook bratwurst, half at a time, over medium heat until brown on all sides. Place bratwurst in a 4- to 5-quart slow cooker. Sprinkle with jalapeño peppers. Add beer.

2 Cover and cook on low-heat setting for 5 to 6 hours or on high-heat setting for 2½ to 3 hours.

3 Using a slotted spoon, transfer bratwurst and jalapeño peppers to a serving platter; discard cooking liquid. Serve bratwurst in hot dog buns and if desired, with mustard.

*Note: Because hot chile peppers, such as jalapeños, contain volatile oils that can burn your skin and eyes, avoid direct contact with chiles as much as possible. When working with chile peppers, wear plastic or rubber gloves. If your bare hands do touch the chile peppers, wash your hands well with soap and water.

Nutrition Facts per serving: 252 cal., 11 g total fat (3 g sat. fat), 50 mg chol.,
988 mg sodium, 20 g carbo., 2 g fiber, 18 g pro.
Daily Values: 1% vit. A, 3% vit. C, 4% calcium, 10% iron
Exchanges: 1½ Starch, 2 Medium-Fat Meat

16 to 20 grams of carbs

cauliflower cheese soup

Everyone on our taste panel just loved the extra flavor punch that the caraway seeds add to this soup.

Prep: 20 minutes Cook: 6 to 8 hours (low) or 3 to 4 hours (high),
plus 15 minutes (high) Makes: 8 side-dish servings

2	cups cubed peeled potatoes
1	cup sliced leeks (3 medium)
6	cups cauliflower florets (1 medium head)
1/4	teaspoon black pepper
2	14-ounce cans reduced-sodium chicken broth
1/2	cup water
8	ounces process Swiss or American cheese slices, torn into small pieces
1/2	teaspoon caraway seeds, crushed

1 In a 3½- or 4-quart slow cooker place potatoes and leeks. Add cauliflower and pepper. Pour chicken broth and water over mixture in cooker.

2 Cover and cook on low-heat setting for 6 to 8 hours or on high-heat setting for 3 to 4 hours.

3 Remove vegetable mixture from cooker. Place half of the vegetable mixture in a blender or food processor. Cover and blend or process until nearly smooth. Return to cooker. Repeat with remaining vegetable mixture.

4 If using low-heat setting, turn to high-heat setting. Stir in cheese and caraway seeds. Cover and cook about 15 minutes more. Stir until cheese is melted.

Nutrition Facts per serving: 174 cal., 7 g total fat (5 g sat. fat), 27 mg chol., 699 mg sodium, 17 g carbo., 3 g fiber, 10 g pro.
Daily Values: 16% vit. A, 60% vit. C, 24% calcium, 7% iron
Exchanges: 1½ Vegetable, ½ Starch, 1 High-Fat Meat

16 to 20 grams of carbs

italian vegetable soup

This flavorful soup is perfect paired with a salad for a light dinner or lunch.

Prep: 20 minutes Cook: 6 to 8 hours (low) or 3 to 4 hours (high) Makes: 6 to 8 side-dish servings

1	9-ounce package frozen cut green beans
1/2	of a 16-ounce package frozen cauliflower
1	14 1/2-ounce can diced tomatoes with basil, garlic, and oregano; undrained
1/2	cup chopped onion (1 medium)
1/2	cup sliced celery (1 stalk)
1/4	cup regular barley
1	clove garlic, minced
1/4	teaspoon black pepper
3	cups reduced-sodium chicken broth
1 1/2	cups reduced-sodium vegetable juice
1/4	cup purchased pesto (optional)

---

1 In a 3½- or 4-quart slow cooker place green beans, cauliflower, undrained tomatoes, onion, celery, barley, garlic, and pepper. In a medium bowl combine chicken broth and vegetable juice. Pour over vegetable mixture in cooker.

2 Cover and cook on low-heat setting for 6 to 8 hours or on high-heat setting for 3 to 4 hours. If desired, top each serving with pesto.

Nutrition Facts per serving: 81 cal., 0 g total fat (0 g sat. fat), 0 mg chol., 520 mg sodium, 17 g carbo., 3 g fiber, 4 g pro.
Daily Values: 19% vit. A, 56% vit. C, 7% calcium, 8% iron
Exchanges: 2 Vegetable, ½ Starch

16 to 20 grams of carbs

mustard-sauced brussels sprouts

A cheesy mustard sauce turns simple Brussels sprouts into a splendid side.

Prep: 20 minutes Cook: 4 to 4½ hours (low) or 2½ to 3 hours (high),
plus 15 minutes (high) Makes: 6 side-dish servings

2	pounds Brussels sprouts (about 8 cups), trimmed
⅛	teaspoon salt
¼	teaspoon black pepper
¾	cup reduced-sodium chicken broth
3	tablespoons spicy brown mustard
½	cup fat-free half-and-half
1	tablespoon cornstarch
⅓	cup shredded Swiss cheese (1½ ounces)

1 Cut any large Brussels sprouts in half. Place Brussels sprouts in a 3½- or 4-quart slow cooker. Sprinkle sprouts with salt and pepper. In a bowl combine chicken broth and mustard. Pour over sprouts in cooker.

2 Cover and cook on low-heat setting for 4 to 4½ hours or on high-heat setting for 2½ to 3 hours.

3 Using a slotted spoon, transfer Brussels sprouts to a serving dish. Cover sprouts with foil to keep warm.

4 If using low-heat setting, turn to high-heat setting. In a small bowl combine half-and-half and cornstarch. Stir into liquid in cooker. Cover and cook about 15 minutes more or until thickened. Whisk cheese into liquid in cooker until smooth. Spoon sauce over Brussels sprouts.

Nutrition Facts per serving: 113 cal., 3 g total fat (1 g sat. fat), 7 mg chol., 290 mg sodium, 16 g carbo., 5 g fiber, 8 g pro.
Daily Values: 21% vit. A, 164% vit. C, 13% calcium, 12% iron
Exchanges: 1½ Vegetable, ½ Other Carbo., ½ Fat

16 to 20 grams of carbs

orange-glazed beets

With a citrusy sauce made from orange marmalade, crème fraîche, and sherry, this is a unique take on beets. Try it with a holiday spread—the dish will add color to the table.

Cook: 6 to 8 hours (low) or 3½ to 4½ hours (high) Makes: 8 to 10 side-dish servings

½	cup water
2½	pounds beets, peeled and cut into 1½-inch pieces
3	medium carrots, peeled and cut into 1½-inch pieces
1	medium onion, cut into thick wedges
½	cup reduced-sugar orange marmalade
2	tablespoons water
1	tablespoon grated fresh ginger
½	cup crème fraîche or sour cream
1	tablespoon snipped fresh chives
1	tablespoon dry sherry (optional)

1 In a 3½- or 4-quart slow cooker place the ½ cup water. In a large bowl combine beets, carrots, and onion. In a small bowl combine orange marmalade, the 2 tablespoons water, and the ginger. Add to vegetables; toss to coat. Spoon vegetable mixture into cooker.

2 Cover and cook on low-heat setting for 6 to 8 hours or on high-heat setting for 3½ to 4½ hours.

3 For sauce, in a small bowl combine crème fraîche, chives, and if desired, sherry. Serve sauce with vegetables.

Nutrition Facts per serving: 130 cal., 6 g total fat (4 g sat. fat), 20 mg chol., 92 mg sodium, 18 g carbo., 4 g fiber, 2 g pro.
Daily Values: 63% vit. A, 9% vit. C, 3% calcium, 5% iron
Exchanges: 1½ Vegetable, ½ Other Carbo., 1 Fat

16 to 20 grams of carbs

creamy cauliflower and corn

This colorful dish is a creamy complement to almost any main course meat, or serve it as an easy side for brunch.

Prep: 15 minutes **Cook:** 5 to 6 hours (low) or 2½ to 3 hours (high) **Makes:** 8 side-dish servings

	Nonstick cooking spray
8	cups cauliflower florets (1 large head)
1½	cups frozen corn
1	10¾-ounce can reduced-fat and reduced-sodium condensed cream of celery soup
1	large onion, thinly sliced
¼	cup evaporated milk
2	tablespoons Dijon-style mustard
⅛	teaspoon cayenne pepper
¾	cup shredded reduced-fat cheddar cheese (3 ounces)
⅓	cup slivered almonds, toasted (optional)

1 Lightly coat a 3½- or 4-quart slow cooker with cooking spray. In a large bowl combine cauliflower, corn, celery soup, onion, milk, mustard, and cayenne pepper. Transfer to prepared cooker.

2 Cover and cook on low-heat setting for 5 to 6 hours or on high-heat setting for 2½ to 3 hours. Stir in cheddar cheese until melted. If desired, sprinkle with almonds.

Nutrition Facts per serving: 121 cal., 3 g total fat (2 g sat. fat), 11 mg chol., 350 mg sodium, 18 g carbo., 3 g fiber, 8 g pro.
Daily Values: 2% vit. A, 82% vit. C, 13% calcium, 4% iron
Exchanges: 1½ Vegetable, ½ Starch, ½ Medium-Fat Meat

16 to 20 grams of carbs

chapter five

21 to 30

grams of carbs

beef and barley soup

Here's a classic, home-style winter warmer. Store extra barley in tightly covered containers up to one year in a cool, dry place.

Prep: 20 minutes   **Cook:** 9 to 11 hours (low) or 4½ to 5½ hours (high)   **Makes:** 6 servings (about 9½ cups)

1½	pounds boneless beef sirloin steak, cut ¾ inch thick
2	14-ounce cans reduced-sodium beef broth
1	14½-ounce can stewed tomatoes, undrained
3	medium carrots, cut into ½-inch slices (1½ cups)
2	small onions, cut into wedges
½	cup regular barley
½	cup water
1	bay leaf
1	teaspoon dried thyme, crushed
2	cloves garlic, minced

---

1 Trim fat from meat. Cut meat into ¾-inch pieces. In a 3½- or 4-quart slow cooker combine meat, beef broth, undrained tomatoes, carrots, onions, barley, water, bay leaf, thyme, and garlic.

2 Cover and cook on low-heat setting for 9 to 11 hours or on high-heat setting for 4½ to 5½ hours. Remove and discard bay leaf.

Nutrition Facts per serving: 252 cal., 5 g total fat (1 g sat. fat), 53 mg chol., 461 mg sodium, 21 g carbo., 4 g fiber, 28 g pro.
Daily Values: 67% vit. A, 7% vit. C, 6% calcium, 20% iron
Exchanges: 1 Vegetable, 1 Starch, 3 Lean Meat

21 to 30 grams of carbs

beef and red bean chili

If you usually make chili with hamburger, give this recipe a go for something different. You'll love the way pieces of succulent pot roast add a robust, meaty angle to the stew.

Prep: 20 minutes Stand: 1 hour Cook: 10 to 12 hours (low) or 5 to 6 hours (high) Makes: 8 servings

1	cup dry red beans or dry kidney beans
2	pounds boneless beef chuck pot roast, cut into 1-inch pieces
1	cup coarsely chopped onion (1 large)
1	tablespoon olive oil
1	15-ounce can tomato sauce
1	14½-ounce can diced tomatoes with mild chiles, undrained
1	14-ounce can reduced-sodium beef broth
1	or 2 chipotle peppers in adobo sauce, finely chopped; plus 2 teaspoons adobo sauce
2	teaspoons dried oregano, crushed
1	teaspoon ground cumin
¾	cup chopped red sweet pepper (1 medium)
¼	cup snipped fresh cilantro

1 Rinse the beans. Place the beans in a large saucepan or Dutch oven. Add enough water to cover by 2 inches. Bring to boiling; reduce heat. Simmer, uncovered, for 10 minutes. Remove from heat. Cover; let stand for 1 hour.

2 Meanwhile, in a large skillet cook half of the meat and the onion in hot oil over medium-high heat until meat is brown. Drain off fat. Transfer to a 3½- or 4-quart slow cooker. Repeat with remaining meat. Add tomato sauce, undrained tomatoes, beef broth, chipotle peppers and adobo sauce, oregano, and cumin to mixture in cooker; stir to combine. Drain and rinse the beans; stir into mixture in cooker.

3 Cover and cook on low-heat setting for 10 to 12 hours or on high-heat setting for 5 to 6 hours. Top each serving with sweet pepper and cilantro.

Nutrition Facts per serving: 269 cal., 6 g total fat (2 g sat. fat), 67 mg chol., 550 mg sodium, 21 g carbo., 8 g fiber, 32 g pro.
Daily Values: 16% vit. A, 48% vit. C, 8% calcium, 30% iron
Exchanges: 1½ Vegetable, 1 Starch, 3 Lean Meat

21 to 30 grams of carbs

beef and chipotle burritos

Chipotle peppers are smoked jalapeños that lend a great smoky flavor to foods. Find them at the supermarket with the other canned chile peppers.

Prep: 20 minutes **Cook:** 8 to 10 hours (low) or 4 to 5 hours (high) **Makes:** 6 burritos

1½	pounds boneless beef round steak, cut ¾ inch thick
1	14½-ounce can diced tomatoes, undrained
⅓	cup chopped onion (1 small)
1	to 2 canned chipotle chile peppers in adobo sauce, chopped
1	teaspoon dried oregano, crushed
¼	teaspoon ground cumin
1	clove garlic, minced
6	9- to 10-inch whole wheat or low-fat flour tortillas, warmed
¾	cup shredded reduced-fat cheddar cheese (3 ounces) (optional)
1	recipe Pico de Gallo Salsa (optional)
	Shredded jicama or radishes (optional)
	Light dairy sour cream (optional)

1 Trim fat from meat. Cut meat into 6 pieces. In a 3½- or 4-quart slow cooker place meat, undrained tomatoes, onion, chipotle peppers, oregano, cumin, and garlic.

2 Cover and cook on low-heat setting for 8 to 10 hours or on high-heat setting for 4 to 5 hours.

3 Remove meat from cooker, reserving cooking liquid. Using two forks, pull meat apart into shreds. Stir enough of the reserved liquid into meat to moisten.

4 To serve, spoon meat just below centers of tortillas. If desired, top with cheese, Pico de Gallo Salsa, jicama, and sour cream. Roll up tortillas.

Pico de Gallo Salsa: In a small bowl combine 1 cup finely chopped tomatoes (2 medium); 2 tablespoons finely chopped onion; 2 tablespoons snipped fresh cilantro; and 1 fresh serrano chile pepper, seeded and finely chopped*. Cover and chill for several hours.

*Note: Because hot chile peppers, such as serrano peppers, contain volatile oils that can burn your skin and eyes, avoid direct contact with chiles as much as possible. When working with chile peppers, wear plastic or rubber gloves. If your bare hands do touch chile peppers, wash your hands well with soap and water.

Nutrition Facts per burritos: 319 cal., 8 g total fat (2 g sat. fat), 54 mg chol., 572 mg sodium, 30 g carbo., 3 g fiber, 29 g pro.
Daily Values: 1% vit. A, 15% vit. C, 6% calcium, 20% iron
Exchanges: 1 Vegetable, 2 Starch, 3 Very Lean Meat, ½ Fat

21 to 30 grams of carbs

country italian beef stew

When the cold wind blows, warm the appetites at your table with this bold beef stew! Here, fennel and parsnips offer a tantalizing change of pace from celery and carrots.

Prep: 25 minutes Cook: 8 to 10 hours (low) or 4 to 5 hours (high), plus 15 minutes (high) Makes: 6 servings

2	pounds boneless beef chuck pot roast
3	medium parsnips, cut into 1-inch pieces
2	cups chopped onions (2 large)
1	medium fennel bulb, trimmed and coarsely chopped (1 cup)
1	teaspoon dried rosemary, crushed
1	cup dry red wine or reduced-sodium beef broth
3/4	cup reduced-sodium beef broth
1	6-ounce can tomato paste
1	teaspoon salt
1	teaspoon finely shredded orange peel
1/2	teaspoon black pepper
4	cloves garlic, minced
2	tablespoons cornstarch
2	tablespoons cold water
3	cups torn fresh spinach

1 Trim fat from meat. Cut meat into 2-inch pieces. Set aside. In a 3½- or 4-quart slow cooker place parsnips, onions, and fennel. Add meat; sprinkle with rosemary. In a medium bowl combine wine, beef broth, tomato paste, salt, orange peel, pepper, and garlic. Pour over mixture in cooker.

2 Cover and cook on low-heat setting for 8 to 10 hours or on high-heat setting for 4 to 5 hours.

3 If using low-heat setting, turn to high-heat setting. In a small bowl combine cornstarch and water. Stir into meat mixture. Cover and cook about 15 minutes more or until thickened. Just before serving, stir in spinach.

Nutrition Facts per serving: 324 cal., 6 g total fat (2 g sat. fat), 89 mg chol., 290 mg sodium, 25 g carbo., 5 g fiber, 36 g pro.
Daily Values: 28% vit. A, 36% vit. C, 7% calcium, 30% iron
Exchanges: 3 Vegetable, ½ Starch, 4 Lean Meat

21 to 30 grams of carbs

beef and brats

The addition of spicy bratwurst brings a new flavor dimension to this American classic.

Prep: 25 minutes Cook: 8 to 10 hours (low) or 4 to 5 hours (high) Makes: 4 servings

1	pound boneless beef round steak, cut 1 inch thick
8	ounces uncooked turkey bratwurst, cut into ³/₄-inch slices
1	tablespoon cooking oil
1	large onion, sliced and separated into rings
1	cup coarsely chopped green, red, or yellow sweet pepper (1 large)
1	teaspoon dried thyme, crushed
¹/₈	teaspoon salt
¹/₈	teaspoon black pepper
2	14¹/₂-ounce cans no-salt-added diced tomatoes, undrained
2	tablespoons quick-cooking tapioca

---

1 Trim fat from meat. Cut meat into 4 serving-size pieces. In a large skillet cook meat and bratwurst in hot oil over medium heat until brown on all sides. Drain off fat. Set aside.

2 In a 3½- or 4-quart slow cooker place onion and sweet pepper. Sprinkle with thyme, salt, and pepper. Add undrained tomatoes and tapioca. Add meat and bratwurst.

3 Cover and cook on low-heat setting for 8 to 10 hours or on high-heat setting for 4 to 5 hours.

Nutrition Facts per serving: 348 cal., 12 g total fat (3 g sat. fat), 99 mg chol.,
703 mg sodium, 21 g carbo., 5 g fiber, 38 g pro.
Daily Values: 4% vit. A, 291% vit. C, 5% calcium, 18% iron
Exchanges: 2 Vegetable, ½ Other Carbo., 5 Very Lean Meat, 2 Fat

21 to 30 grams of carbs

north african beef stew

Cumin, cayenne, cinnamon, and dried fruits give this stew its interesting North African appeal. The serve-along? Couscous, of course—a quintessential Moroccan staple.

Prep: 20 minutes Cook: 7½ to 8½ hours (low) or 3½ to 4 hours (high), plus 30 minutes (high) Makes: 6 servings

1½	pounds lean beef stew meat
2	medium sweet potatoes, peeled, halved lengthwise, and cut into ½-inch slices
1	medium onion, cut into wedges
1	cup water
1	teaspoon instant beef bouillon granules
¾	teaspoon ground cumin
¼	teaspoon cayenne pepper
⅛	teaspoon ground cinnamon
4	cloves garlic, minced
1	14½-ounce can diced tomatoes, undrained
½	cup dried apricots or pitted dried plums (prunes), quartered
	Hot cooked couscous (optional)
¼	cup chopped peanuts

---

1 Cut meat into 1-inch pieces. In a 3½- or 4-quart slow cooker combine meat, sweet potatoes, and onion. Stir in water, bouillon granules, cumin, cayenne pepper, cinnamon, and garlic.

2 Cover and cook on low-heat setting for 7½ to 8½ hours or on high-heat setting for 3½ to 4 hours.

3 If using low-heat setting, turn to high-heat setting. Stir in undrained tomatoes and dried apricots. Cover and cook for 30 minutes more.

4 If desired, serve meat mixture over hot cooked couscous. Sprinkle each serving with peanuts.

Nutrition Facts per serving: 263 cal., 7 g total fat (2 g sat. fat), 67 mg chol., 366 mg sodium, 21 g carbo., 3 g fiber, 27 g pro.
Daily Values: 116% vit. A, 29% vit. C, 7% calcium, 21% iron
Exchanges: 1 Vegetable, 1 Starch, 3 Lean Meat

21 to 30 grams of carbs

hawaiian pork

Did you know you'll get more juice out of fresh lemons if they're squeezed at room temperature? Take them out of the fridge and let them sit on the counter before juicing.

Prep: 30 minutes Cook: 8 to 10 hours (low) or 4 to 5 hours (high), plus 15 minutes (high) Makes: 6 servings

2	pounds boneless pork shoulder roast
1/2	teaspoon salt
1/4	teaspoon black pepper
	Nonstick cooking spray
1	tablespoon cooking oil
1	20-ounce can pineapple tidbits (juice pack), undrained
1	large onion, cut into thick wedges
2	tablespoons grated fresh ginger
1	tablespoon lemon juice
1/2	teaspoon crushed red pepper
2	tablespoons cornstarch
2	tablespoons cold water
2	medium red sweet peppers, cut into bite-sized pieces

1 Trim fat from meat. Cut meat into 1½-inch pieces. Sprinkle meat with salt and black pepper. Lightly coat a large skillet with cooking spray. Cook half of the meat in hot skillet over medium-high heat until brown. Transfer to a 3½- or 4-quart slow cooker. Add cooking oil to skillet. Cook remaining meat in hot oil until brown. Drain off fat. Add meat to cooker. Stir undrained pineapple, onion, ginger, lemon juice, and crushed red pepper into meat in cooker.

2 Cover and cook on low-heat setting for 8 to 10 hours or on high-heat setting for 4 to 5 hours.

3 If using low-heat setting, turn to high-heat setting. In a small bowl combine cornstarch and water. Stir cornstarch mixture and sweet peppers into mixture in cooker. Cover and cook for 15 to 30 minutes more or until sweet peppers are crisp-tender, stirring once.

Nutrition Facts per serving: 319 cal., 11 g total fat (3 g sat. fat), 98 mg chol., 321 mg sodium, 23 g carbo., 2 g fiber, 31 g pro.
Daily Values: 26% vit. A, 147% vit. C, 3% calcium, 13% iron
Exchanges: 1½ Vegetable, 1 Fruit, 4 Lean Meat

21 to 30 grams of carbs

cuban pork tortilla roll-ups

Caramba! Shredded tender pork and onions stuff these tortilla wraps. For even more Caribbean flavor, spoon on Pico de Gallo Salsa (see recipe, page 190).

Prep: 25 minutes Marinate: 6 to 24 hours Cook: 10 to 12 hours (low) or 5 to 6 hours (high) Makes: 8 sandwiches

1/2	cup lime juice
1/4	cup grapefruit juice
1/4	cup water
2	bay leaves
1	teaspoon dried oregano, crushed
1/2	teaspoon salt
1/2	teaspoon ground cumin
1/4	teaspoon black pepper
3	cloves garlic, minced
1	2 1/2- to 3-pound boneless pork shoulder roast
1	large onion, sliced
	Shredded lettuce (optional)
	Chopped tomato (optional)
8	9- to 10-inch whole wheat or low-fat flour tortillas

1 For marinade, in a small bowl combine lime juice, grapefruit juice, water, bay leaves, oregano, salt, cumin, pepper, and garlic. Trim fat from meat. If necessary, cut meat to fit into a 3 1/2- to 5-quart slow cooker. Using a large fork, pierce meat in several places. Place meat in a resealable plastic bag set in a shallow dish. Pour marinade over meat; seal bag. Marinate in the refrigerator for 6 to 24 hours, turning bag occasionally.

2 Place onion in cooker. Add meat and marinade. Cover and cook on low-heat setting for 10 to 12 hours or on high-heat setting for 5 to 6 hours.

3 Remove meat and onion from cooker, reserving cooking liquid. Using two forks, pull meat apart into shreds. Skim fat from liquid. Remove and discard bay leaves.

4 Serve meat, onion, and if desired, lettuce and tomato in tortillas with small bowls of the hot cooking liquid.

Nutrition Facts per sandwich: 354 cal., 11 g total fat (3 g sat. fat), 92 mg chol., 643 mg sodium, 30 g carbo., 3 g fiber, 32 g pro.
Daily Values: 1% vit. A, 17% vit. C, 4% calcium, 17% iron
Exchanges: 2 Starch, 3 1/2 Lean Meat

21 to 30 grams of carbs

pork ribs and beans

When food lovers use terms like "rustic," "hearty peasant fare," and "country French," this dish is the type of simple, honest, and nourishing fare they often have in mind.

Prep: 20 minutes Cook: 8 to 9 hours (low) or 4 to 4½ hours (high) Makes: 6 servings

2½	pounds boneless pork country-style ribs
¾	teaspoon dried rosemary, crushed
¼	teaspoon salt
¼	teaspoon black pepper
½	cup chopped onion (1 medium)
1	15- or 19-ounce can white kidney (cannellini) beans, rinsed and drained
1	15-ounce can black beans, rinsed and drained
1	14½-ounce can diced tomatoes with basil, garlic, and oregano; undrained
¼	cup dry red wine
¼	cup shredded Parmesan cheese (optional)

1 Trim fat from meat. Sprinkle ribs with rosemary, salt, and pepper. Place ribs in a 4- to 5-quart slow cooker. Top with onion, beans, and undrained tomatoes. Add wine.

2 Cover and cook on low-heat setting for 8 to 9 hours or on high-heat setting for 4 to 4½ hours.

3 Using a slotted spoon, transfer ribs and bean mixture to a serving platter. Spoon some of the cooking liquid over meat and beans. If desired, sprinkle with Parmesan cheese.

Nutrition Facts per serving: 289 cal., 9 g total fat (3 g sat. fat), 67 mg chol., 759 mg sodium, 27 g carbo., 7 g fiber, 30 g pro.
Daily Values: 8% vit. A, 11% vit. C, 11% calcium, 21% iron
Exchanges: 1 Vegetable, 1½ Starch, 3 Lean Meat

21 to 30 grams of carbs

hot pepper pork sandwiches

Mexican seasonings add a twist and a kick to this favorite Southern pulled-pork sandwich. Want to turn up the heat even more? Leave the pepper seeds intact.

Prep: 20 minutes Cook: 11 to 12 hours (low) or 5½ to 6 hours (high) Makes: 8 sandwiches

1	2½- to 3-pound boneless pork shoulder roast
2	teaspoons fajita seasoning
1	or 2 fresh jalapeño peppers, seeded, if desired, and finely chopped* or 1 large green or red sweet pepper, seeded and cut into bite-size strips
2	10-ounce cans enchilada sauce
8	whole grain hamburger buns or kaiser rolls, split and toasted

---

1 Trim fat from meat. If necessary, cut roast to fit into a 3½- or 4-quart slow cooker. Place meat in the cooker. Sprinkle meat with fajita seasoning. Add peppers and enchilada sauce.

2 Cover and cook on low-heat setting for 11 to 12 hours or on high-heat setting for 5½ to 6 hours. Transfer roast to a cutting board. Using two forks, shred meat. Stir shredded meat into juices in slow cooker. Using a slotted spoon, spoon shredded meat mixture into toasted buns.

*Note: Because chile peppers, such as jalapeños, contain volatile oils that can burn your skin and eyes, avoid direct contact with them as much as possible. When working with chile peppers, wear plastic or rubber gloves. If your bare hands do touch the chile peppers, wash your hands well with soap and warm water.

Nutrition Facts per sandwich: 262 cal., 9 g total fat (3 g sat. fat), 58 mg chol., 778 mg sodium, 23 g carbo., 3 g fiber, 22 g pro.
Daily Values: 4% vit. A, 6% vit. C, 7% calcium, 18% iron
Exchanges: 1½ Starch, 2½ Lean Meat

21 to 30 grams of carbs

spicy pork and vegetable soup

This sophisticated and tasty soup is packed full of winter vegetables. Fresh spinach added prior to serving adds a touch of color and a boost of nutrition.

Prep: 30 minutes Cook: 10 to 11 hours (low) or 5 to 5½ hours (high) Makes: 6 servings

1	pound lean pork or beef stew meat
1	tablespoon cooking oil
½	cup chopped onion (1 medium)
1	teaspoon paprika
2	cloves garlic, minced
3	cups water
8	ounces winter squash, peeled and cut into ½-inch pieces
3	medium parsnips or carrots, cut into ¼-inch slices (1½ cups)
1	medium sweet potato, peeled and cut into ½-inch pieces
1	8¾-ounce can whole kernel corn, undrained
4	teaspoons instant beef bouillon granules
½	teaspoon salt
¼	teaspoon cayenne pepper
2	cups torn fresh spinach

1 Cut meat into ½-inch pieces. In a large nonstick skillet cook half of the meat in hot oil over medium heat until brown. Transfer meat to a 3½- or 4-quart slow cooker. Add the remaining meat, the onion, paprika, and garlic to skillet. Cook until meat is brown and onion is tender. Drain off fat. Transfer meat mixture to cooker.

2 Stir water, squash, parsnips, sweet potato, corn, bouillon granules, salt, and cayenne pepper into meat mixture in cooker. Cover and cook on low-heat setting for 10 to 11 hours or on high-heat setting for 5 to 5½ hours. Just before serving, stir in spinach.

Nutrition Facts per serving: 231 cal., 7 g total fat (2 g sat. fat), 41 mg chol., 729 mg sodium, 22 g carbo., 4 g fiber, 19 g pro.
Daily Values: 103% vit. A, 29% vit. C, 5% calcium, 8% iron
Exchanges: 1½ Starch, 2 Lean Meat

21 to 30 grams of carbs

green beans, ham, and lentil soup

This soup is flavored with marjoram, which is similar to oregano, but milder in flavor. In a pinch, substitute oregano, but use a little less.

Prep: 15 minutes Cook: 8 to 10 hours (low) or 4 to 5 hours (high) Makes: 6 servings

1¼	cups dry lentils
2	14-ounce cans reduced-sodium chicken broth
2	cups cubed reduced-sodium cooked ham
1	cup chopped carrots (2 medium)
1	9-ounce package frozen cut green beans
1	cup frozen small whole onions
1	cup water
1	teaspoon dried thyme, crushed
½	teaspoon dried marjoram, crushed

1 Rinse and drain lentils. In a 3½- or 4-quart slow cooker combine lentils, chicken broth, ham, carrots, frozen green beans, onions, water, thyme, and marjoram.

2 Cover and cook on low-heat setting for 8 to 10 hours or on high-heat setting for 4 to 5 hours.

Nutrition Facts per serving: 223 cal., 2 g total fat (1 g sat. fat), 20 mg chol., 860 mg sodium, 30 g carbo., 15 g fiber, 22 g pro.
Daily Values: 47% vit. A, 29% vit. C, 7% calcium, 22% iron
Exchanges: 1½ Vegetable, 1½ Starch, 2 Very Lean Meat

21 to 30 grams of carbs

braised lamb with dill sauce

Enjoy tender lamb, tiny new potatoes, and colorful carrots all draped in a creamy dill sauce.

Prep: 20 minutes Cook: 8 to 10 hours (low) or 4 to 5 hours (high) Makes: 6 servings

1½	**pounds tiny new potatoes**
5	**medium carrots, cut into 1-inch pieces**
2	**pounds lean boneless lamb**
1¼	**cups water**
1	**tablespoon snipped fresh dill or 1 teaspoon dried dill, crushed**
½	**teaspoon salt**
¼	**teaspoon black pepper**
½	**cup plain low-fat yogurt**
2	**tablespoons all-purpose flour**

---

1 Remove a narrow strip of peel from center of each new potato. In a 3½- or 4-quart slow cooker place potatoes and carrots. Trim fat from meat. Cut meat into 1-inch pieces. Add meat and water to cooker. Sprinkle with 2 teaspoons fresh or ½ teaspoon dried dill, salt, and pepper.

2 Cover and cook on low-heat setting for 8 to 10 hours or on high-heat setting for 4 to 5 hours. Remove meat and vegetables from cooker, reserving cooking liquid. Cover meat and vegetables and keep warm.

3 For sauce, pour cooking liquid into a glass measuring cup; skim off fat. Measure 1 cup liquid. In a small saucepan combine yogurt and flour. Stir in 1 cup liquid and remaining 1 teaspoon fresh or ½ teaspoon dried dill. Cook and stir over medium heat until thickened and bubbly. Cook and stir for 1 minute more. Season to taste with additional salt and black pepper. Serve meat and vegetables with sauce.

Nutrition Facts per serving: 303 cal., 5 g total fat (2 g sat. fat), 96 mg chol., 327 mg sodium, 27 g carbo., 3 g fiber, 35 g pro.
Daily Values: 256% vit. A, 34% vit. C, 8% calcium, 26% iron
Exchanges: ½ Vegetable, 1½ Starch, 4 Very Lean Meat, 1 Fat

21 to 30 grams of carbs

brunswick-style slow cooker stew

Early Virginia settlers prepared this hearty stew with squirrel meat over an open fire. This updated version features chicken and ham and simmers all day in a slow cooker.

Prep: 20 minutes Cook: 8 to 10 hours (low) or 4 to 5 hours (high), plus 45 minutes (high) Makes: 6 servings

3	medium onions, cut into thin wedges
2	pounds meaty chicken pieces (breast halves, thighs, and drumsticks), skinned
1½	cups chopped reduced-sodium cooked ham (8 ounces)
1	teaspoon dry mustard
1	teaspoon dried thyme, crushed
¼	teaspoon black pepper
1	14½-ounce can diced tomatoes, undrained
1	14-ounce can reduced-sodium chicken broth
4	cloves garlic, minced
1	tablespoon Worcestershire sauce
¼	teaspoon bottled hot pepper sauce
1	10-ounce package frozen sliced okra
1	cup frozen baby lima beans
1	cup frozen whole kernel corn

1 Place onions in a 3½- to 5-quart slow cooker. Add chicken and ham. Sprinkle with mustard, thyme, and pepper. Add undrained tomatoes, chicken broth, garlic, Worcestershire sauce, and hot pepper sauce.

2 Cover and cook on low-heat setting for 8 to 10 hours or on high-heat setting for 4 to 5 hours.

3 Remove chicken from cooker. Replace lid on cooker. When chicken is cool enough to handle, remove chicken from bones. Cut chicken into bite-size pieces. Return chicken to cooker.

4 If using low-heat setting, turn to high-heat setting. Add okra, lima beans, and corn to mixture in cooker. Cover and cook about 45 minutes more or until vegetables are tender.

Nutrition Facts per serving: 270 cal., 6 g total fat (2 g sat. fat), 72 mg chol., 762 mg sodium, 25 g carbo., 5 g fiber, 29 g pro.
Daily Values: 4% vit. A, 31% vit. C, 10% calcium, 15% iron
Exchanges: 2 Vegetable, 1 Starch, 3 Lean Meat

21 to 30 grams of carbs

easy italian chicken

An easy-to-make dinner, this chicken dish goes together in just 10 minutes.

Prep: 15 minutes Cook: 4 to 5 hours (low) or 2 to 2½ hours (high),
plus 15 minutes (high) Makes: 4 to 6 servings

½	**of a medium head cabbage, cut into wedges (about 12 ounces)**
1	**large onion, sliced and separated into rings**
4	**to 6 chicken breast halves, skinned**
½	**teaspoon dried Italian seasoning, crushed**
2	**cups bottled light spaghetti sauce**
2	**tablespoons cornstarch**
2	**tablespoons cold water**
	Grated Parmesan cheese (optional)

1 In a 4½- to 6-quart slow cooker place cabbage and onion. Add chicken. Sprinkle with Italian seasoning. Pour spaghetti sauce over all.

2 Cover and cook on low-heat setting for 4 to 5 hours or on high-heat setting for 2 to 2½ hours.

3 Transfer chicken to a serving platter, reserving sauce. Cover chicken with foil to keep warm.

4 If using low-heat setting, turn to high-heat setting. In a small bowl combine cornstarch and water. Stir into sauce in cooker. Cover and cook about 15 minutes more or until thickened. Spoon sauce over chicken. If desired, sprinkle with Parmesan cheese.

Nutrition Facts per serving: 310 cal., 2 g total fat (1 g sat. fat), 107 mg chol.,
510 mg sodium, 25 g carbo., 5 g fiber, 46 g pro.
Daily Values: 9% vit. A, 58% vit. C, 8% calcium, 14% iron
Exchanges: 1 Vegetable, 1 Other Carbo., 5½ Very Lean Meat

21 to 30 grams of carbs

mexican chicken soup

Chicken soup travels south of the border here, and it's packing plenty of flavor. Black beans and crushed tortilla chips provide color and crunch.

Prep: 20 minutes Cook: 4 to 6 hours (low) or 2 to 3 hours (high) Makes: 6 servings (8 cups)

1¼	pounds skinless, boneless chicken thighs or breast halves
	Nonstick cooking spray
2	10¾-ounce cans reduced-fat and reduced-sodium condensed cream of chicken soup
2	cups water
1	15-ounce can black beans, rinsed and drained
1	14½-ounce can diced tomatoes and green chile peppers, undrained
1	teaspoon ground cumin
	Light dairy sour cream (optional)
	Crushed tortilla chips (optional)

1 Cut chicken into ½- to ¾-inch pieces. Lightly coat a large skillet with cooking spray. In hot skillet cook chicken, half at a time, over medium heat until brown. Place cooked chicken in a 3½- or 4-quart slow cooker.

2 In a medium bowl combine chicken soup, water, beans, undrained tomatoes, and cumin. Pour over chicken in cooker.

3 Cover and cook on low-heat setting for 4 to 6 hours or on high-heat setting for 2 to 3 hours. If desired, top each serving with sour cream and sprinkle with crushed tortilla chips.

Nutrition Facts per serving: 238 cal., 6 g total fat (2 g sat. fat), 84 mg chol., 893 mg sodium, 23 g carbo., 5 g fiber, 26 g pro.
Daily Values: 17% vit. A, 17% vit. C, 5% calcium, 12% iron
Exchanges: ½ Vegetable, 1 Starch, 3 Very Lean Meat, 1 Fat

21 to 30 grams of carbs

deviled chicken and vegetable soup

Deviled refers to a food that is seasoned with piquant ingredients such as red pepper, hot pepper sauce, or as in this dish, mustard. Add more or less to your liking.

Prep: 20 minutes Cook: 8 to 10 hours (low) or 4 to 5 hours (high) Makes: 6 servings

1	pound skinless, boneless chicken thighs
1½	cups frozen whole kernel corn
¾	cup chopped red-skinned potato (1 large)
½	cup chopped onion (1 medium)
½	cup chopped celery (1 stalk)
3	tablespoons Dijon-style mustard
¼	teaspoon black pepper
⅛	teaspoon garlic powder
2½	cups vegetable juice
1	14-ounce can reduced-sodium chicken broth

1 Cut chicken into bite-size pieces. In a 3½- or 4-quart slow cooker combine chicken, corn, potato, onion, celery, mustard, pepper, and garlic powder. Pour vegetable juice and chicken broth over mixture in cooker.

2 Cover and cook on low-heat setting for 8 to 10 hours or on high-heat setting for 4 to 5 hours.

Nutrition Facts per serving: 187 cal., 3 g total fat (1 g sat. fat), 60 mg chol., 672 mg sodium, 21 g carbo., 3 g fiber, 20 g pro.
Daily Values: 35% vit. A, 63% vit. C, 4% calcium, 11% iron
Exchanges: 1 Vegetable, 1 Starch, 2 Very Lean Meat

southwestern chicken stew

Meaty chicken thighs, pinto beans, fire-roasted tomatoes, green chiles, and a perfect blend of seasonings simmer all day for a stew that's all about flavor.

Prep: 15 minutes Cook: 5 to 6 hours (low) or 2½ to 3 hours (high) Makes: 5 servings (5 cups)

1	pound skinless, boneless chicken thighs
1	15-ounce can pinto beans, rinsed and drained
1	14½-ounce can diced fire-roasted tomatoes, undrained
½	cup chopped onion (1 medium)
1	4½-ounce can diced green chile peppers, drained
2	teaspoons ground cumin
1	teaspoon dried oregano, crushed
2	cloves garlic, minced
¼	teaspoon black pepper
⅓	cup light dairy sour cream
¼	cup snipped fresh cilantro

1 Cut chicken into 1-inch strips. In a 3½- or 4-quart slow cooker combine chicken, beans, undrained tomatoes, onion, chile peppers, cumin, oregano, garlic, and pepper.

2 Cover and cook on low-heat setting for 5 to 6 hours or on high-heat setting for 2½ to 3 hours. Top each serving with sour cream and cilantro.

Nutrition Facts per serving: 262 cal., 8 g total fat (2 g sat. fat), 78 mg chol., 791 mg sodium, 23 g carbo., 5 g fiber, 26 g pro.
Daily Values: 15% vit. A, 79% vit. C, 24% calcium, 19% iron
Exchanges: 1½ Vegetable, 1 Starch, 3 Lean Meat

21 to 30 grams of carbs

chicken tostadas

This is a Tex-Mex take on a one-dish meal, as everything—bread, chicken, beans, and salad—all stack up on one plate. Customize this with your own favorite version of salsa.

Prep: 25 minutes Cook: 5 to 6 hours (low) or 2½ to 3 hours (high) Makes: 10 tostadas

2	jalapeño chile peppers, seeded and finely chopped*
8	cloves garlic, minced
3	tablespoons chili powder
3	tablespoons lime juice
¼	teaspoon bottled hot pepper sauce
1	medium onion, sliced and separated into rings
2	pounds skinless, boneless chicken thighs
1	16-ounce can fat-free refried beans
10	purchased tostada shells
1½	cups shredded reduced-fat cheddar cheese (6 ounces)
2	cups shredded lettuce
1¼	cups bottled salsa
¾	cup light dairy sour cream
¾	cup sliced ripe olives (optional)

1 In a 3 ½- to 5-quart slow cooker combine jalapeño peppers, garlic, chili powder, lime juice, and hot pepper sauce. Add onion and chicken.

2 Cover and cook on low-heat setting for 5 to 6 hours or on high-heat setting for 2½ to 3 hours.

3 Remove chicken and onions from cooker, reserving ½ cup of the cooking liquid. Using two forks, pull chicken apart into shreds. In a medium bowl combine chicken, onions, and the reserved ½ cup liquid.

4 Spread refried beans on tostada shells. Top with hot chicken mixture and shredded cheese. Serve with lettuce, salsa, sour cream, and if desired, olives.

*Note: Because hot chile peppers, such as jalapeños, contain volatile oils that can burn your skin and eyes, avoid direct contact with chiles as much as possible. When working with chile peppers, wear plastic or rubber gloves. If your bare hands do touch the chile peppers, wash your hands well with soap and water.

Nutrition Facts per tostada: 317 cal., 11 g total fat (4 g sat. fat), 90 mg chol., 560 mg sodium, 23 g carbo., 5 g fiber, 28 g pro.
Daily Values: 33% vit. A, 21% vit. C, 23% calcium, 12% iron
Exchanges: 1½ Starch, 3½ Lean Meat

21 to 30 grams of carbs

bean soup with chicken and vegetables

Fennel adds a subtle licorice flavor to this dish. The good, hearty soup makes a complete meal with some whole-grain bread.

Prep: 30 minutes Stand: 1 hour Cook: 8 to 10 hours (low) or 4 to 5 hours (high), plus 30 minutes (high) Makes: 8 servings

1	cup dry Great Northern beans
1	cup chopped onion (1 large)
1	cup chopped carrots (2 medium)
1	medium fennel bulb, trimmed and cut into ½-inch pieces
2	cloves garlic, minced
1	teaspoon dried thyme, crushed
1	teaspoon dried marjoram, crushed
¼	teaspoon black pepper
3	14-ounce cans reduced-sodium chicken broth
2½	cups chopped, cooked chicken (about 12 ounces)
1	14½-ounce can diced tomatoes, undrained
2	tablespoons snipped fresh parsley

1 Rinse the beans. In a large saucepan or Dutch oven combine beans and enough water to cover beans by 2 inches. Bring to boiling; reduce heat. Simmer, uncovered, for 10 minutes. Remove from heat. Cover and let stand for 1 hour. Drain and rinse beans.

2 Meanwhile, in a 4- to 5-quart slow cooker combine onion, carrots, fennel, garlic, thyme, marjoram, and pepper. Place beans on top of vegetables in cooker. Add chicken broth.

3 Cover and cook on low-heat setting for 8 to 10 hours or on high-heat setting for 4 to 5 hours.

4 If using low-heat setting, turn to high-heat setting. Stir in chicken and undrained tomatoes. Cover and cook about 30 minutes more or until heated through. Stir in parsley.

Nutrition Facts per serving: 205 cal., 4 g total fat (1 g sat. fat), 39 mg chol., 499 mg sodium, 22 g carbo., 6 g fiber, 20 g pro.
Daily Values: 36% vit. A, 19% vit. C, 9% calcium, 12% iron
Exchanges: 1½ Vegetable, 1 Starch, 2 Very Lean Meat

21 to 30 grams of carbs

indian vegetable soup

Chock-full of nutty garbanzo beans, red-skin potatoes, and chunks of eggplant, this curried soup makes a hearty meal.

Prep: 30 minutes Cook: 8 to 10 hours (low) or 4 to 5 hours (high) Makes: 6 to 8 servings

1	medium eggplant, cut into $\frac{1}{2}$-inch cubes (5 to 6 cups)
1	pound red-skinned potatoes, cut into 1-inch pieces (3 cups)
2	cups chopped tomatoes or one 14$\frac{1}{2}$-ounce can no-salt-added tomatoes, undrained and cut up
1	15-ounce can garbanzo beans (chickpeas), rinsed and drained
1	tablespoon grated fresh ginger
1$\frac{1}{2}$	teaspoons mustard seeds
1$\frac{1}{2}$	teaspoons ground coriander
1	teaspoon curry powder
$\frac{1}{4}$	teaspoon black pepper
4	cups vegetable broth or chicken broth
2	tablespoons snipped fresh cilantro

1 In a 4- to 6-quart slow cooker combine eggplant, potatoes, undrained tomatoes, and garbanzo beans. Sprinkle vegetables with ginger, mustard seeds, coriander, curry powder, and pepper. Pour broth over all.

2 Cover and cook on low-heat setting for 8 to 10 hours or on high-heat setting for 4 to 5 hours. Ladle into bowls and sprinkle with cilantro.

Nutrition Facts per serving: 162 cal., 2 g total fat (0 g sat. fat), 0 mg chol., 889 mg sodium, 30 g carbo., 7 g fiber, 8 g pro.
Daily Values: 7% vit. A, 33% vit. C, 4% calcium, 10% iron
Exchanges: 1$\frac{1}{2}$ Vegetable, 1$\frac{1}{2}$ Starch

21 to 30 grams of carbs

ratatouille soup with beans

Ratatouille is a saucy mix of garden vegetables that originated in the South of France. It makes a great base for this super-pleasing soup.

Prep: 20 minutes Cook: 8 to 10 hours (low) or 4 to 5 hours (high) Makes: 6 side-dish servings (8 cups)

1/2	cup coarsely chopped onion (1 medium)
2	cups peeled eggplant cut into 3/4-inch cubes
2	medium zucchini, halved lengthwise and cut into 1/4-inch slices (2 1/2 cups)
3/4	cup coarsely chopped red sweet pepper (1 medium)
3/4	cup coarsely chopped green sweet pepper (1 medium)
1	15- to 19-ounce can white kidney (cannellini) or Great Northern beans, rinsed and drained
1	14 1/2-ounce can diced tomatoes with basil, oregano, and garlic; undrained
1	14-ounce can reduced-sodium chicken broth
1	cup reduced-sodium vegetable juice
1	2 1/4-ounce can sliced, pitted ripe olives, drained
6	tablespoons shredded Parmesan cheese (optional)

---

1 In a 3 1/2- or 4-quart slow cooker layer in the following order: onion, eggplant, zucchini, sweet peppers, and beans. Pour undrained tomatoes, chicken broth, and vegetable juice over mixture in cooker.

2 Cover and cook on low-heat setting for 8 to 10 hours or on high-heat setting for 4 to 5 hours. Stir in olives. If desired, sprinkle each serving with Parmesan cheese.

Nutrition Facts per serving: 148 cal., 3 g total fat (1 g sat. fat), 6 mg chol., 945 mg sodium, 25 g carbo., 6 g fiber, 10 g pro.
Daily Values: 43% vit. A, 101% vit. C, 15% calcium, 15% iron
Exchanges: 2 Vegetable, 1 Starch, 1/2 Very Lean Meat

21 to 30 grams of carbs

broccoli and corn with bacon

Serve this saucy side dish with grilled or broiled pork chops.

Prep: 25 minutes Cook: 5 to 6 hours (low) or 2½ to 3 hours (high) Makes: 8 side-dish servings

	Nonstick cooking spray
1	16-ounce package frozen cut broccoli
1	16-ounce package frozen corn
1	10¾-ounce can reduced-fat and reduced-sodium condensed cream of chicken soup
1	cup chopped red sweet pepper (1 large)
4	slices low-fat process American cheese, torn into small pieces (4 ounces)
⅓	cup sliced green onions
¼	cup low-fat evaporated milk
¼	teaspoon black pepper
2	tablespoons crumbled crisp-cooked reduced-sodium bacon

1 Lightly coat the inside of a 4- to 5-quart slow cooker with cooking spray. In the prepared slow cooker combine broccoli, corn, chicken soup, sweet pepper, cheese, onions, milk, and black pepper.

2 Cover and cook on low-heat setting for 5 to 6 hours or on high-heat setting for 2½ to 3 hours. Sprinkle with bacon before serving.

Nutrition Facts per serving: 143 cal., 4 g total fat (2 g sat. fat), 14 mg chol., 371 mg sodium, 21 g carbo., 3 g fiber, 8 g pro.
Daily Values: 35% vit. A, 97% vit. C, 18% calcium, 4% iron
Exchanges: 1 Vegetable, 1 Starch, ½ Medium-Fat Meat

21 to 30 grams of carbs

chapter six

Bonus
recipes

chile chicken appetizers

Look for Thai garlic-chile sauce in the Asian foods section of your supermarket or in specialty food shops.

Start to Finish: 15 minutes Makes: 8 servings

4	medium nectarines or peaches
1/2	cup shredded cooked chicken (about 3 ounces)
2	teaspoons snipped fresh cilantro
2	teaspoons bottled Thai garlic-chile sauce or chile sauce

1 Cut nectarines into quarters; remove pits. Carefully scoop out some of the fruit, leaving ¼-inch shells. Chop the scooped-out fruit.

2 In a medium bowl combine chopped nectarines, chicken, cilantro, and chile sauce. Spoon chicken mixture evenly into nectarine shells.

Nutrition Facts per serving: 52 cal., 1 g total fat (0 g sat. fat), 9 mg chol., 26 mg sodium, 8 g carbo., 1 g fiber, 4 g pro.
Daily Values: 5% vit. A, 7% vit. C, 1% calcium, 2% iron
Exchanges: ½ Fruit, ½ Lean Meat

endive leaves with artichoke caviar

Reserve the marinade from the artichoke hearts to infuse the zucchini, tomato, and green onion with tangy flavor.

Prep: 15 minutes   Marinate: 2 to 6 hours   Makes: about 36 appetizers

1	6-ounce jar marinated artichoke hearts
1/2	cup finely chopped zucchini
1/2	cup finely chopped peeled seeded tomato (1 medium)
2	tablespoons chopped green onion (1)
2	tablespoons snipped fresh basil or 1 teaspoon dried basil, crushed
2	cloves garlic, minced
1	teaspoon lemon juice
3	heads Belgian endive

1 Drain artichokes, reserving marinade (to yield about 1/3 cup). Finely chop artichokes.

2 In a medium bowl combine artichokes, zucchini, tomato, and green onion. In a small bowl whisk together the reserved artichoke marinade, the basil, garlic, and lemon juice. Pour over artichoke mixture; toss gently to coat. Cover and chill for 2 to 6 hours, stirring occasionally.

3 To serve, remove cores from Belgian endives. Separate endives into leaves. Drain artichoke mixture. Spoon about 2 teaspoons of the artichoke mixture onto each leaf.

Nutrition Facts per appetizer: 6 cal., 15 mg sodium, 1 g carbo.
Daily Values: 1% vit. A, 4% vit. C
Exchanges: Free

bonus recipes

chunky guacamole

Guacamole is a party favorite any time of year. Lime juice keeps the avocados green and provides a zesty zing.

Start to Finish: 20 minutes Makes: 16 (2-tablespoon) servings

2	medium roma tomatoes, seeded and cut up
¼	cup coarsely chopped red onion
1	to 2 tablespoons lime juice
1	tablespoon olive oil
¼	teaspoon salt
⅛	teaspoon black pepper
1	to 2 cloves garlic, halved
2	ripe avocados, halved, seeded, peeled, and cut up
	Chopped roma tomato (optional)
	Tortilla chips

1 In a food processor combine the 2 cut-up tomatoes, red onion, lime juice, olive oil, salt, pepper, and garlic. Cover and process until mixture is coarsely chopped. Add the avocados. Cover and process just until mixture is chopped. Transfer to a serving bowl. If desired, cover surface with plastic wrap and chill for up to 1 hour. If desired, garnish with additional chopped tomato. Serve with chips.

Nutrition Facts per 2 tablespoons dip: 48 cal., 5 g total fat (1 g sat. fat), 0 mg chol., 40 mg sodium, 2 g carbo., 1 g fiber, 1 g pro.
Daily Values: 4% vit. A, 7% vit. C, 2% iron
Exchanges: 1 Fat

greek-style party pizzettas

You'll find both plain and flavored hummus in the refrigerator case of your supermarket.

Prep: 15 minutes Bake: 9 minutes Oven: 425°F Makes: 16 appetizers

4	7- to 8-inch multigrain or whole wheat flour tortillas
1/2	of a 7-ounce container hummus (about 1/3 cup)
1/2	cup bottled roasted red sweet peppers, drained and chopped
1/2	cup crumbled feta cheese (2 ounces)
1/2	cup shredded mozzarella cheese (2 ounces)
8	pitted kalamata olives, halved
1	teaspoon snipped fresh oregano

1 Arrange tortillas in a single layer on a very large baking sheet. Bake in a 425° oven for 3 to 4 minutes or until crisp.

2 Spread hummus over tortillas; top with roasted red peppers, feta cheese, and mozzarella cheese. Bake about 6 minutes more or until cheese is melted and edges are lightly browned. Sprinkle with olives and oregano. Cut each pizzetta into quarters.

Nutrition Facts per appetizer: 69 cal., 3 g total fat (1 g sat. fat), 5 mg chol., 194 mg sodium, 8 g carbo., 1 g fiber, 3 g pro.
Daily Values: 1% vit. A, 22% vit. C, 5% calcium, 3% iron
Exchanges: 1/2 Starch, 1/2 Other Carbo.

bonus recipes

romas with chèvre and basil pesto

A combination of pesto and chèvre makes this hors d'oeuvre fresh tasting and creamy. Lovely as appetizers, these tomatoes also look great on dinner plates as a delicious side.

Prep: 12 minutes Bake: 7 minutes Oven: 400°F Makes: 20 appetizers

10	roma tomatoes (about 2 pounds), halved lengthwise
1/4	teaspoon dried thyme, crushed
	Salt and black pepper
1/4	cup purchased basil pesto
1/4	cup soft goat cheese (chèvre)
2	tablespoons snipped fresh parsley or basil

1 Sprinkle cut sides of tomato halves with thyme, salt, and pepper. Place tomatoes, cut sides up, in a greased shallow baking pan. Bake in a 400° oven about 5 minutes or until nearly tender.

2 Top tomato halves evenly with pesto and goat cheese. Bake about 2 minutes more or until cheese is softened. Sprinkle with parsley.

Nutrition Facts per appetizer: 31 cal., 2 g total fat (0 g sat. fat), 1 mg chol., 41 mg sodium, 2 g carbo., 1 g fiber, 1 g pro.
Daily Values: 8% vit. A, 10% vit. C, 1% calcium, 1% iron
Exchanges: ½ Vegetable, ½ Fat

fennel and onion dip

Green and red onion power up purchased French onion dip; fennel lends a hint of anise.

Start to Finish: 15 minutes Makes: about 2¼ cups dip (36 servings)

1	**medium fennel bulb**
1	**16-ounce container light dairy sour cream onion dip**
2	**tablespoons finely chopped red onion**
2	**tablespoons thinly sliced green onion (1)**
	Vegetable dippers

---

1 Trim feathery leaves from fennel. Chop enough of the leaves to make 2 tablespoons; set aside. Trim fennel bulb. Chop enough of the bulb to make 1 cup. If desired, cut remaining bulb into strips to use for dippers.

2 In a medium bowl combine the 1 cup chopped fennel, the onion dip, red onion, and green onion.

3 To serve, spoon the dip into a serving bowl. Sprinkle with the reserved 2 tablespoons fennel leaves. Serve with vegetable dippers.

Make-Ahead Tip: Prepare as directed through Step 2. Cover and chill for up to 24 hours. If using fennel leaves, wrap in plastic wrap and chill separately.

Nutrition Facts per 1 tablespoon dip: 19 cal., 1 g total fat (1 g sat. fat), 5 mg chol.,
73 mg sodium, 2 g carbo., 0 g fiber, 1 g pro.
Daily Values: 1% vit. A, 1% vit. C, 3% calcium,
Exchanges: Free

bonus recipes

roasted red pepper dip

Vegetable dippers make this a winning—and healthful—appetizer or snack.

Prep: 10 minutes Stand: 20 minutes Bake: 15 minutes Oven: 425°F Makes: 1½ cups

2	red sweet peppers, or one 7-ounce jar roasted red sweet peppers, drained
1	fresh red chile pepper or 1 to 2 teaspoons bottled chopped red jalapeño pepper
8	ounces soft goat cheese (chèvre) or cream cheese, cut up
2	tablespoons olive oil or cooking oil
1	clove garlic, quartered
2	tablespoons snipped fresh rosemary, basil, or oregano; or 1 teaspoon dried rosemary, basil, or oregano, crushed
	Assorted vegetable dippers (such as broccoli florets, jicama strips, and zucchini slices)

---

1 If using, roast fresh sweet peppers and fresh chile pepper according to directions below. Cut roasted peppers into pieces.

2 In a food processor or blender combine roasted or bottled peppers, goat cheese, oil, and garlic. Cover and process or blend until smooth. Add rosemary; pulse until combined. Transfer dip to a serving bowl.

3 Serve immediately or chill in a tightly covered container for up to two days. Serve with assorted vegetables.

To roast peppers: Halve peppers lengthwise; remove stems, seeds, and membranes. (When working with the chile pepper, wear plastic or rubber gloves so oils in the chile don't burn your skin.) Place pepper halves cut side down on a foil-lined baking sheet. Bake in a 425°F oven for 15 to 20 minutes or until skins are blistered and dark. Carefully bring the foil up and around the pepper halves to enclose. Let stand about 20 minutes or until cool enough to handle. Use a sharp knife to loosen the edges of the skins; gently and slowly peel off the skin in strips. Discard skins.

Nutrition Facts per tablespoon dip: 41 cal., 3 g total fat (2 g sat. fat), 4 mg chol., 35 mg sodium, 1 g carbo., 0 g fiber, 2 g pro.
Daily Values: 36% vit. C, 1% calcium, 2% iron
Exchanges: ½ Medium-Fat Meat

bonus recipes

roasted pepper-cheese mold

Why save such a pretty spread for company? Serve this cheese with crackers to hold over hungry appetites before midweek meals.

Prep: 15 minutes **Chill:** 4 to 24 hours **Makes:** 12 servings

2	3-ounce packages reduced-fat cream cheese (Neufchâtel), softened
3	tablespoons light dairy sour cream
2	tablespoons snipped fresh cilantro
4	teaspoons finely chopped onion
1	small clove garlic, minced
	Dash cayenne pepper
	Dash ground cumin
2	tablespoons chopped bottled roasted red sweet pepper
	Assorted crackers

1 In a small mixing bowl beat the cream cheese and sour cream with an electric mixer on low to medium speed until smooth. Stir in cilantro, onion, garlic, cayenne pepper, and cumin.

2 Line a small bowl or a 6- to 10-ounce custard cup with plastic wrap. Spoon half of the cheese mixture into prepared bowl. Sprinkle with roasted red pepper. Spoon the remaining cheese mixture on top of roasted pepper. Cover and chill for 4 to 24 hours.

3 To serve, unmold cheese mixture onto a serving platter. Serve with crackers.

Nutrition Facts per serving: 43 cal., 4 g total fat (2 g sat. fat), 12 mg chol., 60 mg sodium, 1 g carbo., 0 g fiber, 2 g pro.
Daily Values: 5% vit. A, 8% vit. C, 2% calcium,
Exchanges: 1 Fat

romaine with creamy garlic dressing

You will have some of the salad dressing left over; cover and chill it for up to three days.

Start to Finish: 5 minutes Makes: 4 side-dish servings

½	**cup plain low-fat yogurt**
⅓	**cup bottled reduced-calorie Italian salad dressing**
1	**garlic clove, minced**
4	**cups torn romaine**
¼	**cup shredded Parmesan cheese (1 ounce)**

1 For dressing, in a small bowl combine yogurt, salad dressing, and garlic.

2 Arrange romaine on four salad plates. Drizzle each salad with 1 tablespoon of the dressing. Sprinkle salads with Parmesan cheese.

Nutrition Facts per serving: 60 cal., 3 g total fat (1 g sat. fat), 7 mg chol., 386 mg sodium, 6 g carbo., 1 g fiber, 4 g pro.
Daily Values: 66% vit. A, 23% vit. C, 14% calcium, 4% iron
Exchanges: 1 Vegetable, ½ Lean Meat, ½ Fat

crimson greens and papaya

The peppery kick of coarsely ground papaya seeds in this dressing contrasts with the soothing sweetness of fresh fruit.

Start to Finish: 25 minutes Makes: 8 side-dish servings

1	large papaya
7	cups torn red-tip leaf lettuce and/or mixed salad greens
1	cup shredded radicchio
1	small red onion, thinly sliced and separated into rings
1/4	cup snipped fresh cilantro
3	tablespoons salad oil
1	tablespoon toasted sesame oil*
2	tablespoons lemon juice
2	tablespoons rice vinegar or white wine vinegar
1	tablespoon heat-stable granular sugar substitute
1/8	teaspoon salt

1 Peel, seed, and slice the papaya, reserving 1 tablespoon of the seeds for the dressing.

2 In a large salad bowl combine papaya slices, lettuce, radicchio, red onion, and cilantro; toss gently to mix.

3 For dressing, in a blender or food processor combine salad oil, sesame oil, lemon juice, vinegar, sugar substitute, and salt. Cover and blend or process until smooth. Add reserved papaya seeds; blend or process until seeds are the consistency of coarsely ground pepper. Pour dressing over salad. Toss lightly to coat.

*Note: If toasted sesame oil is unavailable, increase the salad oil to 1/4 cup.

Nutrition Facts per serving: 86 cal., 7 g total fat (1 g sat. fat), 0 mg chol., 44 mg sodium, 5 g carbo., 1 g fiber, 1 g pro.
Daily Values: 23% vit. A, 39% vit. C, 5% calcium, 5% iron
Exchanges: 1 Vegetable, 1 1/2 Fat

bonus recipes

221

ginger-tomato salad

If it's not tomato season, go for the grape-tomato option—these little beauties are bursting with taste even in winter. You'll love the way the cheery gems brighten up a winter meal.

Prep: 15 minutes Chill: 1 hour Makes: 4 side-dish servings

2	tablespoons rice vinegar
1	tablespoon finely minced fresh ginger
1	tablespoon heat-stable granular sugar substitute
1/8	teaspoon salt
2	cups cherry or grape tomatoes

1 In a small bowl whisk together rice vinegar, ginger, sugar substitute, and salt. Add tomatoes; toss gently to coat. Cover and chill for 1 to 4 hours.

Nutrition Facts per serving: 25 cal., 82 mg sodium, 5 g carbo., 1 g fiber, 1 g pro.
Daily Values: 12% vit. A, 30% vit. C, 1% calcium, 6% iron
Exchanges: 1 Vegetable

napa cabbage slaw

A dressing of rice vinegar and toasted sesame oil, tossed with napa cabbage and bok choy, creates a crisper, lighter slaw.

Start to Finish: 15 minutes Makes: 6 side-dish servings

3	cups finely shredded Napa (Chinese) cabbage
1	cup finely shredded bok choy
1/4	of a small red sweet pepper, cut into very thin strips
1/4	cup rice vinegar or white vinegar
1	tablespoon salad oil
1/2	teaspoon toasted sesame oil

1 In a large bowl combine cabbage, bok choy, and sweet pepper.

2 For dressing, in a small bowl whisk together vinegar, salad oil, and sesame oil. Pour over cabbage mixture; toss gently to coat. If desired, cover and chill for up to 2 hours.

Nutrition Facts per serving: 40 cal., 3 g total fat (0 g sat. fat), 0 mg chol., 81 mg sodium, 2 g carbo., 1 g fiber, 1 g pro.
Daily Values: 30% vit. A, 49% vit. C, 6% calcium, 3% iron
Exchanges: 1/2 Vegetable, 1/2 Fat

asian-style asparagus slaw

Tender asparagus spears combine with shredded cabbage and red onion tossed in a sesame oil dressing.

Prep: 10 minutes Cook: 4 minutes Makes: 6 side-dish servings

1	pound asparagus
4	cups very finely shredded green cabbage
1	cup very finely shredded red cabbage
$1/3$	cup very finely shredded carrot
$1/4$	cup snipped fresh parsley
$1/4$	small red onion, thinly sliced
2	tablespoons seasoned rice vinegar
1	tablespoon toasted sesame oil
$1/4$	teaspoon white pepper

1 Snap off and discard woody bases from asparagus. If desired, scrape off scales. In a medium saucepan bring 1 inch of water to boiling. Place asparagus in steamer basket; cover and steam for 4 minutes or until asparagus is crisp-tender. Gently rinse with cool water; drain well. Set aside.

2 In a large bowl combine green cabbage, red cabbage, carrot, parsley, and onion. Add vinegar, sesame oil, and pepper. Toss gently to coat.

3 Divide asparagus spears among six salad plates. Top with cabbage mixture.

Nutrition Facts per serving: 54 cal., 3 g total fat (0 g sat. fat), 0 mg chol., 70 mg sodium, 6 g carbo., 2 g fiber, 2 g pro.
Daily Values: 43% vit. A, 63% vit. C, 4% calcium, 5% iron
Exchanges: 1 Vegetable, $1/2$ Fat

lemon-marinated veggies

Prepare these flavor-infused veggies up to a day ahead to leave time for you to focus on a fancy main course—or to relax and entertain guests.

Prep: 15 minutes Cook: 12 minutes Marinate: 4 to 24 hours Makes: 8 to 10 side-dish servings

1/3	cup olive oil or cooking oil
1/3	cup lemon juice
2	tablespoons snipped fresh basil
1	tablespoon Dijon-style mustard
1	clove garlic, minced
1/8	teaspoon salt
1/8	teaspoon black pepper
8	ounces fresh green beans, trimmed
12	ounces baby carrots with tops, peeled and trimmed
8	ounces fresh mushrooms, stems removed
2	medium red and/or yellow sweet peppers, cut into 1-inch pieces
1	cup cherry tomatoes

1 For vinaigrette, in a screw-top jar combine oil, lemon juice, basil, mustard, garlic, salt, and black pepper. Cover and shake well. Set aside.

2 In a covered large saucepan cook green beans in a small amount of boiling water for 2 minutes. Add carrots; cook, covered, about 8 minutes more or until vegetables are crisp-tender. Drain. Rinse with cold water; drain again.

3 Place beans, carrots, mushrooms, sweet peppers, and cherry tomatoes in a resealable plastic bag set in a large bowl. Pour vinaigrette over vegetables. Seal bag; turn to coat vegetables. Marinate in the refrigerator for at least 4 to 24 hours, turning bag occasionally.

4 To serve, bring vegetables to room temperature. Drain vegetables; arrange on a serving platter.

Nutrition Facts per serving: 95 cal., 6 g total fat (1 g sat. fat), 0 mg chol., 113 mg sodium, 11 g carbo., 3 g fiber, 3 g pro.
Daily Values: 118% vit. A, 105% vit. C, 4% calcium, 4% iron
Exchanges: 1½ Vegetable, 1 Fat

bonus recipes

italian vegetable salad

A bag of frozen mixed vegetables delivers a garden of color without all the cleaning and cooking. Ready-to-go vegetables are the secret to this step-saving salad.

Prep: 10 minutes Chill: 8 to 24 hours Makes: 5 or 6 side-dish servings

1	16-ounce package frozen zucchini, carrots, cauliflower, lima beans, and Italian beans
1/2	cup cubed provolone or mozzarella cheese (2 ounces)
1/4	cup sliced pitted ripe olives
1/4	cup sliced green onions (2)
1/3	cup bottled reduced-calorie Italian salad dressing
2	tablespoons grated Parmesan cheese

1 In a medium bowl combine frozen vegetables, provolone cheese, olives, and onions. Add dressing; toss to coat. Cover and chill for 8 to 24 hours.

2 To serve, sprinkle Parmesan cheese over salad; toss to combine.

Nutrition Facts per serving: 97 cal., 5 g total fat (2 g sat. fat), 10 mg chol., 441 mg sodium, 7 g carbo., 3 g fiber, 5 g pro.
Daily Values: 58% vit. A, 12% vit. C, 14% calcium, 2% iron
Exchanges: 1 Vegetable, 1/2 Medium-Fat Meat, 1/2 Fat

roasted asparagus with gruyère

Slender asparagus stalks and colorful sweet pepper strips lie under a sprinkling of Gruyère cheese to create this stunning side dish.

Prep: 15 minutes Roast: 20 minutes Stand: 2 minutes Oven: 400°F Makes: 6 side-dish servings

2	**pounds fresh asparagus spears**
1	**small onion, cut into thin wedges**
1	**small red or yellow sweet pepper, cut into thin strips**
1	**tablespoon olive oil**
1/4	**teaspoon salt**
1/4	**teaspoon black pepper**
1/4	**cup shredded Gruyère or Swiss cheese (1 ounce)**

---

1 Snap off and discard woody bases from asparagus spears. If desired, scrape off scales. Place asparagus, onion, and sweet pepper in a 15×10×1-inch baking pan. Drizzle with olive oil; toss gently to coat. Spread in a single layer. Sprinkle with salt and pepper.

2 Roast, uncovered, in a 400° oven about 20 minutes or until asparagus is crisp-tender. Transfer to a serving platter; sprinkle with cheese. Let stand 2 minutes until cheese melts.

Nutrition Facts per serving: 73 cal., 4 g total fat (1 g sat. fat), 5 mg chol., 127 mg sodium, 4 g carbo., 2 g fiber, 4 g pro.
Daily Values: 5% vit. A, 94% vit. C, 6% calcium, 4% iron
Exchanges: 1 Vegetable, 1 Fat

bonus recipes

green beans in shallot butter

It's amazing what a scattering of shallots can do to transform green beans into a memorable dish. Try this for a colorful accompaniment to one of the bold, meaty dishes in this book.

Start to Finish: 25 minutes Makes: 8 side-dish servings

1½	pounds green beans
2	tablespoons butter
¼	cup minced shallots (2 medium)
½	teaspoon salt
¼	teaspoon black pepper

1 Place a steamer basket in a large saucepan. Add enough water to come just below bottom of basket. Bring to boiling. Place beans in steamer basket. Cover and steam for 5 to 7 minutes or until beans are crisp-tender.

2 Meanwhile, melt butter in a large skillet over medium-high heat. Add shallots. Cook and stir for 1 minute. Add beans, salt, and pepper to skillet. Cook for 1 to 2 minutes more or until heated through.

Nutrition Facts per serving : 54 cal., 3 g total fat (2 g sat. fat), 8 mg chol., 181 mg sodium, 6 g carbo., 3 g fiber, 2 g pro.
Daily Values: 13% vit. A, 18% vit. C, 3% calcium, 5% iron
Exchanges: 1 Vegetable, ½ Fat

lemon broccoli

This bright broccoli side dish with olive oil, lemon, and garlic pairs beautifully with roast pork tenderloin.

Start to Finish: 25 minutes Makes: 4 side-dish servings

4	**cups broccoli florets (1 pound)**
1	**tablespoon olive oil**
1/2	**teaspoon finely shredded lemon peel**
1/4	**teaspoon salt**
1/4	**teaspoon black pepper**
1	**clove garlic, minced**
	Lemon wedges (optional)

1 Place a steamer basket in a large saucepan. Add enough water to come just below bottom of basket. Bring to boiling. Place broccoli in steamer basket. Cover and steam for 5 to 6 minutes or until broccoli is just tender.

2 Meanwhile, in a large serving bowl combine olive oil, lemon peel, salt, pepper, and garlic. Add broccoli; toss to coat. If desired, garnish with lemon wedges.

Nutrition Facts per serving: 56 cal., 4 g total fat (1 g sat. fat), 0 mg chol., 169 mg sodium, 5 g carbo., 3 g fiber, 3 g pro.
Daily Values: 27% vit. A, 138% vit. C, 4% calcium, 5% iron
Exchanges: 1 Vegetable, 1/2 Fat

broccoli and peppers

Thanks to soy sauce and the nutty intrigue that just one teaspoon of sesame oil imparts, this dish brings a pleasant, Asian-inspired counterpoint to whatever dish you serve.

Prep: 15 minutes Cook: 7 minutes Makes: 12 side-dish servings

3	tablespoons soy sauce
1	tablespoon lemon juice
1	teaspoon toasted sesame oil
8	cups broccoli florets (2 pounds)
2	medium red and/or yellow sweet peppers, cut into strips

1 For sauce, in a small bowl combine soy sauce, lemon juice, and sesame oil. Set aside.

2 Place a steamer basket in a 12-inch skillet. Add enough water to come just below bottom of basket. Bring to boiling. Place broccoli in steamer basket. Reduce heat to medium low. Cover and steam for 4 minutes. Add sweet peppers. Cover and steam for 3 to 4 minutes more or until vegetables are crisp-tender.

3 Transfer vegetables to a serving bowl. Drizzle sauce over vegetables; toss gently to coat.

Nutrition Facts per serving: 32 cal., 1 g total fat (0 g sat. fat), 0 mg chol., 250 mg sodium, 5 g carbo., 2 g fiber, 2 g pro.
Daily Values: 19% vit. A, 129% vit. A, 3% calcium, 3% iron
Exchanges: 1 Vegetable

braised seasoned brussels sprouts

A trio of seeds—mustard, cumin, and fennel—along with fresh ginger, add big, bold flavor to these cruciferous vegetables.

Prep: 15 minutes Cook: 10 minutes Makes: 4 side-dish servings

	Nonstick cooking spray
¹/₂	teaspoon mustard seeds
¹/₂	teaspoon cumin seeds
¹/₂	teaspoon fennel seeds
2	cups halved Brussels sprouts (8 ounces)
¹/₃	cup chicken broth or vegetable broth
2	teaspoons grated fresh ginger
¹/₄	teaspoon salt
1	dried red Thai chile pepper, crushed, or ¹/₄ teaspoon crushed red pepper
1	tablespoon coarsely chopped cashews or peanuts
2	teaspoons sherry vinegar or red wine vinegar

1 Lightly coat a medium saucepan with cooking spray. Heat saucepan over medium-high heat. Add mustard, cumin, and fennel seeds; cook and stir for 30 seconds. Add Brussels sprouts, chicken broth, ginger, salt, and crushed red pepper.

2 Bring to boiling; reduce heat. Simmer, covered, for 10 to 12 minutes or until Brussels sprouts are tender, stirring occasionally. Stir in nuts and vinegar.

Nutrition Facts per serving: 37 cal., 1 g total fat (0 g sat. fat), 0 mg chol., 225 mg sodium, 5 g carbo., 2 g fiber, 2 g pro.
Daily Values: 7% vit. A, 53% vit. C, 3% calcium, 7% iron
Exchanges: 1 Vegetable, ¹/₂ Fat

broiled eggplant with cheese

These quick-to-fix broiled eggplant slices, topped with part-skim mozzarella cheese and oregano, are also easy on the waistline.

Prep: 10 minutes Broil: 8 minutes Makes: 4 side-dish servings

2	tablespoons finely chopped green onion (1)
1	tablespoon olive oil or cooking oil
1	tablespoon balsamic vinegar
2	cloves garlic, minced
	Dash crushed red pepper
1	medium eggplant (about 1 pound)
1/3	cup shredded part-skim mozzarella cheese
1	teaspoon dried oregano, crushed, or 1 tablespoon snipped fresh oregano

1 Preheat broiler. In a small bowl combine green onion, oil, vinegar, garlic, and crushed red pepper. Set aside.

2 Cut eggplant crosswise into 16 slices (about ½ inch thick). Place eggplant on the unheated rack of a broiler pan. Broil 4 to 5 inches from the heat for 8 to 10 minutes or until tender, turning and brushing once with green onion mixture halfway through broiling.

3 Sprinkle eggplant with mozzarella cheese and if using, dried oregano. Broil for 1 minute more. Sprinkle with fresh oregano, if using.

Nutrition Facts per serving: 79 cal., 5 g total fat (1 g sat. fat), 4 mg chol., 51 mg sodium, 8 g carbo., 3 g fiber, 3 g pro.
Daily Values: 4% vit. A, 5% vit. C, 8% calcium, 3% iron
Exchanges: 1½ Vegetable, ½ Medium-Fat Meat, ½ Fat

roasted fennel and onions

Although the fennel stalks look like celery stalks, they're not meant to be eaten. You can, however, save some of the delicate, wispy green fronds for a bright garnish.

Prep: 15 minutes Roast: 35 minutes Oven: 400°F Makes: 6 side-dish servings

2	**medium fennel bulbs**
1	**large onion, cut into 1-inch wedges**
2	**tablespoons olive oil**
1/2	**teaspoon fennel seeds or dried Italian seasoning, crushed**
1/2	**teaspoon salt**
1/4	**teaspoon black pepper**

1 To prepare fennel, cut off and discard upper stalks. Remove any wilted outer layers and cut a thin slice from the fennel base. Wash fennel and cut in half lengthwise. Cut lengthwise into wedges about 1 inch thick. Place fennel and onion in a shallow roasting pan. Drizzle with olive oil; sprinkle with fennel seeds, salt, and pepper. Stir to coat.

2 Roast in a 400° oven for 35 to 40 minutes or until vegetables are light brown and tender, stirring twice.

Nutrition Facts per serving: 75 cal., 5 g total fat (1 g sat. fat), 0 mg chol., 235 mg sodium, 8 g carbo., 3 g fiber, 1 g pro.
Daily Values: 2% vit. A, 19% vit. C, 5% calcium, 4% iron
Exchanges: 1½ Vegetable, 1 Fat

pea pods and onions with dill butter

Dillweed is a member of the parsley family and is often used to enhance seafood, meat, poultry, and vegetable dishes. Here, it makes this side dish simple and sophisticated.

Start to Finish: 15 minutes Makes: 10 to 12 side-dish servings

1	**16-ounce package frozen small whole onions**
2	**6-ounce packages frozen pea pods**
2	**cloves garlic, minced**
3	**tablespoons butter**
1	**tablespoon snipped fresh dill or 1 teaspoon dried dillweed, crushed**
½	**teaspoon salt**
¼	**teaspoon white pepper**
	Fresh dill sprigs (optional)

1 In a large saucepan cook onions in a small amount of boiling water for 2 minutes. Add pea pods and cook for 2 to 3 minutes more or just until tender, stirring occasionally. Drain.

2 Meanwhile, in a small saucepan cook and stir garlic in hot butter over medium heat for 30 seconds. Stir in dill, salt, and white pepper. Drizzle over vegetables, tossing to coat. If desired, garnish with fresh dill sprigs.

Nutrition Facts per serving: 64 cal., 4 g total fat (2 g sat. fat), 9 mg chol., 144 mg sodium, 7 g carbo., 2 g fiber, 2 g pro.
Daily Values: 3% vit. A, 14% vit. C, 2% calcium, 5% iron
Exchanges: 1½ Vegetable, ½ Fat

vegetable primavera

The Italian word "primavera" refers to the use of fresh vegetables, which are featured in this recipe. Squash, carrots, red pepper, and broccoli combine to create a festival of colors.

Start to Finish: 20 minutes Makes: 6 side-dish servings

3	tablespoons reduced-sodium chicken broth
1	tablespoon Dijon-style mustard
1	tablespoon olive oil
2	teaspoons white wine vinegar
	Nonstick spray coating
1½	cups sliced yellow summer squash
1	cup tiny whole carrots
1	cup chopped red sweet pepper (1 large)
3	cups broccoli florets
2	tablespoons snipped parsley

1 In a small bowl combine 1 tablespoon of the chicken broth, the mustard, olive oil, and vinegar. Set aside.

2 Spray a large nonstick skillet with nonstick coating. Preheat the skillet over medium heat. Cook and stir squash, carrots, and sweet pepper in hot skillet about 5 minutes or until nearly tender. Add broccoli and remaining chicken broth to skillet. Cook, covered, about 3 minutes or until broccoli is crisp-tender.

3 Stir in the mustard mixture; heat through. To serve, sprinkle with parsley.

Nutrition Facts per serving: 56 cal., 3 g total fat (0 g sat. fat), 0 mg chol., 114 mg sodium, 7 g carbo., 3 g fiber, 2 g pro.
Daily Values: 75% vit. A, 99% vit. C, 3% calcium, 5% iron
Exchanges: 1½ Vegetable, ½ Fat

go-with-anything tomato sauté

This quick-to-fix sauce of grape tomatoes, shallots, thyme, and fresh mozzarella cheese is terrific over wilted greens.

Start to Finish: 15 minutes Makes: 4 side-dish servings

2½	cups red grape tomatoes, yellow pear-shape tomatoes, and/or cherry tomatoes
	Nonstick cooking spray
¼	cup finely chopped shallots (2 medium)
1	teaspoon snipped fresh lemon thyme or thyme
1	clove garlic, minced
¼	teaspoon salt
¼	teaspoon black pepper
4	ounces fresh mozzarella cheese, cut into ½-inch cubes (1 cup)

1 Halve 1½ cups of the tomatoes; set aside. Lightly coat a large nonstick skillet with cooking spray. Cook and stir shallots, lemon thyme, and garlic in hot skillet over medium heat for 2 to 3 minutes or until shallots are tender.

2 Add all of the tomatoes, the salt, and pepper. Cook and stir for 1 to 2 minutes more or just until tomatoes are warmed. Remove from heat. Stir in mozzarella cheese.

Nutrition Facts per serving: 109 cal., 6 g total fat (4 g sat. fat), 20 mg chol., 237 mg sodium, 6 g carbo., 1 g fiber, 6 g pro.
Daily Values: 25% vit. A, 26% vit. C, 21% calcium, 3% iron
Exchanges: 1½ Vegetable, 1 Medium-Fat Meat

lemon-tarragon vegetables

Grilled or broiled pork, chicken, or fish is an ideal mealtime partner for these lemony herbed veggies.

Prep: 15 minutes Cook: 8 minutes Makes: 4 side-dish servings

8	ounces large fresh mushrooms, halved or quartered
2	small yellow summer squash or zucchini, halved lengthwise and cut into $1/2$-inch slices (2 cups)
3/4	cup bias-sliced celery
1	medium onion, cut into wedges
2	tablespoons chopped bottled roasted red sweet pepper or pimiento
1/2	teaspoon finely shredded lemon peel
1	tablespoon lemon juice
2	teaspoons snipped fresh tarragon or 1/4 teaspoon dried tarragon, crushed
1/8	teaspoon salt

1 In a covered large saucepan cook mushrooms, squash, celery, and onion in a small amount of boiling water about 7 minutes or until vegetables are tender. Drain. Return vegetables to saucepan.

2 Stir in roasted red pepper, lemon peel, lemon juice, tarragon, and salt. Cook and stir about 1 minute or until heated through.

Nutrition Facts per serving: 38 cal., 1 g total fat (0 g sat. fat), 0 mg chol., 95 mg sodium, 7 g carbo., 2 g fiber, 3 g pro.
Daily Values: 4% vit. A, 42% vit. C, 2% calcium, 4% iron
Exchanges: 1½ Vegetable

toasted almond-coconut balls

Keep a stash of these chocolate morsels in the fridge year-round. They'll keep for up to three days. Relatively low in calories, they'll satisfy your cravings without compromising your diet.

Start to Finish: 15 minutes Makes: 12 balls

½	cup toasted slivered almonds
⅓	cup heat-stable granular sugar substitute
⅓	cup unsweetened dried coconut flakes
1	tablespoon unsweetened cocoa powder
2	tablespoons butter, softened
1	tablespoon water
½	teaspoon vanilla

1 Place almonds in a food processor. Cover and process until very finely ground. In a medium bowl combine almonds, sugar substitute, coconut flakes, and cocoa powder. Stir in butter, water, and vanilla.

2 Shape mixture into twelve balls, about 1 inch in diameter. Serve immediately or cover tightly and chill up to three days.

Nutrition Facts per ball: 69 cal., 6 g total fat (3 g sat. fat), 5 mg chol., 22 mg sodium, 3 g carbo., 1 g fiber, 1 g pro.
Daily Values: 3% vit. A, 1% vit. C, 3% calcium, 3% iron
Exchanges: 1½ Fat

tropical berry squares

Strawberry-kiwi-flavored gelatin and rum lend tropical touches to this layered dessert.

Prep: 10 minutes Chill: 6 hours Makes: 9 servings

2	4-serving-size packages sugar-free strawberry-kiwi- or strawberry-flavored gelatin
1½	cups boiling water
1⅓	cups cold water
2	tablespoons rum or water
½	of an 8-ounce container frozen light whipped dessert topping, thawed
1	cup fresh raspberries

---

1 In a large bowl dissolve gelatin in boiling water. Stir in cold water and rum. Cover and chill until partially set (consistency of unbeaten egg whites), about 1 to 1½ hours.

2 Place 1½ cups of the gelatin mixture in a medium bowl; cover and set aside at room temperature. Whisk half of the dessert topping (¼ of an 8-ounce container) into the remaining gelatin mixture until combined. Pour into a 2-quart square baking dish. Cover and chill until almost firm, about 2 hours.

3 Stir raspberries into reserved 1½ cups gelatin mixture. Spoon over top of gelatin mixture in dish. Cover and chill at least 3 hours or overnight. Cut into squares to serve. Top each square with some of the remaining whipped topping.

Nutrition Facts per serving: 48 cal., 1 g total fat (1 g sat. fat), 0 mg chol., 49 mg sodium,
4 g carbo., 1 g fiber, 1 g pro.
Daily Values: 5% vit. C, 1% iron
Exchanges: ½ Other Carbo.

peach melba tea dessert

This ruby red dessert flecked with golden peaches is truly stunning when formed in a gelatin mold. If you don't have a mold, use a 3-quart bowl.

Prep: 10 minutes Chill: 3 hours Makes: 6 servings

2	tablespoons low-calorie artificially-sweetened raspberry-flavored tea mix
1	cup cold water
1	4-serving-size package sugar-free raspberry-flavored gelatin
¾	cup boiling water
	Nonstick cooking spray
1	cup frozen unsweetened peach slices, thawed and chopped
⅓	cup frozen light whipped dessert topping, thawed

1 In a small bowl dissolve tea mix in cold water. Set aside.

2 In another small bowl dissolve gelatin in boiling water. Stir in tea mixture. Cover and chill until partially set (the consistency of unbeaten egg whites), about 1 hour.

3 Meanwhile, lightly coat a 3-cup gelatin mold with cooking spray. Fold chopped peaches into gelatin mixture. Pour into prepared mold. Cover and chill for 2 to 24 hours. Before serving, remove gelatin from mold. Garnish with dessert topping.

Nutrition Facts per serving: 29 cal., 37 mg sodium, 4 g carbo., 1 g fiber, 1 g pro.
Daily Values: 3% vit. A, 3% vit. C,
Exchanges: ½ Other Carbo.

orange-cantaloupe pops

Sometimes after a hearty, slow-cooked entrée, you want to end the meal on a light and fruity note. These cool pops are refreshing, plus they're tons of fun—the kids will love them!

Prep: 10 minutes Freeze: 4 to 6 hours Makes: 10 servings

1	4-serving-size package sugar-free orange-flavored gelatin
½	cup boiling water
2	cups cubed ripe cantaloupe
1	8-ounce carton plain low-fat yogurt

1 In a small bowl combine gelatin and boiling water until gelatin is dissolved. In a blender combine gelatin mixture, cantaloupe, and yogurt. Cover and blend until smooth.

2 Pour cantaloupe mixture into ten 3-ounce ice-pop molds or paper cups. If using paper cups, cover the cups with foil. Cut a small slit in the center of each foil cover; insert a wooden stick into each cup. Freeze pops for 4 to 6 hours or until firm.

3 To serve, remove pops from ice-pop molds, or remove foil from paper cups and tear paper away from pops.

Nutrition Facts per serving: 29 cal., 1 mg chol., 47 mg sodium, 4 g carbo., 2 g pro.
Daily Values: 22% vit. A, 20% vit. C, 4% calcium
Exchanges: ½ Other Carbo.

almond cream with berries

This recipe is wonderfully versatile. Another time, use a different variety of berry such as raspberries or blueberries.

Start to Finish: 15 minutes Makes: 4 servings

½	of an 8-ounce package reduced-fat (Neufchâtel) cream cheese, softened
3	tablespoons heat-stable granular sugar substitute
½	cup light dairy sour cream
¼	teaspoon almond extract
¼	teaspoon vanilla
1	cup sliced strawberries

1 In a small mixing bowl beat cream cheese and sugar substitute with an electric mixer on medium speed until fluffy. Beat in sour cream, almond extract, and vanilla until combined.

2 Spoon into dessert dishes. Top with strawberries.

Nutrition Facts per serving: 127 cal., 9 g total fat (6 g sat. fat), 31 mg chol., 132 mg sodium, 7 g carbo., 1 g fiber, 5 g pro.
Daily Values: 13% vit. A, 35% vit. C, 9% calcium, 1% iron
Exchanges: ½ Other Carbo., 2 Fat

strawberry-citrus slush

Many Americans don't get enough fruit in their diets. Here's a yummy, sweet-tart way to help you join the force of healthy eaters!

Start to Finish: 10 minutes Makes: 3 servings

6	ounces frozen unsweetened whole strawberries (about 1$^{1}/_{3}$ cups)
1	12-ounce can low-calorie grapefruit carbonated beverage
1	cup ice cubes
2	teaspoons heat-stable granular sugar substitute
$^{1}/_{4}$	teaspoon orange extract or lime extract (optional)

1 In a blender combine strawberries, carbonated beverage, ice cubes, sugar substitute, and if desired, orange extract. Cover and blend until smooth. Serve in wine glasses.

Nutrition Facts per serving: 20 cal., 23 mg sodium, 6 g carbo., 1 g fiber
Daily Values: 1% vit. A, 39% vit. C, 1% calcium, 2% iron
Exchanges: ½ Other Carbo.

spiced baked custard

Sugar substitute keeps this old-fashioned dessert in an allowable meal plan.

Prep: 10 minutes Cook: 30 minutes Oven: 325°F Makes: 4 servings

3	beaten eggs
1½	cups milk
⅓	cup heat-stable granular sugar substitute
1½	teaspoons vanilla
½	teaspoon ground allspice

1 In a small mixing bowl combine eggs, milk, sugar substitute, and vanilla. Whisk until combined. Place four 6-ounce custard cups in a 2-quart square baking dish. Divide egg mixture among custard cups; sprinkle with allspice. Place baking dish on oven rack. Pour boiling water into baking dish around custard cups to a depth of 1 inch.

2 Bake in a 325° oven for 30 to 45 minutes or until a knife inserted near the center of each cup comes out clean. Remove cups from water. Cool slightly on a wire rack before serving. (Or cool completely in cups; cover and chill until serving time.)

Nutrition Facts per serving: 101 cal., 4 g total fat (1 g sat. fat), 161 mg chol., 97 mg sodium, 7 g carbo., 0 g fiber, 8 g pro.
Daily Values: 12% vit. A, 6% vit. C, 17% calcium, 7% iron
Exchanges: ½ Milk, ½ Medium-Fat Meat, ½ Fat

bonus recipes

spiced cantaloupe

Lime juice imparts this dish with some tang while nutmeg gives it a hint of celebration. Serve it to guests who are watching their diets.

Start to Finish: 10 minutes Makes: 4 servings

2	**cups cubed cantaloupe**
2	**tablespoons lime juice**
1	**tablespoon heat-stable granular sugar substitute**
¼	**teaspoon ground nutmeg**

1 In a medium bowl combine cantaloupe, lime juice, sugar substitute, and nutmeg; toss gently to combine. Spoon into dessert dishes.

Nutrition Facts per serving: 30 cal., 13 mg sodium, 8 g carbo., 1 g fiber, 1 g pro.
Daily Values: 55% vit. A, 53% vit. C, 1% calcium, 1% iron
Exchanges: ½ Fruit

bonus recipes

double berry delight

When fresh strawberries come into season, smother them with a brandy-spiked raspberry topper for a total berry indulgence!

Start to Finish: 10 minutes **Makes:** 4 servings

1/4	cup sugar-free raspberry preserves
1	tablespoon water
1	tablespoon brandy
1 1/3	cups quartered strawberries

1 In a small saucepan combine preserves and water. Cook and stir over medium-low heat until preserves are melted. Remove from heat. Stir in brandy.

2 Divide strawberries among dessert dishes. Drizzle with raspberry mixture.

Nutrition Facts per serving: 34 cal., 1 mg sodium, 9 g carbo., 1 g fiber
Daily Values: 47% vit. C, 1% calcium, 1% iron
Exchanges: ½ Fruit

spicy baked oranges

You'll be amazed at how three simple ingredients can come together to make such a tasty, healthful dessert.

Prep: 10 minutes Bake: 8 minutes Oven: 400°F Makes: 6 servings

3	**medium oranges**
3	**tablespoons chopped pecans**
1/2	**teaspoon pumpkin pie spice**

1 Peel oranges. Cut into 1/4-inch slices. Remove any seeds.

2 Place orange slices in a 2-quart square baking dish. In a small bowl combine pecans and pumpkin pie spice. Sprinkle over orange slices.

3 Bake in a 400° oven for 8 to 10 minutes or until heated through.

Nutrition Facts per serving: 55 cal., 3 g total fat (0 g sat. fat), 0 mg chol., 0 mg sodium, 8 g carbo., 2 g fiber, 1 g pro.
Daily Values: 3% vit. A, 58% vit. C, 3% calcium, 15 iron
Exchanges: 1/2 Fruit, 1/2 Fat

warm spiced peaches

When fresh peach season rolls around, remember this sweet and spicy bake. Pluck a little basil from the garden to add a fresh, minty finish.

Prep: 15 minutes Bake: 5 minutes Oven: 350°F Makes: 4 servings

3	medium ripe peaches, peeled and sliced
2	teaspoons heat-stable granular sugar substitute
½	teaspoon ground cinnamon
½	teaspoon finely shredded orange peel
½	teaspoon vanilla
¼	teaspoon ground nutmeg
2	teaspoons snipped fresh basil or 1 teaspoon snipped fresh mint

---

1 In a medium bowl combine peaches, sugar substitute, cinnamon, orange peel, vanilla, and nutmeg; toss gently to combine. Divide peach mixture among four 5-inch individual quiche dishes or 10-ounce custard cups.

2 Cover and bake in a 350° oven for 5 to 10 minutes or just until warm. (Or loosely cover and microwave on 100% power [high] for 1 to 1½ minutes or just until warm.) Sprinkle with basil.

Nutrition Facts per serving: 32 cal., 8 g carbo., 1 g fiber, 1 g pro.
Daily Values: 6% vit. A, 9% vit. C, 1% calcium, 2% iron
Exchanges: ½ Fruit

bonus recipes

index

metric information

The charts on this page provide a guide for converting measurements from the U.S. customary system, which is used throughout this book, to the metric system.

Product Differences

Most of the ingredients called for in the recipes in this book are available in most countries. However, some are known by different names. Here are some common American ingredients and their possible counterparts:

- All-purpose flour is enriched, bleached or unbleached white household flour. When self-rising flour is used in place of all-purpose flour in a recipe that calls for leavening, omit the leavening agent (baking soda or baking powder) and salt.
- Baking soda is bicarbonate of soda.
- Cornstarch is cornflour.
- Golden raisins are sultanas.
- Green, red, or yellow sweet peppers are capsicums or bell peppers.
- Light-colored corn syrup is golden syrup.
- Powdered sugar is icing sugar.
- Sugar (white) is granulated, fine granulated, or castor sugar.
- Vanilla or vanilla extract is vanilla essence.

Volume and Weight

The United States traditionally uses cup measures for liquid and solid ingredients. The chart below shows the approximate imperial and metric equivalents. If you are accustomed to weighing solid ingredients, the following approximate equivalents will be helpful.

- 1 cup butter, castor sugar, or rice = 8 ounces = ½ pound = 250 grams
- 1 cup flour = 4 ounces = ¼ pound = 125 grams
- 1 cup icing sugar = 5 ounces = 150 grams

Canadian and U.S. volume for a cup measure is 8 fluid ounces (237 ml), but the standard metric equivalent is 250 ml.

1 British imperial cup is 10 fluid ounces.

In Australia, 1 tablespoon equals 20 ml, and there are 4 teaspoons in the Australian tablespoon.

Spoon measures are used for smaller amounts of ingredients. Although the size of the tablespoon varies slightly in different countries, for practical purposes and for recipes in this book, a straight substitution is all that's necessary. Measurements made using cups or spoons always should be level unless stated otherwise.

Common Weight Range Replacements

Imperial / U.S.	Metric
½ ounce	15 g
1 ounce	25 g or 30 g
4 ounces (¼ pound)	115 g or 125 g
8 ounces (½ pound)	225 g or 250 g
16 ounces (1 pound)	450 g or 500 g
1¼ pounds	625 g
1½ pounds	750 g
2 pounds or 2¼ pounds	1,000 g or 1 Kg

Oven Temperature Equivalents

Fahrenheit Setting	Celsius Setting*	Gas Setting
300°F	150°C	Gas Mark 2 (very low)
325°F	160°C	Gas Mark 3 (low)
350°F	180°C	Gas Mark 4 (moderate)
375°F	190°C	Gas Mark 5 (moderate)
400°F	200°C	Gas Mark 6 (hot)
425°F	220°C	Gas Mark 7 (hot)
450°F	230°C	Gas Mark 8 (very hot)
475°F	240°C	Gas Mark 9 (very hot)
500°F	260°C	Gas Mark 10 (extremely hot)
Broil	Broil	Grill

*Electric and gas ovens may be calibrated using celsius. However, for an electric oven, increase celsius setting 10 to 20 degrees when cooking above 160°C. For convection or forced air ovens (gas or electric), lower the temperature setting 25°F/10°C when cooking at all heat levels.

Baking Pan Sizes

Imperial / U.S.

9×1½-inch round cake pan
Metric 22- or 23×4-cm (1.5 L)

9×1½-inch pie plate
Metric 22- or 23×4-cm (1 L)

8×8×2-inch square cake pan
Metric 20×5-cm (2 L)

9×9×2-inch square cake pan
Metric 22- or 23×4.5-cm (2.5 L)

11×7×1½-inch baking pan
Metric 28×17×4-cm (2 L)

2-quart rectangular baking pan
Metric 30×19×4.5-cm (3 L)

13×9×2-inch baking pan
Metric 34×22×4.5-cm (3.5 L)

15×10×1-inch jelly roll pan
Metric 40×25×2-cm

9×5×3-inch loaf pan
Metric 23×13×8-cm (2 L)

2-quart casserole
Metric 2 L

U.S. / Standard Metric Equivalents

⅛ teaspoon = 0.5 ml

¼ teaspoon = 1 ml

½ teaspoon = 2 ml

1 teaspoon = 5 ml

1 tablespoon = 15 ml

2 tablespoons = 25 ml

¼ cup = 2 fluid ounces = 50 ml

⅓ cup = 3 fluid ounces = 75 ml

½ cup = 4 fluid ounces = 125 ml

⅔ cup = 5 fluid ounces = 150 ml

¾ cup = 6 fluid ounces = 175 ml

1 cup = 8 fluid ounces = 250 ml

2 cups = 1 pint = 500 ml

1 quart = 1 litre

Yes, You Can!

2 years for the price of 1
Only $16.97

Plus $3 postage and handling.

Take control with a **FREE** YEAR of the only magazine that celebrates your healthy lifestyle—*Diabetic Living!*

Every issue of **Diabetic Living**™ is like getting an entire cookbook (70+ recipes per issue!), exercise handbook and health guide—all rolled into one. Here are the benefits of this offer:

1. One Bonus-Year of *Diabetic Living* **Magazine**

2. Yes-You-Can Main Dishes
Dive into the good-tasting comfort food you crave! Tex-Mex Sloppy Joes. Meat Loaf like Mom's. Glazed Pork Roast. All the flavor—and good for you, too!

3. Yes-You-Can Desserts
Go ahead—treat yourself! Double Chocolate Brownies. Homemade Apple Pie. Lemon Cheesecake Mousse. So, so good…the only thing missing is the fat.

4. Yes-You-Can Snacks
Feeling hungry? Grab some Crispy Parmesan Chips. Mango-Strawberry Smoothies. Peanut Butter Cereal Bars. Dozens of tasty, healthy treats you can whip up in a flash.

5. Yes-You-Can Fitness Tips
Walking, yoga, water sports—even kickboxing! Every issue brings you fun, safe ways to feel healthy and look fit…your workout won't feel like work at all!

6. Yes-You-Can Health Info
We comb through thousands of medical reports to bring you up-to-the-minute advances in diabetes research. If it affects your health, you'll know it first.

7. Yes-You-Can Stories of Real People
We'll introduce you to everyday people…difference-makers who have looked diabetes square in the eye and said, "Yes, I can!" You can, too!

8. Yes-You-Can Info You Can Trust
Every article, every recipe, every health tip is checked and double-checked by the doctors and health pros on our Editorial Advisory Panel. So you know it's right.

9. 100% Unconditional Money-Back Guarantee
If *Diabetic Living* doesn't show you all you CAN do…with great recipes, fitness tips and health info, just let us know. We'll refund every penny. No questions asked.

To take advantage of this special offer, RSVP today at:
www.bhg.com/diabeticliving_offer1